# LAND & LEISURE

## Concepts and Methods in Outdoor Recreation

# LAND & LEISURE

## Concepts and Methods in Outdoor Recreation

*Edited by*

David W. Fischer
*University of Waterloo*

John E. Lewis
*Wilfrid Laurier University*

George B. Priddle
*University of Waterloo*

**maaroufa press** inc

Chicago

**Maaroufa Press**
**Geography Series**
**Eric Moore,**
**Advisory Editor**

*For Jan,*
*Penny, and Ruth*

## ACKNOWLEDGMENTS

To many an edited book is a relatively simple task. To the editors of this book, who now know better, the task has been time consuming yet very challenging. It is recognized, however, that without the interest and help of many individuals *Land and Leisure* would not have been possible. Our thanks, therefore, go to the students enrolled in recreation courses in Geography and Planning at the University of Waterloo and Wilfrid Laurier University who have critically assessed the value and usefulness of numerous articles on the topic; to Jan Fischer for her diligence in preparing the manuscript; to Lillian Peirce for her repeated typing of the text; and, to the two universities for their general cooperation.

Finally, we acknowledge the enthusiasm and cooperation of Ted Tieken, Publisher, Maaroufa Press, whose experience in the publishing field is evidenced in the many decisions pertaining to the reader.

In conclusion, the editors share all responsibilities for any deficiencies or inadequacies associated with this work.

DAVID W. FISCHER
JOHN E. LEWIS
GEORGE B. PRIDDLE

## List of Contributors

Arthur A. Atkisson, Health Sciences Center,
    University of Texas

William R. Burch, Jr., Department of Sociology
    and Forestry, Yale University

Marion Clawson, Resources for the Future, Inc.,
    Washington, D.C.

Robert K. Davis, Department of Economics, Johns Hopkins
    University

B. L. Driver, School of Natural Resources,
    University of Michigan

Frank C. Edminster, Soil Conservation Service,
    U.S. Department of Agriculture

Herbert J. Gans, Center for Urban Education,
    Columbia University

Jack L. Knetsch, Development Advisory Service,
    Harvard University

John V. Krutilla, Resources for the Future, Inc.,
    Washington, D.C.

Wilbur F. LaPage, Northeastern Forest Experiment Station,
    Durham, New Hampshire

Barry Lentnek, Department of Geography,
    Ohio State University

Eugene Mattyasovsky, Department of Urban and Regional
    Planning, University of Toronto

P. H. Montgomery, Soil Conservation Service,
    U.S. Department of Agriculture

Peter H. Pearse, Department of Economics,
    University of British Columbia

Harvey S. Perloff, Resources for the Future, Inc.,
    Washington, D.C.

Richard Lee Ragatz, Department of Urban Planning,
    University of Oregon

Ira M. Robinson, City and Regional Planning,
    University of Southern California

Paul O. Rudolf, North Central Forest Experiment Station,
    St. Paul, Minnesota

Elwood L. Shafer, Jr., Northeastern Forest Experiment
    Station, Upper Darby, Pennsylvania

Ernst W. Swanson, Emeritus, Department of Economics,
    North Carolina State University

Gordon D. Taylor, Travel Industry Branch,
    Office of Tourism, Ottawa

Bryan Thompson, Department of Geography,
    Wayne State University

Clarke W. Thomson, Department of Geography,
   Brock University

S. Ross Tocher, School of Natural Resources,
   University of Michigan

James R. Trail, Department of Geography,
   Ohio State University

Carlton S. Van Doren, Department of Recreation Resources,
   Texas A & M University

Lowdon Wingo, Jr., Resources for the Future, Inc.,
   Washington, D.C.

# contents

x

# INTRODUCTION

Leisure has come to be a vital force in our lives. A contributor to this book underlines this statement by saying that "the way leisure is used affects a culture as much as or more than the 'productive' work of the culture." In this sense, leisure represents an opportunity for self-expression outside or apart from our work efforts.

Within the larger framework of leisure, outdoor recreation is assuming a greater role. At one time or another each of us is a participant in some kind of outdoor recreation whether actively or passively as our tastes and whims dictate, or as such opportunities present themselves. As increased amounts of leisure time contribute to our growing demands for outdoor recreation, larger amounts of resources of varying diversity and quality are required to meet those demands. With this in mind, it is clear why the planning and managing of recreational resources is of personal interest to everyone. Such efforts determine the quality of our recreational experiences and provide the range of opportunities available to us when we are outdoors.

The rapid growth of outdoor recreation has led to overuse of facilities with subsequent abuse of quality to sites and recreation experiences. Losses of this nature, coupled with the demands for new recreational areas, have accelerated interest in the planning and management of outdoor recreation.

The post-World War II surge in the use of recreational areas found the few hard-working recreation professionals unprepared to meet the demands placed upon them. Furthermore, outdoor recreation was taught and studied by only a handful of academics in separate departments such as sociology, geography, zoology, and economics; it was only just beginning to be recognized as a separate field of study in the universities.

Recreation decisions depending upon a single discipline should be rare. Nevertheless, policy has often been formed by a single discipline operating in concert with a recreation agency. Such agencies used grants and other means to reinforce single discipline solutions which were sold by creating a demand for them. This procedure effectively ignored other concepts and methods and promoted a narrowly-defined solution. At best, such efforts created questionable consequences; at worst, they ignored major social factors.

The watershed in outdoor recreation came with the work of the U.S. Outdoor Recreation Resources Review Commission which published a set of Study Reports in 1962. The Commission was largely composed of individuals from government, universities, and business. This group contributed its wide range of experience to provide the first broad and in-depth studies in outdoor recreation. The results of these studies are now history, for they signaled the beginning of an era when recreation issues would be dealt with openly and across a wide range of professional interests.

Today, the study of outdoor recreation resources is fully recognized as a profession in its own right. Interest is being manifested at the college level with increasing numbers of students opting for careers in recreation. But while the demand for training in recreation is on the increase, the field itself is still quite fragmented. The paradox of the current situation for instructors as well as planners is that while much is being written about outdoor recreation, there is no one published source that brings together the diverse set of results that has been developed. New findings are scattered among a wide variety of sources, seemingly unknown and unrelated to the journals and reports read by any one profession.

One of the results of this apparent lack of effort, to date, to integrate into one body all of the concepts and methods used in outdoor recreation is a form of circular thinking in which those in each discipline feel that their approach is definitive. Because they believe it definitive, they are reluctant, even unwilling, to broaden their views to embrace other theories—some of which may question their assumptions. It follows that because no efforts are made to broaden their beliefs, they continue to think of them as definitive. Only by experimenting with concepts and methods from all participating disciplines can the limitations of this current cycle of thinking be broken.

By creating a book that will introduce the reader to basic cornerstones of recreational land use—spatial, behavioral, economic, and physical analyses—we hope that a dialogue between different professionals and students can occur. It is our feeling that an intelligent understanding of these four areas of investigation is necessary for two reasons: (1) to have a basic understanding of these types of investigations and (2) to be able to see the relevance of these various types of disciplinary inputs to the overall study of outdoor recreation. It is for these reasons that our book brings together in one place the concepts and methods from the various disciplines that have contributed to the understanding of outdoor recreation.

This book has several objectives. It is designed to show students the basic ideas which have emerged over the last decade to help shape recreation decisions. Reading and reflecting on these selections should help students grasp the complexity surrounding the planning and management of recreational resources. The book focuses on "how to do it." The editors' experiences in "teaching-learning" have suggested that students desiring a foundation in recreation enjoy learning the basic concepts and methods as a base for understanding recreation. The concern for both concepts and methods is twofold: initially, the emphasis is on concepts that have utility in the formation of theory; attention then turns to the methods derived from such theory that are useful for planning and management. Concepts and methods are inseparable, and much misunderstanding can occur if they are divorced.

To aid in understanding the scope and structure of this book we have summarized the flow of ideas that link together the five Parts. The social values of the recreation planners and users are the basis of the spatial patterns that emerge. The behavioral aspect of recreation is interpreted through the activities users pursue at the sites and users' responses to the amenities such sites provide. Valuing the behavior of recreationists by using their travel patterns and attitudes to construct the demand for recreation facilities aids planners in determining what sites should be provided and where they should be located. Valuation also provides the basis for a possible fee structure in order to reduce the impacts of congestion and trampling. The environmental impact of recreation is a problem for planners and managers to understand and alleviate through site selection and layout, which in turn reflects the social values of the planners and affects the social values of the users.

As indicated before, the book is divided into five Parts. Part One is designed to give the student an overview of the magnitude of the problem of outdoor recreation and to provide him with a meaningful framework within which to consider the more specific and technical concepts and methods which are discussed in the following Parts.

The introductory overview of some of the problems inherent in leisure and outdoor recreation is followed by Part Two which is composed of readings, somewhat more specific in content, that discuss the patterns and flows of recreational users. These selections, in particular, are highly representative of analysis that is spatially oriented.

Part Three deals with some of the behavioral aspects of recreation. While behavioral assumptions have been widespread in recreational literature, we would like to point out that little work in outdoor recreation has been done by behavioral scientists. Instead, such work has been done by those trained in such physical disciplines as biology, forestry, and geography. Not until recently have these disciplines incorporated behavioral studies into their research, and the consequences are vital to anyone who would contribute to the field of outdoor recreation.

Part Four consists of selections on the economics of outdoor recreation. The readings included were carefully chosen for their content as we realized that many of those reading this book will have had no more than an introductory semester of economics. Although some may find the selections difficult, it is our hope that they will take the necessary time to understand and grasp them.

Part Five deals with the all important consideration of the environmental impact of recreational land use. To date, little attention has been given to this topic, much to the chagrin of many land managers. For, in truth, much misuse and abuse of the environment have occurred in the name of recreation. As with other Parts, we were somewhat restricted by a lack of space and, as a consequence, some valuable materials dealing with landscape evaluation techniques have not been included. Such studies attempt to bring together the physical and the human as they consider how man evaluates his leisure time environment.

The book as originally conceived was much longer. Unfortunately, due to production considerations, several excellent articles had to be deleted. We hope, however, that this circumstance will be compensated for by the lists of Further Readings which follow and end each Part. These lists were carefully compiled and consist of material that has proven to be most useful to the editors in the study and practice of outdoor recreation. All of the materials, Further Readings included, have been of assistance not only to ourselves, but to our students, as well.

## Uses of the Book

*Land and Leisure* is intended primarily for use in college curricula, although it should also be helpful to professional planners. The book has been designed for a general course in outdoor recreation, be it within a single discipline such as geography, or within a multi-disciplinary course. The readings can be used as a basic text or as a supplement; they can also be used in conjunction with additional readings of particular interest to the instructor.

Many different course outlines and student experiences combined to form the basis of the contents. It is hoped that the selections we have included are of general interest. Readings of a purely professional nature that were too difficult for undergraduates have not been included.

*Land and Leisure* has a definite social science orientation. In the past, most instructors and planners in outdoor recreation have come from a background in the applied biological and physical sciences. It was felt, therefore, that an emphasis on the social sciences had considerable merit.

Further Readings are suggested to guide students into a deeper understanding of the disciplines that have marked the study of outdoor recreation. In addition, short statements written by the editors preface the chapters. These statements serve not only to introduce the reader to a chapter's particular relevance, but also to elucidate its relevance to preceding materials.

Finally, the stress on concepts and methods is designed to give students, regardless of their areas of concentration, a basic understanding of the essentials of outdoor recreation from a multi-disciplinary point of view. If students and instructors enjoy reading this book as much as we enjoyed preparing it, our efforts will have been more than justified.

# Part One
## LEISURE AND RECREATION: SOCIAL VALUES AND APPROACHES

## PREFACE

With increasing leisure time and mobility the demand for recreational space is increasing dramatically. How can this increase be accommodated? What is the social carrying capacity of existing recreational spaces? What additional facilities are needed and how and where should they be provided? Prior to answering such questions, an appreciation of the social forces that create and drive recreational demand is necessary.

A basic premise of many recreational studies is the belief that creating or managing recreation areas automatically provides for social needs. It is essential that an appreciation be gained not only of the social utility of recreation but of its limitations as well. Increasing concern for social welfare, added to the pressures of limited public budgets, has demonstrated to recreation planners that if recreation is indeed accommodating social need then serious consideration must be given to identifying and measuring the nature and magnitude of its human satisfactions.

Transmitting social information in a form that is acceptable to managers, planners, and politicians is a major problem for recreationists. This situation exists because so much of recreational data is subjective—recreation has to do with the intrinsic issues of human values and the quality of life.

Part One considers an underlying issue of all recreation research—namely, its social value. It should also give the reader a means of answering two important questions: (1) how does a particular study of recreation fit into the overall body of recreation studies, and (2) how can facts and values be separated and yet accommodated in the planning process?

CHAPTER

# 1 HOW MUCH LEISURE NOW AND IN THE FUTURE
## Marion Clawson

No one is more cognizant than Marion Clawson of what increasing leisure implies for outdoor recreation. Clawson, as one of the first social scientists writing in the area of leisure and recreation, suggests that both the timing and size of the periods of leisure of individuals in a society will influence recreation values, patterns, behavior, and impacts. The future imprint of these forces upon our recreational resources has yet to be fully demonstrated.

Two considerations dominate a discussion of leisure: (1) the way leisure is used affects a culture as much as or more than the "productive" work of that culture, and (2) the amounts and forms of leisure in the United States have been changing rapidly and will change further in the future.

## CHARACTERISTICS OF LEISURE

There has been considerable confusion in discussions of leisure, apparently because there is not a universally accepted definition of the term. Man requires time each day to exist and to subsist; beyond the necessary minimum for these purposes, his time is discretionary, where greater choice is possible. By leisure, we mean all time beyond the existence and subsistence time. In order to maintain life, man must sleep, ingest food, and have some time for personal hygiene; this is what we mean by time to exist. In the modern world, we must also work at a job or jobs in order to obtain income, at least in most cases; this is what we mean by time to subsist. Like all definitions, there is some fuzziness around the edges, but not too much, we hope. Sometimes it is difficult to tell whether a man is working for subsistence or engaging in activity primarily for sheer enjoyment, and time spent in eating may be simply for existence or also partly for pleasure.

So defined, leisure closely resembles discretionary income, a concept which economists find very useful even though there is some ambiguity about some items that might be included in it. Leisure has well been called "choosing time," because one can choose what to do with it, over a wider range than he can choose how much time to use for existence or subsistence.[1]

Reprinted from *Leisure in America*, Monograph No. 4 of the American Academy of Political and Social Science (April, 1964): 1–20, by permission of The American Academy of Political and Social Science and the author. One section of the original article has been deleted and the notes renumbered.

In our view, leisure does not connote idleness. Among some groups in the United States today, among larger groups in our country in earlier times, and in large parts of the world today, there is much idleness. People do essentially nothing, not because this is what they choose, but because they lack the money, the ideas, the opportunity, or the energy to *do* something, either for work or for fun. As we shall point out later, total leisure in the United States today is higher than it has been in the past and will be much higher in the future, but it is altogether possible that sheer idleness is less today than formerly and will be still less in the future.

Moreover, discretionary time, like discretionary income, can be committed to the hilt—or overcommited. The man or woman whose club, reading, television, and other interests are so numerous as to conflict for available discretionary time is the counterpart of the man whose monthly payments for auto, television, boat, high-fidelity phonograph, and other luxury or semiluxury goods exceed his discretionary income—in extreme cases, exceed his total income. A man may have a great deal of leisure, in the sense we use the term, and yet be harried by the pressure of things he wants to do but lacks the time for. He may think he is harried, yet he certainly does not have the pressing existence and subsistence demands on his time that our forefathers had to meet if they and their families were merely to live.

More specifically, we include as leisure all time not spent in sleep, at work, in school, or in necessary personal chores. As we have noted, there is a small area of fuzziness around some of these items. One study found that 20 percent of professional and managerial workers would choose to use an extra two hours a day, if by some miracle they had it, for their job; presumably they found this more interesting than any other discretionary use of time.[2] Some question may also be raised about school, but, in this modern age, it is mostly an essential form of investment in one's self, to permit later subsistence on a satisfactory level. Some persons, of course, get further education for pure enjoyment. The line between work and leisure is less clear for preschool-age children and for housewives. But all these marginal cases do not touch the basic distinction between leisure and nonleisure.

If leisure is time available for choosing, recreation is one major activity chosen for such available time. Although leisure and recreation are highly associated, they are distinctly different concepts.

In the opinion of many, leisure is primarily the opportunity for self-expression. As we shall point out later, many people today are part of a socially ordered life in work and in personal lives. But, in their leisure hours, they may—within the limits of their income, knowledge, and tastes—do as they please. One may choose television, another bridge, another reading, and so on; one may wish to work in his garden, another to go the ball game, and another for a hike. The range of activities possible in our modern society is almost infinite; one authority listed over 500 different kinds of recreation, which by no means included all known kinds of recreation, and did not attempt to include many other kinds of personal activity.[3]

## TIMING AND PIECES OF LEISURE

. . . Leisure may be looked at in a different way: when does it occur, and how large are the individual pieces?

Some leisure is daily—a little before work or school, possibly a little during the lunch period, but mostly in late afternoon or evening, after work and before bed. The worker and the student experience this pattern; the housewife may have a little more during the day, less at evening. The total hours per day are limited, often to four or less, and even this is broken into several pieces in most cases. As a result, the activities that can be carried on are distinctly circumscribed.

Other leisure is weekly in its pattern. For students and workers, it is the days out of school or off work—Saturdays and Sundays mostly, but sometimes other days for some workers. On these days, not only do the regular daily personal chores reduce the time that might otherwise be leisure but often other personal or household chores are allowed to pile up during the week to be liquidated on these days. But it may be possible to undertake activities now that are impossible on work days. Attendance at certain kinds of parks and recreation areas is very much heavier on weekends than on weekdays, for instance.

Still other leisure is vacation time. For students, this may extend through the whole summer. For workers, as we have noted, it is likely to be a few weeks, usually in the summer also but increasingly at other seasons. For a relatively long period, the time demands of school and job are set aside, but the demands for existence remain. Obviously, many kinds of activities are possible in such time periods that were out of the question in the shorter free periods. In particular, travel to some vacation spot and the many kinds of activities common there are now possible. Full enjoyment of the vacation free time often requires relatively much more money than does full enjoyment of other free time. For many families, it is desirable or essential to send children to special summer camps for part of the vacation period, often at considerable cost.

The timing and size of pieces of leisure are obviously still different for the preschool child and for the retired person. The demands of existence remain, even though subsistence does not require time. The time demands of existence are often necessarily greater for the very young and the older persons—they move slower and require more. They can become, especially for older persons, almost the whole of life—although work does not take time, mere living takes all of it, so that none is left for purposeful leisure pursuits.

In the next section, we present some statistical estimates of total time, nationally, in the past and at present, in these various categories. It will be seen that the proportions have changed greatly and promise to change still more in the future.

5

## A NATIONAL TIME BUDGET

In spite of some deficiencies in data, a national time budget can be estimated, as shown in Table 1 and in Figure 1.[4] In 1950 there were 151.7 million people in the United States, each of whom had twenty-four hours each day, for 365 days of the year, or a grand total of 1,329 billion hours for all the people in the nation. Based on numbers of people in each age and occupation group and upon typical patterns of daily activity, a total budget of time was prepared for 1950, also for 1900, and estimates were made for 2000; the figures for the year 2000 are based upon a projected population of slightly over 330 million persons.

| Use of Time | 1900 | 1950 | 2000 |
|---|---|---|---|
| Total time for entire population | 667 | 1,329 | 2,907 |
| Sleep | 265 | 514 | 1,131 |
| Work | 86 | 132 | 206 |
| School | 11 | 32 | 90 |
| Housekeeping | 61 | 68 | 93 |
| Preschool population, nonsleeping hours | 30 | 56 | 110 |
| Personal care | 37 | 74 | 164 |
| Total, accounted for above | 490 | 876 | 1,794 |
| Remaining hours, largely leisure | 177 | 453 | 1,113 |
| Daily leisure hours | 72 | 189 | 375 |
| Week-end leisure hours | 50 | 179 | 483 |
| Vacation | 17 | 35 | 182 |
| Retired | 6 | 24 | 56 |
| Other, including unaccounted | 32 | 26 | 16 |

**TABLE 1.** *National Time Budget and Time Division of Leisure, 1900, 1950, and 2000 (Billions of Hours Annually)*

In these, as in any other projections of the future, there is obviously much uncertainty; the reality may differ considerably from our best estimate today. A very comprehensive and careful analysis of future economic growth in the United States concludes that the total economy will move forward, that employment will keep pace with economic growth, and that natural resource scarcities will not, in general, inhibit such growth, at least up to the year 2000.[5] Technological change has characterized the American economy in the past and will continue to characterize it in the future; although we cannot now know exactly what will happen, we can be fairly sure that technological change will continue. Past technological change has often brought severe problems of economic dislocation, yet, on the whole, it has improved the lot of the common man. We think it highly

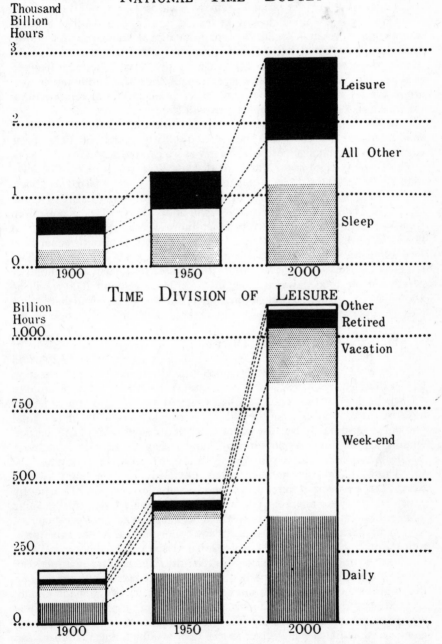

**FIGURE 1.** *National Time Budget and Time Division of Leisure, 1900, 1950, and 2000*

probable that future technological change, while bringing its problems of adjustment, will likewise bring its general rewards.

Changes in employment and in leisure must also be kept in a larger framework of general social change. Educational standards will almost surely continue to rise; the differential in income between the well and the poorly educated may widen in the future. Occupational structure is likely to change, especially under technological impact. But these and other changes are not likely to invalidate the trends in total leisure nor to remove either the problems or the opportunities they will bring.

In these specific estimates, an average work week of about sixty hours was estimated for 1900 and one of about forty hours for 1950; these conform to the actual situation, as nearly as we can judge. An average work week of twenty-eight hours was estimated for 2000; this is materially lower than the estimate in the comprehensive resource study referred to above.

At each of these major periods, by far the largest single use of time was for sleep. The average adult sleeps eight hours daily; older people sleep somewhat more and children very much more. Work at a job, school, and housework take another substantial amount of time, as does personal care. Deducting these from the total available hours gives a remainder, which largely conforms with our definition of leisure. In 1900 it was about 27 percent of the total national time; in 1950, 34 percent; in 2000 it will be about 38 percent. These changes are in part due to differences in daily living pattern, but far more are due to difference in age and occupation of the total population.

More striking than these changes in total leisure are those in leisure at different periods. Retired leisure has risen most since 1900—a fourfold increase by 1950, with a further more than doubling by 2000; vacation leisure doubled from 1900 to 1950; we project it will increase by fivefold in the second half of the century (it had doubled by 1960). Weekend leisure has risen and will rise in the future, partly because of a larger total population and partly because of fewer work days per week. Daily leisure, while rising in total as population changes, has nevertheless become a smaller fraction of total leisure through a larger fraction of total time.

These changes in national totals obviously include many diverse trends, as between different age and occupation groups. The poorly educated may be unemployed, with much idleness and little genuine leisure; the same may be true of workers displaced by technological change who cannot readjust to new employment opportunities. At the same time, well-trained, able, experienced professional and managerial personnel may be so much in demand as to have little leisure. These differences between groups are highly important, particularly in the social sense. But the data on the total for the whole population give some measure of the magnitude of the national problem and opportunity in leisure, irrespective of these variations among groups within it. Time availability is highly important in commercial activities which cater to leisure hours, including equipment and supplies for leisure; it is also important for social or group services aimed at meeting the leisure needs of the population. There was a relatively small but important summer resort business for the wealthy in 1900; the vacation "industry" in 1950 was vastly different in clientele, in total size, and in specific activities; in 2000 it will be still different in major ways. The same is true of weekend leisure and, to a lesser extent, of daily leisure. The dramatic rise in retired leisure will have major economic and social impact. It seems highly likely that available time, plus expected available discretionary income, will create a demand for goods and services, and this in turn will create private business organizations to provide the desired goods and services. But it is also highly probable that the same available time will create other demands for public services of many kinds—parks, playgrounds, education for fun, and many others.

Some very rough estimates of time spent in outdoor recreation, at public places or events, and in travel for fun along highways suggest that roughly 3.5 percent of national leisure time in 1960 was spent in these activities.[6] This excludes time spent in one's own yard or in other individually provided outdoor recreation, and, of course, it excludes all indoor recreation. While it may seem very low, it should be recalled that most daily leisure is spent in other activities, as is a great deal of weekend leisure; moreoever, in much of the United States, outdoor recreation is largely confined to relatively short seasons. By comparison, less than one quarter of one percent of the much smaller total leisure in 1900 was used for the same outdoor recreation activities; by 2000 possibly as much as 8 or 10 percent of total leisure will be so used.

## SOCIAL ORDERING OF INDIVIDUAL LEISURE

Although leisure is "choosing time"—an opportunity for self-expression—in fact, individual leisure is highly ordered by society as a whole. This is true as to amount of leisure, its timing, and the activities in it.

Modern life is more ordered, timewise, than was life in earlier periods. Mumford has put it very well:[7]

> The clock, not the steam-engine, is the key machine of the modern industrial age. For every phase of its development the clock is both the outstanding fact and the typical symbol of the machine: even today no other machine is so ubiquitous. . . . the effect of the mechanical clock is more pervasive and strict: it presides over the day from the hour of rising to the hour of rest. When one thinks of the day as an abstract span of time, one does not go to bed with the chickens on a winter's night; one invents wicks, chimneys, lamps, gaslights, electric lamps, so as to use all the hours belonging to the day. When one thinks of time, not as a sequence of experiences, but as a collection of hours, minutes, and seconds, the habits of adding time and saving time come into existence. Time took on the character of an enclosed space: it could be divided, it could be filled up, it could even be expanded by the invention of labor-saving instruments. . . . Abstract time became the new medium of existence. Organic functions themselves were regulated by it: one ate, not upon feeling hungry, but when prompted by the

9

clock: one slept, not when one was tired, but when the clock sanctioned it. . . . The gain in mechanical efficiency through coordination and through the closer articulation of the day's events cannot be overestimated: while this increase cannot be measured in mere horse-power, one has only to imagine its absence today to foresee the speedy disruption and eventual collapse of our entire society. The modern industrial regime could do without coal and iron and steam easier than it could do without the clock.

Society as a whole, operating through one or another of many diverse social mechanisms, determines the timing of a great many activities of individuals. School and work hours are established on a group basis, with very little or no choice for the individual. These, with the demands for existence (sleep and personal chores), determine not only how much leisure but *when* the individual will have it. Moreover, a great deal of his leisure activity is also socially determined; if he wants to look at a particular television program or if he wishes to attend a baseball or football game, he must do so at the time set by others, for the convenience of substantial segments of the public. As Mumford has noted, the gains are very great; the situation is not unlike that of highway traffic regulation—by giving up our right to drive on either side of the road or through red lights, we gain in speed and safety. But the socially ordered nature of leisure time must also be stressed.

Society also operates, through a variety of mechanisms, to make some uses of leisure socially acceptable and others less so or definitely unacceptable. Of course, this has always been true, and it seems probable that the modern city, with the anonymity it offers to all but the flagrantly nonconformist, offers greater freedom than did the rural countryside and small town, where everyone knew all about everyone else, especially about his deviations from the straight and narrow path. At the same time, the great rise in free time, especially for the young and the old, makes social-control mechanisms both more important and perhaps more necessary. If the Devil finds mischief for idle hands, presumably the potentialities for mischief rise at least as rapidly as the time available for it increases. Many students of society have been much concerned over the wise use of widespread public leisure.

## USES OF LEISURE

Although leisure is choosing time—within socially determined limits—the attitudes of people toward their leisure activities differ greatly. At one extreme are what might be called "unfun"—activities undertaken out of boredom, or for escape, or because of lack of better opportunities. One may go fishing or play poker primarily to escape one's wife, for instance. A study of youth leisure activities in Washington suggests that many youths, especially from lower income homes, watch television on this basis. This use of leisure is perhaps simply the least-worst use of time.

On a different level are leisure activities undertaken positively, because one genuinely wants and enjoys them. There may well be variations in satisfactions among these, of course, and the dividing line between them and unfun is not sharp and clear. At still a different level are those activities one does not undertake at all but would like very much to do or those which one does to a limited extent and would like to do very much oftener. In the same youth study, many young people, especially from lower income families, wanted to go water skiing and horseback riding and to attend legitimate theater very much more frequently than they were able to do.

What one actually does with his leisure is affected by many factors, of which available income is surely one important one; what he would do if he could is also affected by many factors, again with available income in the forefront. The relationship between what one actually does and what one wishes he could do runs a wide gamut, a continuum, from those activities which one often does but would prefer not, to those which one both does and likes, to those which one rarely does but would like very much to do. Both business and social organizations which seek to serve the leisure time of individuals should seek to ascertain the likes as well as the actions and the reasons for divergence. It may well be true that actual experience would materially modify attitudes toward some activities now indulged in infrequently—the image may be more attractive than the reality would prove.

There has been a great rise in outdoor recreation in recent years. Data are available for certain kinds of public areas only; at various federal and state park and forest areas, attendance has risen roughly about 10 percent annually for many years.[8] This is a rate more than five times the rate of increase in total population—if there has been a "population explosion," there has been a recreation explosion five times as violent. Camping, water sports, and numerous other outdoor activities have experienced particularly rapid growth; they have generally been on a family rather than on an individual basis. The past increases in attendance have been possible only because areas of parks have increased. The outlook is for material further increases in outdoor recreation over the next generation or longer, and these, too, will require a lot more land and water area for their satisfaction.

At the same time that outdoor recreation has increased so much, participation in many cultural activities has risen also. Attendance at concerts and at art museums has experienced equally rapid increases, for instance. Many thousands of people, of all ages, participate in many self-expression cultural activities. Reading is certainly at an all-time high, in spite of talk that Johnny can't read. Even the television, often downgraded by the high-brows, probably represents a materially improved use of leisure over street-corner loafing.

One would be hard put to measure the "quality" of use of leisure. Standards of excellence are certainly an individual matter, and data are often scanty or unreliable. Yet, one can venture the judgment that the quality of leisure activities has improved in recent years, that people use

11

leisure more purposefully and to better advantage now than a generation ago. This is not to deny vast possibilities for further improvement.

## WHAT OF THE FUTURE?

How much leisure shall we have, or should we have, in the future? How will it be divided, or should it be divided, as between daily, weekly, vacation, and retired? What will people do with it, and what should they do with it? These obviously are not easy questions nor is it possible to give firm and unequivocal answers to them.

Total leisure nationally will depend in part upon total numbers of people in the nation, their age, and their position in the life cycle. We have presented some indications of these matters, following general practice among economists and demographers, always with the assumption of no catastrophic war. We shall have many more people in 2000—more than 300 million, almost surely; the young and the old will be relatively more numerous; there will be many youths not yet in the labor force and many elderly retired, each of which will demand leisure pursuits in relative abundance. The questions here relate primarily to exact magnitudes, because—always in the absence of major war—there is little question as to the general trend.

Much more choice is possible as to the length of the average work week. As we have noted, this will be primarily a group choice—labor unions, large employers, and perhaps the federal government. One basic choice is between work, with attendant output of goods and services, and leisure. Severe and prolonged unemployment would surely build greater pressures for shorter work weeks, to spread employment, than would booming prosperity. There is a real possibility, however, that the nation might make a *de facto* choice on this point without ever facing up explicitly to the policy issues involved. That is, competition among unions for better deals for their members might take the form of pressure for shorter work weeks, either as longer paid vacations, shorter regular weeks, or otherwise, and these might be granted, in part, in ways that would in time materially shorten the work week without anyone really having chosen the final result.

An equally important issue, in our judgment, concerns the form of added leisure, if any—that is, the size and timing of the pieces. To dramatize the alternatives, let us assume that a decision were made to shorten, over a period of time, an average work week of forty hours by 20 percent. This might be done by cutting the work day from eight to six and one-half hours, leaving untouched all other hours of work; or by cutting the working days per week from five to four, again leaving everything else untouched; or by granting one week paid vacation in each of three quarters of the year, one month in the fourth quarter, and six months every five years; or by some combination of these.[9] Each of these, if adopted alone, would almost exactly reduce the average work week from forty hours to thirty-two. One need think only a moment to visualize how differently these added amounts of leisure would be used and what effect they would have upon the user, his family, and the whole community. The range of alternative uses would become wider the larger the individual pieces of leisure.

From my viewpoint, increased daily leisure would be largely "wasted"; the recipient would use it, but his life would not be greatly enriched thereby, and at the end of a year, he would have a hard time recalling what he had done with it. Weekly leisure might be more effectively used, but this would run headlong into established patterns of life on the part of other members of the family—school children, especially. The longer weekends would surely be a major force toward living further from one's job, especially if one traveled a good deal anyway. If one were away from home a good bit anyway, and if he worked only four days a week, his family could live where they chose within a 200-mile or greater radius of his office; he could come in Monday (or Tuesday) morning, have his own living quarters in the city, and travel home again Thursday (or Friday) night. But increased leisure on an annual basis, and especially longer periods of leisure at longer intervals, would have much greater opportunities for travel, education, public service, and other activities as well as for sheer play. It, too, would surely have a major impact upon community activities and business. These issues are not simply academic or intellectual. Some labor unions are already pressing for shorter average or standard work weeks; many have successfully sought longer paid vacations. Pressure in these directions may remain relatively low, or it might increase sharply, under conditions (such as massive and persistent unemployment) where it would gain general public acceptance. We do not either condemn or endorse increased leisure or any particular form of it; what we are doing is pleading for careful consideration and rational decision, from a broad public or national viewpoint as well as from the interests of the individuals or groups directly involved.

One final point should be made: in the future, availability of time may be a more limiting factor on man's activities in the United States than will availability of income. The consensus of economic forecasters is for a rough doubling of real income per capita by 2000—more than $4,000 then compared with more than $2,000 now. This will mean family incomes, in terms of present prices, averaging $15,000 to $20,000—with, of course, many much higher as well as many lower. Whatever one means by "affluent society," this is surely nearer it than anything the world has known or knows today. Money will still limit activities, but time availability will increasingly enter as a limiting factor, as well as money, or instead of money. Economic growth can increase real income per individual, but it cannot add to total time and may increase demands on available time. We have long been concerned with national income—meaning national income as measured in money; should we not now become equally concerned with national time, measured as a resource and as the vital ingredient of life?

## NOTES

[1] G. Ott Romney, *Off the Job Living—A Modern Concept of Recreation and Its Place in the Postwar World* (New York: A. S. Barnes, 1945).

[2] Alfred C. Clarke, "Leisure and Occupational Prestige," *American Sociological Review* 21, no. 3 (June, 1956). Also reprinted in Eric Larrabee and Rolf Meyersohn, *Mass Leisure* (Glencoe, Ill.: Free Press, 1958).

[3] George D. Butler, *Introduction to Community Recreation*, 3rd ed. (New York: McGraw-Hill, 1959), Chap. 14.

[4] Mary A. Holman, "A National Time-Budget for the Year 2000," *Sociology and Social Research* 46, no. 1 (October, 1961).

[5] Hans H. Landsberg, Leonard L. Fischman, and Joseph L. Fisher, *Resources in America's Future* (Baltimore: The Johns Hopkins Press, 1963).

[6] Unpublished studies by the author.

[7] Lewis Mumford, *Technics and Civilization* (New York: Harcourt, Brace, 1934).

[8] Marion Clawson, *Statistics on Outdoor Recreation* (Washington, D.C.: Resources for the Future, 1958).

[9] This was outlined briefly in Marion Clawson, *The Dynamics of Park Demand* (New York: Regional Plan Association, 1960). See page 22, where my debt to Edgardo Contini, of Victor Green and Associates, is acknowledged.

CHAPTER

# 2

## OUTDOOR RECREATION AND MENTAL HEALTH
### Herbert J. Gans

Although social considerations are extremely difficult to quantify and incorporate into the management process, the recreation planner should at least be made aware of them. There is a very real danger that in the search for a better life something like outdoor recreation may be grasped as a balm for all social ills. This chapter by Herbert Gans warns us that there have been no reliable empirical studies of the relationship between outdoor recreation and mental health or illness and it raises many questions that remain unanswered as to the real social value of recreation.

## THE PROBLEM—AN HISTORICAL SURVEY

The overall topic of this essay is the relationship between outdoor recreation and mental health. Whether or not such a relationship exists is a question that has been discussed in America for many years, and some light can be shed on the answer by a brief consideration of the conditions under which the question was first raised.

The deliberate planning and development of outdoor recreation in America, at least in its cities, date back to the middle of the last century, when Frederick Law Olmsted began to call for the establishment of urban parks. Olmsted was the sickly son of a well-to-do Connecticut merchant, who was advised for health reasons to spend as much time outdoors as possible. After some years of farming, a trip to Europe stimulated his interest in landscape architecture, and for the rest of his life he designed and supervised the construction of city parks, beginning with New York's Central Park in 1857. His interest in parks developed at a time when cities of the eastern United States were growing by leaps and bounds, pushing back the rural areas beyond the reach of the city dwellers, especially the large majority who lived in tenements.

Olmsted was raised in a small New England town, and like a number of other reformers of the period he was horrified by the rapid expansion of

Reprinted from U.S. Outdoor Recreation Resources Review Commission, *Trends in American Living and Outdoor Recreation*, Study Report 22 (Washington, D.C.: U.S. Government Printing Office, 1962), pp. 233–42, by permission of the author. This article has been extensively edited for this volume and the notes renumbered.

urban slums. He was upset not only by the overcrowding and the poor quality of housing but also by the social and cultural patterns which he observed in the slums. Olmsted felt that these conditions were inevitable consequences of city living and argued that if city dwellers could only spend some of their leisure time outdoors, their existence would be more bearable. He conceived of parks as urban facsimiles of rural landscapes, which would provide "tranquility and rest to the mind." [1] Less sensitive and temperate observers than Olmsted described parks—and later, playgrounds as well as other forms of recreation—as veritable cure-alls which would isolate young people from and immunize them against the delinquency, alcoholism, prostitution, and crime that abounded in the slums. Many of the other phenomena which they described as evils we today would consider as fairly typical aspects of working-class and lower-class family and neighborhood life. However, these advocates of recreation had grown up in middle-class, small-town surroundings and could not accept alternative ways of living. Consequently, they tried to use outdoor recreation to convert the lower-class city dweller to the patterns of their culture.

Olmsted and the other advocates of outdoor recreation did not use the term "mental health," but their statements imply that the provision of outdoor recreation would lead directly to mental health. In later years, when the term mental health became popular, the virtues of outdoor recreation were reformulated in mental-health terms. The implied relationship between outdoor recreation and mental health was never seriously questioned, because the people who advocated outdoor recreation were so firmly convinced of the health-giving virtues of rural life and the desirability of defending rural and small-town America against the surge of immigrants that there was no need for evidence. The skeptic needed only to look at the slums of New York, Boston, or Philadelphia, in which trees, grass, and fresh air were rare indeed, while crime and mental illness flourished.

In our day, however, the answer to the old question is no longer self-evident, for the development of various forms of outdoor recreation has not done away with the traditional urban evils. This brief historical survey is not intended to suggest that the nineteenth-century answer to the question is necessarily wrong or that it was once correct but is now wrong, or that it was all a result of Olmsted's poor health. What I am saying is that the traditional answer was developed by a culturally narrow reform group which was reacting to a deplorable physical and social environment and rejected the coming of the urban-industrial society. As a result, it glorified the simple rural life and hoped to use outdoor recreation as a means of maintaining at least some vestiges of a traditional society and culture. Given these conditions and motivations, no one saw fit to investigate the relationship between outdoor recreation and mental health empirically.

## THE NATURE OF LEISURE AND RECREATION

Before it is possible to discuss the relationship of outdoor recreation and mental health, it is necessary to define some terms. Leisure and recreation can be defined in many ways; leisure is usually thought of as a temporal concept, denoting the time not given to work, maintenance, and sleep; recreation, as the behavior patterns which fill this time. I want to define the terms somewhat differently, relating them in a way that I think is useful not only for understanding the phenomena involved but also for policy-making purposes. By leisure or leisure behavior I mean the activity, or inactivity, which people pursue during their spare time. By recreation I mean the artifacts, facilities, and institutions which people employ for leisure behavior. Outdoor recreation is one such facility; the television set, arts and crafts, and the vacation resort are others. Some recreation facilities are provided by governmental agencies; these are usually thought of as public recreation. Others are provided by semipublic, private, or commercial agencies, and many if not most are purchased commercially, but used privately in or near the home.

Recreation is thus considered a means to leisure behavior. Leisure behavior is subjective, and leisure cannot be planned, or planned for. All that government and commercial agencies can do is to plan recreation facilities, with the intent, and hope, that they will be attractive enough for people to use them in leisure behavior.

This distinction is important for two reasons. First, it emphasizes the fact that the mere provision of outdoor recreation is not enough, for if recreation is not used, it does not provide the satisfactions of leisure. Second, it stresses a particular value judgment that one should not plan any person's leisure behavior. Leisure is satisfying and desirable only when it is chosen freely and spontaneously; for if it is not, it cannot be leisure. Conversely, recreation should be planned for deliberately.

## THE NATURE OF MENTAL HEALTH AND MENTAL ILLNESS

The concepts of mental health and mental illness are much more difficult to define than recreation or leisure. Mental health, or positive mental health, as it is sometimes called, is especially difficult to define, because any definition must include some vision of the good life and the good society, and there are many differences of opinion about the nature of both.

One of the thorniest problems is the evaluation of class differences. Many definitions of mental health employ a middle-class concept of the good life and the good society, implying therefore that the divergent ways of other classes, especially of the working class and the lower class, are pathological, rather than simply different. One way of resolving this dilemma, at least for me, is this definition: mental health is the ability of an individual as an occupier of social roles and as a personality to move toward the achievement of his vision of the good life and the good society.[2] Such a definition leaves room for cultural differences in the determination of the good life.[3] It also suggests that mental health is a social rather than an individual concept, because if society frustrates the movement toward the good life, the mental health of those involved may be affected.[4]

## LEISURE AND MENTAL HEALTH

It seems to me that the opportunity to obtain and the ability to indulge in satisfying leisure behavior are part of the good life, however that is defined by various American subcultures.

By satisfying leisure behavior I mean here the kind of activity that provides the individual with physical and emotional relaxation, reduction of fatigue, restoration of energy lost elsewhere, and general recreation without ill effects. I add this last phrase—without ill effects—to suggest two qualifications. First, I would not consider the destructive acts of a person bent on self-destruction as satisfying leisure behavior. Pathological gambling, heavy alcohol use, or high-speed auto racing under conditions of extreme risk may satisfy the seeker of self-destruction, but I would not consider his leisure behavior satisfying. I do not consider gambling, drinking, or even auto-racing as pathological recreation facilities, however, since they can also be used for satisfying leisure behavior. Second, socially destructive leisure behavior is also excluded from the definition of satisfying leisure behavior. Teen-agers may enjoy racing jalopies at high speed, even with much danger to themselves; but if they create driving hazards to others, their leisure behavior is antisocial. The determination of what is antisocial is not easy to make, and one must be careful not to surrender to the temptation of describing leisure behavior one does not like as antisocial, or for that matter, as bad for mental health. For example, use of the mass media and most forms of commercial entertainment has traditionally been considered undesirable by the advocates of outdoor recreation, but the available evidence does not indicate that normal use of these facilities is in any way antisocial or pathological.[5]

If satisfying leisure behavior as I have defined it is part of the good life, it would follow that it is also a constituent part of mental health. Therefore, the recreation facilities which help to make leisure satisfying are necessary for the achievement of mental health. . . .

## OUTDOOR RECREATION AND MENTAL HEALTH

My basic assumption . . . is that satisfying leisure behavior is a part of the good life and therefore a constituent part of mental health. Consequently, the recreation facilities which help to make leisure satisfying are necessary for mental health. However, I do not believe that recreation generally, or outdoor recreation specifically, can by itself bring about or materially aid in the bringing about of mental health, that it can cure or prevent mental illness, or that there are significant relations between outdoor recreation, physical fitness, and mental health.

The assumption behind these questions is that the mere act of being outdoors and participating in outdoor recreation can have a fundamental therapeutic effect on people and can resolve emotional and social problems that have developed at work or indoors. I have not seen any data that would lead me to suspect that this fundamental therapeutic effect exists.

Strenuous outdoor activity will engender physical fitness, but so will indoor activity in a gymnasium or a dance class. Moreover, whatever muscular or endocrinal effects physical exercise may have, and however much it may provide relaxation and a change from a sedentary routine, I doubt whether it can ever do more than bring about what the TV commercials call temporary relief of other problems. At best, it is a form of escape and, as such, good leisure behavior. Likewise, I do not think that being outdoors is responsible for whatever differences in stability and mental health exist between urban and rural people. If rural people are indeed mentally healthier, and I doubt this, I would imagine it to be due to other factors, such as the farmer's freedom and lack of occupational pressure. However, that would apply only to the family farmer, and if so, probably not to today's farmer, because changes in agriculture have made his existence problematic. It certainly would not be true of the migrant farm laborer.

The assumption which underlies these negative answers is that the outdoors and outdoor recreation cannot have any fundamental independent effect on people and that in order for outdoor recreation, or any other form of recreation, to have positive effects, there must be predispositions within the individual or the family toward these effects. In other words, outdoor recreation can provide satisfying leisure behavior if people are predisposed to enjoy such recreation.

The advocates of outdoor recreation have written voluminously and passionately about the joys of being outdoors, the gratifications that come with camping, hiking, the enjoyment of greenery, fresh air, and the communion with nature. They suggest that such activities produce something close to a religious experience, and presumably this leads to the belief that outdoor recreation can directly affect mental health.

I am sure that there are people for whom being outdoors provides very deeply felt emotional satisfactions, but I suspect that their outlook on life predisposes them to such intense feelings. I have known other people who derive similar benefits from walking through the streets of Manhattan, Paris, or Florence, and I have also known some people—residents of a densely populated urban tenement area in Boston—who, when taken out to Cape Cod by a settlement houseworker, were utterly bored and wanted to get back as quickly as possible to the physically and socially dense surroundings of their own neighborhood. They come from a culture which does not prepare them for being alone and for becoming immersed in nature, just as people who like to commune with nature come from a culture which rejects the hustle and bustle of urban-industrial society.

Those who cannot endure the physical beauties of the Cape Cod landscape and those who are really happy only out of doors are representatives of minority subcultures. For the large majority of Americans, participating in outdoor recreation is an enjoyable form of leisure behavior which provides a change of scenery, both physical and social, and offers an opportunity to relax, forget the daily routine, and explore new environments. This is due partly to the satisfactions that come from being outdoors and partly to the fact that most people get outdoors only during their leisure hours, whether evenings, weekends, or vacations. My studies in a suburban community suggest that the pleasures of being outdoors are as satisfying in a small backyard as they are in the majestic environment of a national-park landscape, although only systematic research would show if they are of equal intensity or duration. In any case, since being outdoors is identified with leisure time in American society, it is difficult to say to what extent the outdoors and to what extent predispositions toward leisure are responsible for the satisfactions to be derived from outdoor recreation. This topic, too, deserves systematic study.[6]

## SOME PLANNING AND POLICY IMPLICATIONS

I have argued that satisfying leisure behavior is necessary, but not sufficient, for mental health and that satisfying leisure behavior is best produced by making available those recreation facilities which will appeal to people's leisure predispositions, that is, their leisure preferences, anticipated and unanticipated, present and future. Insofar as recreation can aid in the maximization of mental health, this is best done by providing those recreation facilities that are in demand and that are likely to be in demand in the future. This means that recreation planning must adopt a user-oriented approach, to find out what its consumers want now and what they are likely to accept in the way of as yet untried facilities. The first is easily done, but the latter requires experiments with innovations in order to see whether or not they will be accepted. Also, like other reform-oriented agencies, recreation planners must restrain themselves from giving people what they clearly do not want, even though the planner may feel strongly that they should want what he wishes to provide.

Unfortunately, little is known about leisure behavior and leisure preferences, partly because the reform orientation discouraged any interest in studies of these subjects. The data gathered by the Outdoor Recreation Resources Review Commission in its "National Recreation Survey," [7] and the study "Participation in Outdoor Recreation" [8] are therefore of immense importance for future recreation planning—local, state, and regional as well as national—all over the country.

Let me conclude with a little speculation about contemporary leisure behavior trends and their implications for the planning of outdoor recreation. The speculation is based on a fairly exhaustive survey of user behavior and preference studies concerning public recreation.[9] From the little evidence that is available, it is clear that considerable changes have been taking place in leisure behavior in the post-World War II era. Not only have rising incomes and educational levels reduced total inactivity, but there has also been a reduction, if not in amount of time, then in the relative importance of indoor spectator activity. People still watch TV and go to the movies, but when time and money permit it, they make much greater use of outdoor facilities of all kinds.

Perhaps the most important such change has come as a result of the ability of the white working and lower-middle class to move to suburbia.

This has stimulated an interest in gardening on a large scale, and for many people this is an extremely important form of leisure behavior. Car ownership and the changes in working conditions that make it possible for almost everyone to take vacations also have important consequences for leisure behavior. Many people still spend their vacations at home, but an increasing number take to the road and participate in sightseeing, picnicking, swimming, boating, camping, and a variety of other activities that can be conducted by a family with a car. In the future these trends are likely to increase, creating further demand for open space and outdoor recreation facilities.

Proper recreation planning must concern itself not only with the amount but also with the kinds of open space and facilities that will be needed. Here again there is some conflict between the traditional prescriptions of the recreation movement and the demands of the users. Because open space was and still is considered as a substitute for the departed rural idyl, the advocates of open space and outdoor recreation have stressed the need for more urban, suburban, and regional parks and for wilderness areas suitable for hiking, camping, nature study, and the like. As I read the available studies of the use of open space, the demand for these facilities and activities is quite small. What most people seem to want most urgently is not communion with nature, but the opportunity for individual and family activity of a not too strenuous or too primitive nature which can be conducted outdoors. Close to home, they want beaches and swimming pools, picnic areas, zoos, and areas suitable for a Sunday afternoon drive. Almost every study which has interviewed people about leisure-activity preferences has shown that the most frequent demand, and the first mentioned, is for swimming facilities. As the work week is reduced and the opportunity for week-end trips increases, they will want even more of these facilities, as well as places where they can spend a couple of days outdoors. They will want resorts or large park areas where the majority can stay in comfortable motels or cabins and where the minority who want to rough it can camp out. Incidentally, more people will also want summer homes or cottages in mountain areas, or near bodies of water, thus putting heavy pressure on the use of such land for private development.

If my hunches about trends in user behavior are correct, the metropolitan areas of our country will need a much larger number of parks that provide for the kinds of activity I have mentioned. These parks must be located near man-made or natural bodies of water, and they should offer nature's beauty as well as some of the conveniences usually associated with resorts or vacation areas. Ideally, they should offer a variety of outdoor recreation, commercial entertainment, restaurants, cafés, museum and zoo facilities, as well as the features usually found in a park. In urban areas, small parks, playgrounds, and swimming pools are badly needed in the dense residential sections of our cities, especially in neighborhoods where low-income people live in apartments, without cars, and without either the time or money for trips and vacations. Conversely, there will be less need for the traditional kind of park in suburban areas, where gardens as well as private and public pools are available. Lewis Mumford and Leonard Duhl have also insisted on the need for more lover's lanes, and I concur with their recommendation. More areas for Sunday drives will be needed, either in or near the cities, but easily accessible, and without the traffic congestion that characterizes most such areas now.

The demand for national and state park acreage is already much greater than the supply, and more parks are obviously needed. If the use of such space follows present patterns, people will visit these areas for day trips and weekend outings, and if they are on vacation, they may stop over for a few days, perhaps as part of a longer trip to visit relatives or friends. Traffic studies show that the main attractions in these parks are famous landmarks, scenic drives, areas for swimming, picnicking, and fishing, and sites where families can camp out or stay at motels and cabins. We need to know much more than we do about how many people are likely to use such parks, how far they will drive to get to them for weekend trips and for longer vacations, and exactly what parts of the parks they will want to use most frequently and intensely.

The increase in vacation trips and reductions in the cost of travel will also create greater demands for commercial resort areas, such as Cape Cod, Atlantic City, or Miami Beach. These have traditionally been too costly except for the very rich, but this pattern is changing, and the very rich are escaping to various Caribbean islands and other areas outside the American continent. Commercial resort areas are popular because they combine the enjoyment of the outdoors with the glamour and excitement of the more urban entertainment facilities—and with comfort. Public recreation planning has traditionally scorned such resort areas, but as the demand for them increases significantly, they must be considered as open space to be planned for in conjunction with more public—and more pastoral—acreage. Incidentally, I suspect that in the future, outdoor recreation planning will also have to consider vacations that have a distinctively urban destination, that is, visits to such metropolises as New York, Chicago, San Francisco, and New Orleans. These offer historic and architectural attractions as well as entertainment facilities and a cosmopolitan atmosphere. They are likely to draw people who seek a temporary respite from the quiet life of the suburbs.

The use patterns I have speculated about differ considerably from emotionally quiet, physically active, and solitary use of parks, reservations, and wilderness areas that is recommended by the recreation movement. There will also be an increasing demand for the use of wilderness areas, but even so, it will be numerically modest in comparison to the demand for other kinds of outdoor recreation. This creates a real planning problem, which gets right at the heart of the difference between the reform-oriented and the user-oriented approaches. The advocates of wilderness areas have traditionally valued these areas because they are not overrun by people; they have placed higher priority on the land than on people. They have done so partly because they love such areas—and they are worth loving; partly because they feel there is a desire to save such areas from what they feel to be the negative influences of man-made forms, be they urban

22

settlements or private and public resort areas; partly because these areas are symbols of a pioneer era in American life with which they identify strongly; and partly because there is a need to conserve large land areas for future, and as yet unanticipated, recreation and agricultural requirements.

The planning problem is whether the value of conserving the wilderness for future generations is equal to the value to be gained by opening it up to higher-density recreation use now. Such a decision requires cost-benefit studies which measure the benefits of opening these areas for high-density use against the costs of giving up the wilderness.[10] These benefits and costs are not easy to measure or even to estimate, but without a systematic consideration, it is easy to make a wrong decision. One of the temptations is to fall back on the mystique that is associated with such areas and to argue that the "pure" pleasure of a few nature lovers is more desirable—and possibly more intense—than the irreverent, sometimes gaudy and seemingly less intense satisfactions of a large number of sightseers and campers. Intensity of pleasure is hard to measure, and often the reaction against higher-density use is simply a way of maintaining the areas for enjoyment by the reverent and more statusful few. Conversely, while decisions about use should be made on a democratic basis, planning only for present use commits scarce and irreplaceable resources for all time and deprives future generations of freedom of choice. Even so, I think planning for clearly established needs of today is more important than concern over needs unknown or needs hypothecated for the distant future. After all, we cannot know how future generations will spend their leisure hours, but we can know, and solve, the pressing problems of our own time.

Whether the planning concerns city parks or wilderness areas, the most desirable planning approach, both from a mental-health and a general welfare perspective, is one which seeks first to provide the various types of users with the facilities they now use and prefer. Afterward, there is also a challenge to develop new kinds of facilities and activities, to anticipate future wants, and to encourage people to develop new kinds of leisure behavior in years to come—including perhaps that quasireligious communion with nature and the productiveness which the advocates of outdoor recreation have recommended for so long.

## NOTES

[1] F. L. Olmsted, *Public Parks and the Enlargement of Towns* (Cambridge, Eng.: Riverside Press, 1870), p. 23.

[2] This definition owes much to Marie Jahoda, *Current Concepts of Positive Mental Health* (New York: Basic Books, 1958).

[3] The definition would have to be qualified to leave out self-destructive or socially destructive visions of the good life.

[4] It is true, however, that some people can adapt to such frustrations without overt ill effects, although this may be due as much to the availability of group supports as to individual personality configuration and strength.

[5] See for example, Joseph Klapper, *The Effects of Mass Communication* (Glencoe, Ill.: Free Press, 1960).

[6] This might be investigated by a study of the outdoor leisure behavior of people whose work is outdoors and requires considerable physical activity. Such a study might show that the leisure predisposition, rather than the environment, has the primary beneficial effects.

[7] Outdoor Recreation Resources Review Commission, *National Recreation Survey*, Study Report 19 (Washington, D.C.: U.S. Government Printing Office, 1962), prepared by the staff on the basis of data collected by the Bureau of the Census, U.S. Department of Commerce.

[8] Eva Mueller and Gerald Gurin, assisted by Margaret Wood, *Participation in Outdoor Recreation*, U.S. Outdoor Recreation Resources Review Commission, Study Report 20 (Washington, D.C.: U.S. Government Printing Office, 1962).

[9] See Herbert J. Gans, "Recreation Planning for Leisure Behavior," Chapter 3.

[10] For an attempt to develop such an approach, see *A User-Recreation Planning Method* (Loomis, Calif.: National Advisory Council on Regional Recreation Planning, 1959).

# 3

# URBAN GROWTH AND THE PLANNING OF OUTDOOR RECREATION

**Harvey S. Perloff**
**Lowdon Wingo, Jr.**

The field of outdoor recreation has been plagued by the lack of a useful conceptual framework for recreation planning and research. The chapter by Harvey Perloff and Lowdon Wingo provides such a framework. Although they profess to be concerned with the urban environment, the systems framework they suggest is a suitable one within which to organize all recreational planning and research, to determine the relevance of a particular study, or to suggest critical gaps in the existing literature and hence directions for further work. Systems thinking is a prerequisite to understanding outdoor recreation.

## INTRODUCTION

The future of outdoor recreation in the United States is closely bound up with the forces which are shaping our metropolitan civilization. Our material wealth proliferates; our genius for innovation augments our leisure; our numbers and our wants press upon the land; and in measure appropriate to these, our collective search for recreation intrudes itself among our major national purposes. New problems have emerged, some from the special requirements inherent in the nature of recreation, others from the changing characteristics of urban living—the concentration of people and activities in great urban regions, the spilling out of urban development over the land, the needs for psychic renewal generated by the tempo and environment of urban life. A special brand of tough-minded planning based on a new perspective of outdoor recreation and its interconnections with other important areas of national concern is called for.

What is the "problem" of outdoor recreation? It is something quite different today from what it was two generations ago when the main

Reprinted from U.S. Outdoor Recreation Resources Review Commission, *Trends in American Living and Outdoor Recreation*, Study Report 22 (Washington, D.C.: U.S. Government Printing Office, 1962): 81–100, by permission of the authors. This article has been extensively edited for this volume and the notes renumbered.

The authors wish to acknowledge a large debt to their colleagues at Resources for the Future, Inc., Irving K. Fox and Marion Clawson, for their helpful comments and criticisms.

concern of government was to secure for the public and posterity a magnificent endowment of irreplaceable landscape resources. This concern fathered not only the national parks system,[1] but also Chicago's Lake Front, San Francisco's Golden Gate Park, and the Charles River Park in Boston; it is manifest today in the political tug of war over the proposed Chesapeake and Ohio Canal Park along the Potomac River.

By contrast, today's problems do not center on the acquisition of the unique and dramatic resources for the public, but on the broad availability of outdoor recreation for enjoyment by everyone and often; nearby open areas for weekend visits by moderate-income urbanites are more characteristic of our recreation needs than the annual trip to a far away area of unforgettable beauty by the fortunate persons who can get there.

In one sense, the existence of the problem is a measure of the achievement of the material Utopia toward which Western civilization has been moving for two centuries. Freedom and wealth have made vast populations demanders after space, and sun, and air, and water, and the simple grandeur of nature, and we are increasingly conscious that the supply of things—brought together in a recreation environment—is painfully limited.

Future historians may find that the most enduring property of this metropolitan civilization is congestion—an increasingly awkward relationship between space in its many guises and our demands upon it. This is true of transportation and of buildings; it is no less true of outdoor recreation.

The central dilemma of outdoor recreation planning is how to ameliorate its special forms of congestion so that the regenerative qualities of nature in the open can be enjoyed without discrimination by those who possess the appetite for its rewards.

Planning for recreation is an extraordinarily difficult intellectual and political task. It would be demanding enough if we could concentrate our attention and our efforts on the building of recreation into a sensible scheme of environmental planning for the metropolitan region; here we would face all of the usual problems associated with the fragmentation of government in the metropolitan region and, expressly, with the lack of technique for broad-scaled, region-wide planning. But this parochial view is no longer tenable: in their search for opportunities for recreation, urban dwellers now travel across states with the same ease with which a generation ago they crossed counties. Geography is no barrier, and the demand for recreation spreads out across the national landscape from all of the urban regions. One dimension of affluence and leisure is mobility, and it is the mobility of the urban populations across the nation which elevates outdoor recreation to the status of an important national problem. The current picture of outdoor recreation as a national problem is one of unsatisfied demands and satiety side-by-side, of a capricious patchwork of facilities whose performance when measured against the needs of a great urban civilization is melancholy indeed.

How should a problem of this sort be tackled? Our experience has made it clear that the hallowed processes of planning by bits, spurts, and crises can achieve little. We need new tools not only to cope with the problems, but especially to expand and deepen our understanding of outdoor recreation as a systematic form of behavior in our society. One of these tools, which has come to be known as "systems analysis," [2] promises to throw some light on the kinds of problems which one encounters in recreation planning. In the pages that follow, we have tried to think through in a very general way how to apply a systems approach to the problems of outdoor recreation, in the hope of saying something useful about how planning for outdoor recreation might be improved. . . .

## The Big Issue in the Planning of Outdoor Recreation

Outdoor recreation has a number of inherent properties which make its planning very difficult: some are typical of the planning of any community service or facility;[3] others relate more to the character of regionwide services, such as drainage, water distribution, sewerage, and transportation; still others develop simply because of the differences in scope and complexity between planning for urban populations and the planning that goes on within the urban community. The difficulties encountered at each level tend to amplify the rest in a way that makes the planning of outdoor recreation a complex exercise indeed. . . .

The initial dilemma for the outdoor recreation planner is posed by the lack of guidelines for decisions. No market mechanism exists by which public preferences can direct the allocation of community resources into recreation, or among the various recreation alternatives. There is no more consumer sovereignty here than in public education or public health—if anything, there is probably less. He is thrown back on budgetmaking as the allocating mechanism—a political process where ultimately ballots rather than dollars vote. Political allocation is probably more egalitarian than the market—its decisions are not weighted by income distribution—but it can be so erratic and imprecise that the final allocation may be only a distorted parody of what the community wants and needs. Services depending on long-range public investments are especially sensitive to these imperfections, a circumstance which has been one of the most persuasive warrants for long-range comprehensive planning in urban areas. Given the prime objectives of all general governmental services, a basic investment program dimensioned over the long run can be laid out to permit political allocation against an orderly background of information and programs. The long-range comprehensive plan is essentially a device for organizing and ordering the investment claims upon the public purse without which political allocation can be largely a result of mere reaction to "squawk" and brute power.

However, the potentialities of long-range planning are currently not being realized. There are many reasons for this. One of the central reasons has to do with the manner in which city planning is handled. The relationship of comprehensive physical planning to the needs, wants, and demands of urban populations has always been a special issue for the city planner. But his actual scope has fallen far short of "comprehensiveness."

27

His responsibility has been partial in the sense that he has been expected to plan the physical facilities without having any role in specific functional programs. At best he can only assure that the capacity to produce a given output will be available. A tendency to exclude the variability of functional programs from his considerations has been a direct consequence of his separation from the operating end of the public services. Having, on the other hand, no direct mechanism, such as a market indication, to inform him about what people want has led him to make assumptions about objectives. This condition, in which he has only limited responsibility for the services produced and few direct and intimate links with what people want and need, has impelled him to rest his case on what people ought to want, such as the orderly, the efficient, the beautiful.

Now, however, we are beginning to understand that the performance of governmental programs can only be measured in terms of what people want of them. We are beginning to see public programs as behavioral systems—with key elements grounded in continually changing views of what is desirable and needed and with public pressures building up around what is available as against what is expected and aspired for—a constant back and forth flow of action and reaction. Such a viewpoint calls for particular kinds of information—the kinds of information which are rarely available at the present time. At the most general levels, the special frameworks of economists, sociologists, and psychologists are essential to identify the characteristics of behavior systems. At the level of data we need information of a special sort on the wants, needs, demands, behavioral patterns, and responses of the various population subgroups, since it follows that we are more likely to be concerned with program effectiveness than with simple concepts of efficiency. . . .

The freedom with which people move about the region in pursuit of outdoor recreation greatly complicates its planning: meeting recreation needs may begin with the urban community, but sooner or later the planning horizon must stretch far beyond the city limits. The effective production of a public service depends on a responsible relationship between the government producer and the private consumers. By these terms the modern metropolitan area—with its alkanized suburbs and its penchant for ignoring state boundaries—is in an impossible position. Nowhere is there lodged responsibility to cope with such transcendent needs of the region as transportation, water and sewerage, air pollution, and now, outdoor recreation. Numerous solutions have been experimented with, ranging from metropolitan government through special purpose authorities, and though such solutions may have had beneficent consequences for some kinds of metropolitanwide public services, there is no showing that the problem of outdoor recreation has proven amenable to these approaches. . . .

It is evident that outdoor recreation cannot be viewed purely as a local matter. The nature of the demands and the distribution of the resources virtually compel the local community to act irresponsibly with respect to the interests of the larger community. The real challenge is the design of a broad system of recreation facilities which will exploit each region's resources for outdoor recreation for the kinds of demands which will confront it. This involves overcoming jurisdictional barriers, but it also requires a clear view of the equities involved—if arbitrary restriction is to be struck down as a legitimate device, equal care must be taken to assure that the costs and deprivations are distributed in some rough correspondence to the benefits. Certainly the problem is not laid to rest merely by penetrating the jurisdictional barriers, but to penetrate them—or to rise above them—is an essential condition for the planning of outdoor recreation for the latter part of this century.

Thus, the planning of outdoor recreation involves problems which transcend even the difficult issues of modern city planning. Where the planning of urban services generally encounters its most severe difficulties, there also the planning of outdoor recreation will meet with special problems. However, the overcoming of these problems for city planning generally is no assurance of an effective recreation program. There are special problems which are unique to and innate in outdoor recreation as a human and social activity which must be overcome. The solution of the problems that it has in common with city planning is necessary, but it is not sufficient for an effective program of outdoor recreation services. The content of recreation behavior involves us in one of the most complex and difficult areas of public policy. Why this is so is suggested by a more detailed look at some of the demand and supply features of outdoor recreation.

The relationship of recreation users on the demand side to recreation resources on the supply side, as already noted, is anything but direct. Mobility is the hard fact in the problem of political jurisdiction, but it has a more important dimension, also. The geographical range of people pursuing their recreation inclinations is great and growing, not only because of more time and money but especially because new recreation appetites have been stimulated. A dozen years ago, for example, skindiving was the exclusive property of a small number of daring underwater explorers; in the seaboard cities today, one can purchase skindiving equipment in the better stocked drugstores. Certainly a crucial effect of mobility is its propensity to bring into range of the individual's curiosity new recreation alternatives and new experiences. The inverse of this, however, is that the clientele for any activity or facility tends to become more and more geographically diffuse.

Demand has another dimension also. The problem for the planner is not only how many people, as a case in point, propose to spend time camping this summer, but how many people propose to camp, for example, in Yosemite Park on July 4. The potential market for Yosemite's limited services is nationwide, and, depending on how millions of people make their vacation decisions, the demand on any one day can be crushing. So far, it seems that aggregate recreation behavior may be somewhat more unstable than most forms of consumption simply because the market is so vast, the alternatives have high degrees of substitutability for consumers, and fad, fashion, and the "snowball effect" can exert decisive effects at any one moment.

The increasing tenuousness of the relationship between the users and the providers of outdoor recreation facilities has special policy requirements. The great burdens which this vast and mobile demand for recreation opportunities can thrust upon unusually desirable resources and facilities immediately raise questions about how to ration them so that they can be used at a level which will still offer a valuable recreation experience to the user, and at the same time to protect them from the permanent damage or destruction which consistent overexploitation would impose. Under these circumstances there is always a danger that the rationing techniques will be injudicious—that they will be inordinate and so waste valuable services, that they will be discriminatory and leveled against groups whose needs are great, that they will be irresponsible and unresponsive to the needs of the larger community. The prospects for such behavior are sufficiently great to evidence a need for a new definition of public responsibilities in the field of outdoor recreation. An effective system of recreation will require a consistency of policy which current arrangements seem incapable of achieving.

One other complication needs to be recorded—the relationship between activities and facilities. If outdoor recreation were a basically uniform public service, such as the distribution of water or the provision of fire protection, it would involve a comparatively simple set of policy problems. Actually, what we call "outdoor recreation" is an extremely heterogeneous bundle of activities whose relationships to recreation facilities are likewise imprecise. The questionnaire used in the "National Recreation Survey" [4] lists some 23 activities ranging in generality from "playing outdoor games or sports" to "water-skiing," but in fact the list is almost endless. Some of these activities depend on very specialized facilities, such as "mountain climbing with gear" or skiing; others can be engaged in with facilities of a more general character. This complex and slippery relationship of facilities to activities is amplified by the fact that most users tend to be recreationally unspecialized; they may not only engage in any of a number of activities, but may substitute among these with considerable freedom. The technical characteristics of production among the services of outdoor recreation are complicated enough, but the characteristics of demand, given the extremely elastic behavior of a large fraction of the consumers, are even more complex. To plan a system of facilities around demands of this .sort will most certainly tax existing techniques and viewpoints to their limits.

Finally, space compounds the complex relationships between the demand for outdoor recreation services and the facilities supplying them. Facile substitution among kinds of facilities and among different kinds of recreation activities is complicated by the ease with which the consumer can make locational substitutions—another consequence of mobility. If facilities in one area are congested and unappealing, one can gain access to more desirable facilities in other areas. To the extent that facilities are easily accessible, high quality facilities are likely to experience excessive demands while lesser facilities go underutilized. The natural consequence of this is a really gigantic propensity for "peaking." How to satisfy this, or to rearrange it, is a strategic problem facing the planner.

For all of these reasons the long-range planning for outdoor recreation is extraordinarily difficult. Where it is comprehended in the planning of cities and metropolitan regions, it partakes of all of the main problems to which they are heir. Beyond this, the very nature of outdoor recreation itself as a form of individual and social behavior not only defies conventional policy approaches, but eludes conventional forms of analysis. A proper ordering of these issues would undoubtedly begin with repairing the deficiencies in the analytical framework, so that a probing of the main features of outdoor recreation quite properly follows.

## OUTDOOR RECREATION CONCEIVED IN "SYSTEMS" TERMS

All the difficulties described above, coupled with the evident shortcomings of the present approaches to planning outdoor recreation, argue the need for a new planning and policy framework—a system, if you will—which brings into perspective the recreation behavior of urban populations, the evolving needs and demands, and the requirements and potentialities on the supply side. Hopefully, such a systematic analysis and resynthesis will define some of the indispensable specifications for the planning of outdoor recreation. To carry out such a procedure requires that we specify the key elements and describe how they interact. If we can identify the casual relationships between the system and the environment-at-large which may affect the operation of the system, we can seek out interventions to achieve the kinds and levels of performance we want. Fully aware of all the pitfalls, we attempt here to suggest some central features of such a "systematic" approach to outdoor recreation. While some rather obvious things need to be included to describe the elements, there is a gain in trying to see the picture whole.

### The Elements: Recreation Publics, Activities, Facilities

The core elements of outdoor recreation can be viewed in terms of people—or more specifically, various recreation "populations"—the outdoor recreation activities in which they participate, and the inputs from the public sector—the facilities—which make their activities possible. In this context, people are seen as possessing characteristics which are associated with common features of their recreation behavior: populations can be broken down into groups, homogeneous in large degree, and exhibiting consistent recreation tendencies, or propensities. These recreation propensities are the basic links between populations and the outdoor recreation activities which are available to them. In fact, the demand at any moment for outdoor recreation—as a public service—can be construed as the summing of the recreation propensities of the population. Activities and outdoor recreation facilities are related by the degree to which the technological requirements of activities can be met by the characteristics of the facilities. Two steps, then, need to be taken: first, to investigate the nature of the elements of the system—population groups, outdoor recreation activities, and the facilities for outdoor recreation; then to explore the interactions among them.

*Population groups as elements.* Analysis of the total population in terms of reasonably consistent groups[5] can isolate the major variables in the system; "mix" effects can be distinguished from structural effects in the recreation behavior of large groups. We know, for example, that the recreation behavior of the wealthy is different from that of the poor, that the young engage in activities shunned by the elderly, that males enjoy uses of their leisure time having little appeal to females. Any shuffling of the proportions of rich and poor, young and old, male and female, will show up as changes in the aggregrate recreation behavior of the community, without anyone actually changing at all. On the other hand, some kinds of changes do result from alterations in the recreation patterns of large groups in the population; these are structural effects, which can be isolated by eliminating "mix" as the source of variation.

The first step, then, is to disaggregate the population into groups which are reasonably homogeneous by criteria discussed below. These outdoor recreation groups are the basic units of the system, and are so drawn as to exhaust the population: every member of any population will fall into one of the boxes. Under this condition any change in group behavior identified by the criteria can be described as a shift among outdoor recreation classes and structural changes are defined out of the problem. The prediction of recreation behavior is then achieved by the process of assigning the members of a population to the outdoor recreation groups through estimates (1) of the characteristics of the new population increments and (2) of the probabilities that individuals will shift among the outdoor recreation classes in the interim.

The classifying criteria must, of course, be significantly associated with recreation behavior, otherwise the reliability of the forecasts will be no greater than that associated with random choice. The predictive power of this framework, hence, depends on analysis of the factors dominant in the patterns of recreation behavior. Position in the life cycle, socioeconomic status, subjective preference patterns, and location appear to be the influential factors in recreation behavior although we would do well to keep our eye on a residual, or "all others" class of factors.

Certainly one's position in the family or life cycle has a substantial influence on the outdoor recreation activities in which he is likely to engage. Families with small children tend to exploit recreations in which all can jointly participate; young, single males are predisposed toward more active, more challenging, and perhaps more competitive activities; elderly retired couples frequently seek reasonably passive, but gregarious recreation activity. In this sense where one stands in life has an important effect in setting out the bounds within which recreation behavior is likely to take place.

Socioeconomic status is equally obvious as a variable in how people make choices about the use of leisure time.[6] This variable has a number of dimensions: an income effect is clearly distinguishable—rich people can simply afford more expensive forms of recreation than the less affluent; there is also a class effect—certain recreations have prestige associations which influence recreation behavior; education effects, leisure time effects, and a number of others are present, but these elements will tend to be strongly intercorrelated so that the broad differential of socioeconomic status has an importance of its own.

The subjective preference patterns of individuals are effective determinants, also. This includes all of those personal proclivities we refer to as tastes, ranging from inscrutable psychic predispositions to physical endowment. Personal history, especially of one's youth, conditions later uses of leisure. It is also a fact that one enjoys doing the things he does well, so that training and skills are big factors in personal preferences for outdoor recreation.

Location in its broadest sense has a special set of effects depending on the level of interest. At the regional level, uniquely local patterns in the use of leisure are apparent. To some extent they stem from tradition, but in greater degree from major differences in regional endowments—it is no accident that winter sports are more popular in New England than in the Southwest. At another level, the influence of location results from conditions of accessibility: location determines the time-and-money-costs of gaining access to facilities, a major factor in the total costs for some types of activity. Other important criteria could be used to disaggregate the population, but a set of outdoor recreation classes built on these criteria would go far toward a reliable framework with which to predict recreation behavior.

*Activities as elements.* The second set of elements is the broad array of outdoor recreation activities which people will pursue when opportunity permits. These reflect the output of any system of recreation, and so exhibit a significant difference between recreation and the other sectors of public production. Most public services are produced for instrumental reasons; they are actually intermediate inputs into other production processes. Fire protection and transportation systems are most certainly oriented to sustaining the complex of production activities in the community. Here the government is playing its role of investment in social overhead to improve the efficiency of the city as a vast productive plant. Another set of government products are not intermediates, but are enjoyed as final goods. Outdoor recreation, like education and cultural preoccupations, is an end product which is wanted, needed, and demanded for its own sake. Its consumers view it as a crucial ingredient in the total quality of life, as providing a tone to experience which infuses day-to-day living with a special individual quality. Outdoor recreation has as many forms and is as complex as human play and esthetic satisfaction are capable of being. This quality of diversity and complexity is essential to outdoor recreation, and needs to be kept central in plans and policies. To meet some concept of demand by pruning away the luxuriant opportunities for individualism generally inherent in recreation would be a spurious solution.

In the system we are describing, activities are the fulcrum which fixes the overall relationship of the recreation propensities of outdoor recreation groups to the array of facilities which are in different degrees available to users. They relate in specific ways to the behavior patterns of the outdoor recreation groups and each has certain requirements for the nature of the facilities that support it. To make these relationships clear, outdoor recreation activities can be classified by some specific criteria.

Skill requirements set apart some activities from others in signal fashion. Some make strong demands on the physique, skills, and experience of their devotees. Mountain climbing is an extreme example, but this is true of skiing and swimming also. Participation in (and demand for) such activities will be limited to those properly equipped to participate in them. Others require little of participants, such as picnicking or walking, and their potential demand is limited only by other factors. Certainly skill requirements do distinguish in an important way among these activities.

The role of group participation is a useful differential also. Some activities are basically solitary. Trout fishing is an excellent example; nothing is more superfluous than a second fisherman at a trout pool. Other activities invite joint enjoyment, and some—group games—positively require it.

Personal expenditure requirements are likewise significant in their variation among activities. At one extreme, yachting and polo require tremendous investments in the appropriate paraphernalia; at the other, walking and picnicking require virtually none.

Seasonal and climatic orientations differentiate among activities in ways that influence the distribution of demand throughout the year and among the regions. Winter sports and hunting are clear examples of seasonal specialization. Others, not directly limited by seasonal conditions, nevertheless tend to be modified by climatic conditions. Fewer people probably hike in winter than in summer, and open swimming and sunbathing are abandoned when temperatures are below 70 degrees.

Many activities are highly specialized in terms of the kinds of facilities they require, while others are quite undifferentiated in this respect. Hunting depends on an unimproved natural environment; pleasure boating requires the construction of marinas. Some activities can be enjoyed under conditions of extreme density, as in the intensive use of public beaches on hot summer days; others, such as hunting, are essentially space-extensive. Many activities have special resource requirements to be met by the native endowment of a facility. Mountain climbing needs mountains; but even hiking needs a natural endowment of topography, flora, and fauna to absorb and stimulate the hiker. Each activity has its own requirements which must be met by facilities before the activity can be carried out. The nature of these requirements is an important link between those activities which people are likely to want and those which can be provided.

Other features characterize the differences between outdoor facilities, but the ones set forth have the virtue of being highly selective in terms of who participates, when, where, and how much. These activity classes have the role in the system of linking the demand side of the picture—populations, outdoor recreation groups, and their recreation propensities—to the supply side, consisting of the array of facilities which public policy provides.

*Facilities as elements.* From the policy point of view, facilities for outdoor recreation have several key characteristics which influence the manner in which the system operates. A facility may be highly specialized in use, so that one, or at best, a few activities can be carried on in it. Unspecialized facilities permit several activities to be enjoyed concurrently by different users, where the activities are themselves unspecialized. A facility may be "multiple-purpose" in the sense that it is arranged to permit a number of specialized and unspecialized activities to be carried on simultaneously. The facility can be viewed as an intermediate product in the production of outdoor recreation services, which are consumed when the facility is used. Since the technology of this product is an essential feature of the system, it is useful to examine the nature of the inputs.

The concept of land is too gross for our concern, because two aspects of land have unique consequences for the use of facilities: space, in a simple geometric sense, and the resource endowment that goes with it. Space as the effective quantity of the land input frequently involves some complex dimensions: length more than area is important in the recreation capacity of a public beach, and similarly, of streams for canoeing and fishing; unobstructed area is crucial for space-extensive games, and other spatial features may influence the way in which we measure the input of space into a facility. Whatever the resource endowment of the facility, however, simple area has an important relationship to capacity for most activities. Resource endowment—all of those features which especially suit an area for specific kinds of outdoor recreation—is the qualitative dimension of the space input. Scenic qualities, availability of bodies of water, or of game and fish, all relate to activities for which the land might be used.

A second type of input embraces capital investment in improvements. Capital inputs have special significance for facilities which are not highly endowed with natural resources and for those adapted to some highly specialized recreation activities. Cities have, on occasion, developed parks from old sanitary fills with heavy expenditures for compacting, topsoil, and landscaping, for example, and so have substituted capital for deficient endowment. Golf courses are highly specialized facilities involving a substantial investment in reshaping the topography, in landscaping, and in the special installations which the sport requires. Capital investment frequently substitutes for space where land prices are high: Chicago reclaimed much of its recreation lakefront from Lake Michigan at great cost, for example. Finally, capital is often used to increase the intensity with which parks of high demand or limited area can be used. In general, investment in recreation capital has the effect of increasing the degree of specialization of a facility, and may involve a wide range of projects from hiking trails to artificial lakes.

Although location does not fit the role of an input, it is so critical a factor affecting the ability of a facility to produce services valued by a recreation clientele that its omission here would leave the analysis incomplete. The primary effect of location (or accessibility) is exhibited in the intensity with which a facility is used. In the following section, we examine the special role of location in greater detail.

## The Interactions among the Elements: The System at Work

A systems-analysis approach to a problem requires a focus on the relationships which connect the elements of the system and which are the pathways by which changes are communicated among the elements. Effective public policy must work its purposes through these relationships. If the problem is seen to be one of relating a set of demand conditions to a set of supply conditions, these interactions stand in the place of the market. If the problem is basically construed as a matter of minimum standards of welfare, the interactions are the mechanism by which such an objective must be achieved. Both views might, of course, be applied.

The outstanding feature of a system is the interdependence of its parts, and interdependence is abundantly apparent in the complex array of outdoor recreation demands, activities, and facilities across the nation. This can best be seen in terms of the spatial features of the interactions. The demand for Yosemite's extraordinary services begins in Boston, Little Rock, Sioux Falls, and Coeur d'Alene just as effectively as in Los Angeles or San Francisco, and when urban Californians preempt its services for their local recreations, they clearly do so at the expense of its ability to serve the vacationing Bostonian. In the same way in which the national economy can be described and analyzed in terms of its subnational parts, so the total production and consumption of the services of outdoor recreation in the various parts of the nation constitute a unitary system whose facilities extend from the great western national parks down to the local park systems in the cities. The thread which knits this system together is the demand of recreation[7]—its magnitude, its mobility, its variety.

If this is—as is suggested here—a vast, interdependent behavioral system, there are some rather revolutionary implications for public policy in outdoor recreation. In the first place, substantial elements of the demand for local facilities may actually arise outside of the community—a large proportion of local recreation services may actually be exported. Then, because of the leakages to the rest of the system, local recreation objectives may be very difficult to achieve. But the obverse is true also; parts of the system outside of the community may absorb so much of the local demand for outdoor recreation that a modest local program might easily meet the unsatisfied wants in the community. The central conclusion is unavoidable —the performance of any local outdoor recreation program is strongly conditioned by the performance of the total system of outdoor recreation. How this system works and how performance levels evolve and change require some exploration before planning and policy requirements can take form.

*Location, intensity of use, and quality in outdoor recreation.* People engaging in outdoor recreation use space. How much they use—and what kind—depends on the characteristics of the specific activity. Picnickers use a small area around a table or fireplace; hikers occupy that much of a trail which permits comfortable walking; hunters preempt virtually all of the area within easy range of their weapons. In addition, the space actually used is surrounded by a penumbra of space which, varying with the activity and the user, plays an important role in the evaluation of the recreation experience. At one end of the scale the amount of space may be so restricted that the conduct of the activity and the value of the recreation experience are seriously impaired; at the other the marginal value of additional space to the user for the activity is negligible. Family picnicking may be a frustrating experience if strangers are similarly picnicking ten feet away, yet a family exclusively occupying an acre of ground for its picnic would probably not value an additional acre very highly. At some point within this penumbra of accessory space a point exists where the quality of the experience will begin to decline very rapidly with any further reduction in the amount of space available to the user for the activity in which he is engaged. The relationship of this point to the core, or minimum, space requirements varies greatly among activities and among individuals; nevertheless, its existence is the crucial fact, suggesting a positive relationship between the quality of the recreation experience and the amount of space—within these limits. Further, since the amount of space per unit is the reciprocal of density, the relationship between the density of use of a facility and the quality of the individual experience is negative within these limits: as the number of persons using the facility at any one time increases, at some point the quality of the "product"—the recreation experience—will begin to decline very rapidly. This is the congestion effect in outdoor recreation—a key factor in the performance of the system and its parts.

Density—the number of users employing a facility for a given activity simultaneously—is related to the broader concept of intensity of use. A high intensity of use is associated with a high volume of demand; a high density of use is associated with the peaking characteristics of demand as measured by "load factor," the ratio of average to maximum demand. Density and intensity are loosely related; neither necessarily implies the other, but in reality the characteristics of demand for most activities are such that little violence is done to truth to assume that high intensity implies high density.

Intensity is introduced here because of its relationship to a more general concept of demand, and our objective at this point is to indicate the manner in which demand, the nature of the facility, and performance are

37

intimately interrelated. Two characteristics of a facility determine its level of output: the first involves the kinds of services which a facility is equipped to produce, such as canoeing, hiking, and swimming. A double-pronged effect is apparent here. The space requirements, capital investment, and natural endowment establish a set of capacities for the facility (where capacity is anchored to the concept of minimum space requirements for an activity). Then, this output addresses a specific market, a group of users whose recreation propensities can be served by it. The nature of the product, in short, identifies the output in its quantitative and qualitative terms.

The second dimension is embraced by the concept of location—where the facilities are located with respect to their consuming publics. Location affects the performance of a facility because distance influences the recreation decisions of the consumer. Normally, a consumer will use a given facility at a rate related to its distance from his home: the more remote it is, the less he will tend to use it. Or, given several comparable facilities, all other things being equal, he will use the nearer more frequently than—or to the exclusion of—the more remote.

Although these relationships seem simple and straightforward, they are actually quite complex in practice. Distance is the prime barrier to the consumption of outdoor recreation services, many of which are free goods in situ. In order to enjoy these services, the user must overcome this barrier; he must transport himself to the facility, and this involves him in cost calculations. It not only costs money to make the trip to the facility and return, but it takes time. Since his supply of both is not unlimited, he must always measure the satisfaction of the anticipated experience against the values of other experiences which alternative uses of his time and money would have made possible. In short, distance is a measure of the dominant private costs confronting the consumer of outdoor recreation services. Transportation costs are not necessarily the only costs to a user of a given activity, but they do distinguish between the facilities producing the activities in an important way—particularly when the key element of time is weighed in the balance.

If all of the persons demanding the services pertinent to an activity can be accommodated at the near facility at a density consistent with an unimpaired satisfaction from the experience, the other facilities may not be used at all. The case is more likely however, that the capacity of the facility or the volume of demand would result in congestion—i.e., densities at which the quality of the service is substantially impaired. For any user there will be a point in the decline of the quality of the experience where its value to him will be less than the private costs, or opportunity costs, of realizing the experience. When this happens he will cease to be a demander.

The preceding case will hold only in the absence of effectively competing facilities. Where alternative, if more remote facilities are available, the user will tolerate the decline in quality only to the point where the value of the differential in quality between the nearest and the next nearest is equal to or greater than the increment in the distance costs associated with the more remote of the two. For any number of facilities located in specific ways with respect to a market or clientele, this relationship will hold. Thus, given the nature of the demand side of the market for an activity, as well as the number, sizes, and locations of facilities producing the relevant services, there is an equilibrium distribution of users among the facilities such that the quality of the service at any facility is valued by the user at the private costs associated with it. If all users valued the quality of service in the same way, and had common sets of private costs, there would be no economic problem, and where the number of users exceeded the capacity constraints some form of rationing would be required. As is more realistically the case, private costs vary tremendously, and uniformity in the manner in which people appraise and evaluate quality in the recreation experience is an untenable assumption. The aggregate of demand is a summation across a mix of demanders who vary with respect to the private costs of the experience and quality valuation, so that, although the equilibrium condition is pertinent, it is also subject to the nature of the demand "mix."

The simple case of uniform facilities and a single activity does not really restrict the system, for the conclusions are easily expanded into the whole system by the competition among activities for space among the facilities—especially in the long run—and by the ease of substitution among activities which characterizes the consumer. It is true that some activities have very tenuous interconnections in the system—the demand for participation in polo probably has very little impact on the system—but these are at the margin of the problem and need not concern us greatly.

The central conclusion here is that all outdoor recreation facilities are tied together in a system in which changes, general or localized, tend to have impacts on many or all of the other facilities in the system. In the short run, the expansion of one facility will set in motion a wavelike set of impacts in the system. In the first instance, those facilities for which it is an easy substitute will experience a reduction in the intensity with which they are used, or, obversely, an appreciation of the quality of the services produced. In the second instance, more remote facilities which are easy substitutes for the first set will have the same experience, and in this fashion the effects of the change are propagated throughout the system. There is a qualification of this process, since it assumes that all facilities operate within congestion ranges initially: the rise in quality of the services at the one location induces an appropriate consumer response. Where the quality of service is not materially affected by the expansion, no consumer can materially improve his position by changing the place at which he consumes his services and the impact is dampened, or even totally absorbed by the excess capacity.

These then are some of the central economic characteristics of the system of outdoor recreation. It consists of facilities which produce the services of outdoor recreation, services whose quality declines (or whose implicit prices rise) with increasing density, and hence with intensity. These facilities turn out specific products at given locations. Further, the system includes a set of consumers with propensities to engage in certain kinds of recreation, budgets in both money and time, knowledge of alternatives, and an inclination to act rationally to maximize their net satisfactions. The location of all of the facilities and the residential locations of the users determine the distance costs, which relate the behavior of the consumers to the nature of the products of the various parts of the system. The scale of consumer behavior here is dominated by the severe peaking of demand and the extremely low load factors.[8]

The policy problem now becomes somewhat simpler in the overall. The government is the producer of a service which it may not always care to price, but generally prefers to offer as a free good. However, the use of the service carries with it private costs which exert something of a price effect on the behavior of the consumer. How can an investment-allocating mechanism be constructed for such a system?

*The nature of consumer demand for outdoor recreation.* Since it is the behavior of consumers which powers the system, some of its main features are worth exploring for a clearer picture of how this behavior is likely to change in response to external developments and especially to changes elsewhere in the system, such as those induced by changes in public policy. Demand in the economic sense refers to the manner in which people in an aggregate will use their resources to satisfy their subjective preferences. . . .

The peculiarity, then, of outdoor recreation as a province of economics is that the consumer must engage in "double-budget" calculations; he must spend a time-income and a money-income, the size of which is determined by the wage bargain. There are, accordingly, private costs associated with every form of recreation, no matter how free it is in money terms; at the very least an activity "costs" the amount of time necessary to engage in it. This peculiarity produces some special characteristics in individual demand. At one extreme, one may have a very large money-income and a very limited amount of leisure time to allocate, so that the real constraint on his demand is the availability of time; at the other, an unemployed laborer may well have a large leisure-time-income, but virtually no money-income, so that his consumption possibilities among outdoor recreations are limited by the amount of money he can afford to spend. When one sums up these possibilities across the population, the aggregate demand for outdoor recreation will have its own dynamics compared to other demand sectors, and will tend to respond to secular changes in the economy in a quite different way. . . .

The accounting framework has provided an indispensable technique for assembling and organizing our information about the money economy, and it seems clear that for purposes of outdoor recreation it needs to be expanded to take into consideration the "time economy." We not only need information about how many people will have incomes between, say, $5,000 and $10,000 per year at any given time, but the distribution of leisure incomes within this class and how each is arranged in time. In its simplest form, this accounting system might take the form of a set of boxes organized by income class along one axis and by "leisure class" along the other. Each box would contain the number of consuming units, or users, within that income and leisure class. Summed across one axis the accounts would produce income distribution; summed the other way, the distribution of leisure. Because the accounts are exhaustive, it will require all changes to be completely accounted for—there are no leaks in the data system. . . .

We now have before us the operating characteristics of the system of outdoor recreation. Turning toward the facilities, or the supply side of the system, we observe that the quality of the services and the intensity with which a facility is used are closely linked together and these, in turn, are linked to the accessibility characteristics of the facility. The demand side is built on the significance of time as a cost dimension, and on access costs as the parameters integrating supply and demand. . . .

## Guidelines for Planning and Policy

A soaring demand for leisure time activities and the systemic character of outdoor recreation are the dominant ingredients of this new challenge to the ingenuity of planners and decisionmakers at every level of government. By the criteria of our social wants the invisible hand of the market is a defective guide; short-run political decisionmaking, however, too frequently disregards critical interdependencies so that policy is dissipated in execution or vitiated by side effects so negative that sought after social benefits are swallowed up by uncounted social costs. What is needed then is a carefully designed process for planning the development of the outdoor recreation system which can meet these tests:

1. It must perform a market-type function of investing the consumer with a more effective sovereignty over the allocation of the resources that go into the system;

2. It must equip the system with a mechanism to assure the realization of the appropriate social benefits; and

3. It must exploit fully the internal interdependencies of the system as well as its interconnections with other sectors of public and private activity.

In the final section of this essay we set down some tentative suggestions on the type of approach which might be appropriate for the development and performance of such a process.

The most conspicuous issue emerges from the very nature of the growing demand, its scope, and its origins. The rate of growth is truly remarkable, and it takes its basic character from the processes of urbanization which gave it birth. Contrast these considerations with a public policy in outdoor recreation which has been distinguished by a preoccupation with the natural resources of the landscape to the extent that the development and distribution of the elements of this system bear only a fortuitous relationship to the geography of demand. This bias has by implication chosen the kinds of activities to be supported and the publics to be served without admitting the proliferating demand and the pressing social needs to any primacy in the setting of objectives and in the choice of means; policy formulations which begin—and frequently end—with the delimitation of areas of extraordinary landscape qualities are from the very beginning ill-adapted to serve any concept of popular recreation needs. Measured against demands and needs of urban populations these resources are generally in pitifully short supply; furthermore, the intensity at which they are used frequently requires regulation to avoid ecological damage to the resource itself.

The dimensions and character of demand strongly assert the need to shift our basic policy in outdoor recreation away from its excessive emphasis on resource-based activities and in the direction of a dominant role for user-oriented forms of recreation. The evolving need is not so much for more Yosemites, Grand Canyons, and Okefenokees as it is for millions of acres of just plain space endowed in many cases with only perhaps modest landscape and topographical interest, but richly and imaginatively developed—this is the basic shift in approach that is called for by the logic of the present-day situation. Without this, it is hard to see how outdoor recreation facilities are to withstand the deluge of demand building up in our cities. Conserve our national recreation and landscape resources, yes; but do not confuse this conservation objective with the powerful objective of meeting the recreation needs of the nation. What is needed is a new strategy for recreation policy which is urban-oriented—that is, oriented toward serving the great majority of the national population—in its articulation with urban needs, developmental in its constantly improving levels of performance, and carefully integrated with the whole array of public activities which afford a joint payoff for the production of recreation services. . . .

In short, the emphasis of an urban-oriented system of recreation rests heavily upon an extensive supply of space permanently located within comparatively easy access of its market.[9] It requires policy coordination among such urban functions as transportation and open space programs. Finally, it requires institutional devices and information flows to permit a continuing adjustment of the supply of recreation opportunities to the changing dimensions of demand.

That a recreation program should be developmental is merely another way of saying that it should have some special dynamic qualities. In the first place, it must be capable of responding smoothly to changes in demand. As the region grows, so should the capacity of the system; as the mix of outdoor recreation groups undergoes alteration, so should the system permit the fulfillment of new demands and wants. As there is no ceiling on the absorption of education, of spiritual self-fulfillment, or culture, so recreation needs ever expanding horizons if it is to serve its humanizing function well. Hence, such a system should be developmental in the sense that it attains progressively higher levels of performance and proliferates the kinds of recreation opportunities available to all groups within the region. . . .

The nature of the national system of outdoor recreation imposes responsibility on government at all levels to respond to this general problem in a large-scale, integrated way. Mechanisms by which consumers can register their wants, by which consumer horizons can be expanded and enriched, by which the government, with its sights fixed on longrun developmental goals, can respond sensitively and smoothly to changes in user demands need to be developed. It is not sufficient, however, for the public to key its programs solely to tracking demand. It must more and more take on the creative role of being an imaginative risk taker along the whole developmental front of outdoor recreation; failing this, our system of facilities a generation from now could consist almost exclusively of scenic views from highways, 60 million picnic facilities and campgrounds, and very little else. In short, the institutions which we need must have a dual capacity of informing themselves about—and responding to—what people want and need, and of building into their programs an increasingly rich array of opportunities for recreation diversification and individuation. . . .

## NOTES

[1] Cf. John Ise, *Our National Park Policy* (Baltimore: Johns Hopkins Press, 1961).

[2] A concise description of systems analysis and its role in decisionmaking can be found in the National Academy of Sciences-National Research Council, *Conference on Transportation Research* Publication 840, Washington, D.C. (1960), pp. 61–63. Our "systems approach" seeks to identify the strategic relationships, not to quantify them. It is the logical exercise which must precede systems analysis.

[3] See especially Herbert J. Gans, "Recreation Planning for Leisure Behavior: A Goal-Oriented Approach," unpublished Ph.D. dissertation, University of Pennsylvania, 1957. Gans's dissertation is possibly the most thoroughgoing study of the role of public policy in the production of public recreation services. Although it centers on recreation as a problem for the city planner, its insights have illuminated many aspects of the role and responsibility of government in the provision of recreation services.

[4] U.S. Outdoor Recreation Resources Review Commission, *National Recreation Survey,* Study Report 19 (Washington, D.C.: U.S. Government Printing Office, 1962), prepared by the Commission staff on the basis of data collected by the Bureau of the Census (Form Rec. IV-4).

[5] One approach to the analysis of demand by characterizing "user groups" is described in National Advisory Council on Regional Recreation Planning, *A User-Resource Recreation Planning Method* (Loomis, Calif.: National Advisory Council on Regional Recreation Planning, 1959).

[6] See especially Eva Mueller and Gerald Gurin, assisted by Margaret Wood, *Participation in Outdoor Recreation: Factors Affecting Demand among American Adults*, U.S. Outdoor Recreation Resources Review Commission Study Report 20 (Washington, D.C.: U.S. Government Printing Office, 1962).

[7] Marion Clawson has pioneered in the development of demand analysis in outdoor recreation in his *Methods of Measuring the Demand for and Value of Outdoor Recreation,* Reprint no. 10 (Washington, D.C.: Resources for the Future, 1959).

[8] Load factor: The ratio of average demand for all periods to peak period demand.

[9] For the New York metropolitan region alone in 1985, and by conservative standards, it is estimated that 1,100 square miles of permanent open space will be needed to add to the existing 600 square miles, the total of which comprises 25 percent of the region's total land area. See Regional Plan Association, *The Race for Open Space* (New York: Regional Plan Association, 1960), p. 9, Table 1.

# FURTHER READING

## Leisure and Recreation: Social Values and Approaches

Davis, L. S., and W. R. Bentley, "The Separation of Facts and Values in Resource Policy Analysis," *Journal of Forestry* 65, no. 9 (September, 1967): 612–21.

Doell, C. E., *Elements of Park and Recreation Administration* (Minneapolis: Burgess, 1963).

Driver, B. L., ed., *Elements of Outdoor Recreation Planning* (Ann Arbor, Mich.: University Microfilms, 1968).

Dunn, E. S., Jr., *Economic and Social Development: A Process of Social Learning* (Baltimore: Johns Hopkins Press, 1971).

Loy, J. W., and G. S. Kenyon, *Sport, Culture and Society* (New York: Macmillan, 1969).

Perloff, H. S., ed., *The Quality of the Urban Environment* (Baltimore: Johns Hopkins Press, 1969).

*Recreation Research* (New York: National Recreation and Park Association, 1966).

U.S. Department of Agriculture, Northeastern Forest Experiment Station, *Recreation Symposium Proceedings 1971* (Washington, D.C.: U.S. Government Printing Office, 1971).

*U.S. Outdoor Recreation Resources Review Commission Reports* (Washington, D.C.: U.S. Government Printing Office, 1962).

Study Reports:

3. *Wilderness and Recreation—A Report on Resources, Values and Problems.*

5. *The Quality of Outdoor Recreation: As Evidenced by User Satisfaction.*

10. *Water for Recreation—Values and Opportunities.*

19. *National Recreation Survey.*

20. *Participation in Outdoor Recreation: Factors Affecting Demand Amongst American Adults.*

21. *The Future of Outdoor Recreation in Metropolitan Regions of the United States.*

22. *Trends in American Living and Outdoor Recreation.*

23. *Projections to the Year 1976 and 2000: Economic Growth, Population, Labour Force and Leisure, and Transportation.*

26. *Prospective Demand for Outdoor Recreation.*

27. *Outdoor Recreation Literature: A Survey.*

Whyte, W. H., *The Last Landscape* (New York: Doubleday, 1968).

# Part Two
PATTERNS OF
RECREATIONAL
RESOURCE USE

## PREFACE

The development and use of recreational resources in both urban and rural areas is, in part, a function of accessibility. Increases in disposable income and leisure time, together with improvements in technology, have resulted in greater mobility for the recreationist. Recreational travel has itself become an important form of recreation. As a result, greater attention is being devoted to the provision of quality transportation modes and related facilities as well as to the provision of recreational resources. Transportation for different types of activities and locations varies considerably. The most common form of transportation required is for travel to and from the recreation site. In many cases there are specific demands for on-site transportation as well.

Good accessibility and suitable transportation facilities have several implications for the planner and manager of recreation facilities and resources. He must recognize that access will influence the level of use a particular recreation resource will receive. By understanding this, the recreation planner can encourage or discourage the use of a particular resource. For example, the decision of where to locate a park in relation to an urban center would be better made if the recreation planner knew the travel patterns of the urban inhabitants.

Other implications of recreational travel for the recreation planner and resource manager relate specifically to the travel experience. Since driving and touring attract many individuals, it is important that consideration be given to the location, design, and management of roads so that the scenic and cultural features of the adjacent landscape can be experienced and enjoyed.

The objective of this Part is to outline some of the concepts and methods used in analyzing the patterns of recreational travel and resource use. Although Part Two concentrates on explaining the existing patterns and flows of recreationists, the reader should be aware of the implications for the future development of recreation facilities and opportunities.

# 4

# RECREATIONAL TRAVEL: A REVIEW AND PILOT STUDY
## Bryan Thompson

This chapter by Bryan Thompson is an excellent introduction to the importance of determining travel patterns of recreationists. He uses the traditional method of the gravity model to determine why individuals in Ontario travel to certain parks within the provincial parks system.

This paper has a dual purpose: first, to examine the methods that have been used for analyzing patterns of recreational travel, and second, to conduct a pilot study to examine the flow of campers to a sample of Ontario provincial parks.

The models examined are the gravity model, the intervening opportunities model, and the systems theory model. Basically, although there are many variations, the gravity model relates recreational travel to population, attractiveness of the recreational area, and distance (or time). The intervening opportunities model assumes that the traffic generated between a population area and a recreational area is directly related to the number of opportunities closer (in travel time) to the population area than the recreation area. The last model, the systems model, uses theory borrowed from the electrical engineering literature.

Data obtained from a sample survey by the Ontario Department of Lands and Forests were used for analyzing recreational travel patterns to a sample of Ontario parks. The assumption was that camper traffic flow is related to city population ($P$), city-park distance ($D$), and park capacity ($C$) as indicated by the number of campsites. The Department of Highways IBM 7040 Computer was used to calculate the exponents for $P$, $C$, and $D$. A number of tentative conclusions are drawn from an evaluation of the residuals. These conclusions relate to park location, park size, spacing of parks, and the size and socioeconomic structure of cities. Limitations of and suggested refinements in the gravity model are outlined, along with suggestions for experimentation with the intervening opportunities approach and the systems theory approach.

The paper concludes by emphasizing the need for creating and preserving a recreational environment possessing quality.

Man spends his leisure time in many ways. One of the most popular

Reprinted from "Recreational Travel: A Review and Pilot Study," *Traffic Quarterly* (October, 1967): 527–42, by permission of the *Traffic Quarterly* of the Eno Foundation for Transportation Inc. and the author.

forms involves participation in various types of outdoor recreation. Unquestionably the demand for outdoor recreational facilities will increase as an expanding population enjoys more leisure time while becoming more affluent and more mobile.

The recreational component of vehicular flow has grown enormously over the last fifteen years in Canada, and the jammed roads leading out of and into the Metropolitan Toronto area on a summer weekend attest this fact. One form of outdoor recreation is camping, and this increase in recreational traffic flow has brought with it a commensurate increase in the demand for camping facilities. To meet this demand, the Parks Branch of the Ontario Government has developed numerous parks throughout the Province (91 in 1965), to accommodate day-visitor trips, and short- and long-term camping trips. Viewed from the standpoint of a highway department, these parks generate traffic flows which must somehow be incorporated into the highway system. In matters of highway planning, the ability to predict these flows with some degree of confidence is desirable. Further to this, research is needed to provide definitive answers to the following basic questions. How does the demand for recreation at a particular park decrease as distance from the park increases? How can the attraction of a park be evaluated? What socioeconomic factors affect recreational travel habits? When answers to the preceding questions are forthcoming, highway officials will be in a better position to improve existing roads, plan new roads, and locate new parks.

One purpose of this paper is to review some of the techniques that have been used for analyzing recreational travel. A second purpose is to examine one form of recreational travel, that of campers to Ontario provincial parks, and to develop an exploratory and simplified model for simulating the flow of campers between the major centers of population and a sample of Ontario parks.

## GRAVITY MODEL

The gravity model has been used successfully for predicting travel between two areas.[1] This model, an analogue of Newton's Law of Gravity, states that the trip volume between area $i$ and area $j$ can be expressed as:

$$Tij = KP_iP_jD_{ij}{}^x$$

where $Tij$ = the number of people traveling between area $i$ and area $j$
   $Pi$  = population of area $i$
   $Pj$  = population of area $j$
   $Dij$ = the distance between area $i$ and area $j$
   $K$ and $x$ are constants

Volk used the gravity model in his analysis of travel to national parks in the United States.[2] To measure the effect of distance, he computed the per capita visits from each state to each park and plotted the results against distance to the park on a log-log scale.[3] This relationship showed that factors other than distance influence the degree of participation in outdoor recreation.[4] Volk went on to use a multiple regression technique to study the effects of median income, degree of urbanization, and mobility on park attendance.[5] In all cases, distance accounted for at least 60 percent of the total variation, and in some cases the effect was as high as 90 percent. Income and urbanization were so closely linked that they were considered as one variable, and together they explained an additional 3 to 16 percent of the variation.

Schulman, working on a smaller scale than Volk, collected data on visitors to five of the twenty parks in the Indiana state park system.[6] A license plate study provided the necessary origin-destination data, since Indiana license plates are prefixed by the county number. The form of the equation fitted to these data was:

$$Tij = \frac{Ti}{\sum_{j=1}^{n} \frac{Rj}{Dij}x} \cdot \frac{Rj}{Dij}x$$

where $Tij$ = the corrected number of trips from County $j$ to Park $i$. A correction factor was needed since the model tends to either over- or underestimate the total number of trips attracted to a park. The correction factor for Park $i$, for example, was a ratio of the observed and calculated number of trips to Park $i$ from all residential areas

$Rj$ = a measure of the number of recreational trips generated from County $j$

$Ti$ = the total number of automobile trips attracted to Park $i$ from all residential areas

$Dij$ = the road distance between County $j$ and Park $i$

$x$ = the value of the exponent for $Dij$

An analysis of the pattern of visits indicated a rapid drop-off in the number of visitors beyond a certain distance.[7] "The trips from in-state counties tend to be undercalculated (greater percentage of positive errors) while the trips from out-of-state counties tend to be overcalculated (greater percentage of negative errors)." [8]

A study by Crevo of weekend recreational travel to two parks in Southeastern Connecticut incorporated time-distance into the model.[9] Neither of the parks is used for camping, but rather for bathing, boating, and picnicking. Zones were constructed around the parks and the ratio of actual to theoretical trips was calculated for each zone.[10] This figure was then plotted against the travel time in minutes from origin zone centroids to the parks. The resulting scatter of points indicated that a curve of the exponential form was the best fit.

A modified version of the gravity model was used for forecasting traffic growth in the county of Dorset, England.[11] Traffic was measured in two classes: "native," which was related to resident population, and "holiday visiting," which was related to the national records of vehicles licensed. To calculate the percent of traffic ending in Dorchester, Whitehead modified a formula developed by Tanner.[12] Tanner had proposed that the number of journeys should fall off with increasing distance according to a low inverse power for short distances and a high inverse power for long distances, a function of the form $x^{e-\lambda x}$. The equation used was:

$$Q = \frac{\kappa . P_1 \cdot P_2 \, e^{-\lambda x}}{n_x}, \text{ where:}$$

$Q$ = traffic flow between two population centers
$P_1 \; P_2$ are populations of two towns distance $x$ apart
$K$, $\lambda$, and $n$ are constants

Whitehead modified the $P_1 \cdot P_2$ relationship since he felt that it was unreasonable to assume that if populations are doubled, the traffic will increase fourfold. He also used a time measurement in place of distance.

The gravity model was used to analyze patterns of camper travel in Michigan parks. Like Crevo, Van Doren used a time-distance measure, but also introduced a measure of park attraction into his model.[13] The assumption was that park attraction is related to the park's physical attributes and the type of recreational activities offered. The general form of the equation was:

$$Nij = K \, Pi \, Aj \, Tij^a$$
where $Nij$ = the number of campers at Park $j$ from County $i$
$Pi$ = county population
$Tij$ = time-distance between Park $j$ and County $i$
$Aj$ = measure of park attraction
$K$ and $a$ are constants

The gravity model has been used successfully in the analysis of recreational travel patterns. Its application can be quickly learned and it is readily adapted to computer programming. However, there are many problems associated with its use. For example, human behavior involves more complex sets of forces than argument by analogy to a physical law will bring to light. Yet the model may lead to a greater understanding of human behavior since residual analysis, for example, often will yield insights into behavioral variations.

Another problem arises in assigning an exponent of unity to population. Hauser found that people in large cities have a lower propensity to go camping than do people in small cities.[14] Furthermore, the socioeconomic structure of a city also is related to the degree of activity in outdoor recreation.[15] Problems also arise in measuring the attractiveness of a recreational area. How are factors such as park size, aesthetic qualities, and types of facilities to be weighted? Distance poses yet another problem. Measurement is an easy matter, but how well does distance measure the friction effect? A number of studies have substituted a time measure for distance. Furthermore, the distance people will travel is also a function of the availability of alternative recreational opportunities. Under this assumption, the greater the number of alternative and competing opportunities close to the city, the less the need people have to travel large distances for participation in outdoor recreation.

## THE INTERVENING OPPORTUNITIES MODEL

The importance of intervening opportunities has been alluded to in a number of studies of recreational travel, but any rigorous testing is lacking. Adams found that the traffic arriving at Algonquin Park from Northern Ontario and Quebec was less than expected; that is, relative to the populations of the areas.[16] An abundance of camping and other outdoor recreational opportunities in Northern Ontario and Quebec was proposed as an explanatory factor. Similarly, Volk, in explaining the patterns of visits to Rocky Mountain National Park, submitted that the reason for the disproportionately high number of visits to the Park from the Great Plains and the Midwestern states compared with the low number from the Western states was a function of the greater number of opportunities in the West.[17]

Simply stated, the intervening opportunities model assumes that the probability of a trip originating in area $i$ and terminating in area $j$ will be directly related to the total number of opportunities in area $j$ and inversely related to the number of opportunities closer (in travel time) to area $i$ than area $j$.[18] Stated mathematically, the model is expressed as follows:

$$Vij = Vi \left( e^{-LV} - e^{-L(V+Vj)} \right)$$

where $Vij$ = trips originating in zone $i$ and terminating in zone $j$
$Vi$ = trip origins in zone $i$
$V$ = number of possible destinations lying closer (travel time) to zone $i$ than to zone $j$
$Vj$ = number of possible destinations in zone $j$
$L$ = empirically derived factor varying with trip type
$e$ = base of natural logarithms

The intervening opportunities model appears to have potential for the study of recreational travel patterns. There is little doubt, for example, that the number of campers visiting a park from a city in Southern Ontario is related to the number of camping facilities located between the park and the city.

## THE SYSTEMS THEORY MODEL

Using theory borrowed from electrical engineering literature, Ellis has developed a method for analyzing flow between population centers and the parks of Michigan.[19]

The systems theory model . . . assumes that each *component* can be modeled separately—the parameters of individual components appear in formulae *specific* to the behavior of the class of component to which it belongs—and it also takes into account the specific interconnection pattern of the system under study. These features, again, are indicative of the strength and weakness of the method. It provides a very satisfying procedure from the behavioral point of view, but also requires specific behavioral knowledge to model the components—or at least good *postulates* regarding behavior. The theory of the system (*sic*) approach appears in the electrical engineering literature, and small-scale applications have been shown to apply to non-physical systems.[20]

The gravity model has been used successfully in the analysis of recreational travel patterns. However, it suffers because of an assumed applicability throughout an entire system. The systems theory model avoids the problem by individual modeling of the system components, and the intervening opportunities model replaces the distance measure with a measure of alternative or competing opportunities.

## CAMPERS FROM CITIES IN SOUTHERN ONTARIO: A PILOT STUDY

The densely settled areas of Southern Ontario pose major problems in terms of present and future flows of recreational traffic. As an initial phase in the research, ten cities and ten parks were selected for study (see Figure 1). Randomness was deliberately sacrificed in the selection of cities in order to focus on the major centers of traffic generation (see Table 1).

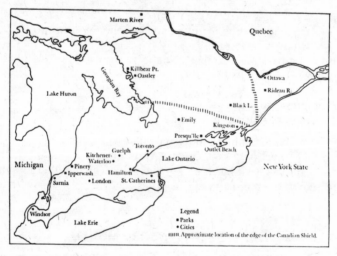

**FIGURE 1.** *Approximate Locations of the Cities and Parks Used in the Analysis of Travel Patterns of Southern Ontario Campers*

| City | Approximate Population in 1963 (in 000's) |
|------|-------------------------------------------|
| Metropolitan Toronto | 1652 |
| Hamilton | 376 |
| Ottawa | 302 |
| London | 171 |
| Windsor | 112 |
| Kitchener-Waterloo | 104 |
| St. Catharines | 86 |
| Sarnia | 51 |
| North Bay | 42 |
| Guelph | 41 |

**TABLE 1.** *Cities Used in Camper Study*

The choice of parks also was biased since most of the parks are located in the southern part of Ontario (see Table 2). Presumably these parks will generate a higher proportion of short-distance camping trips than will the parks in the northern parts of the Province since long-distance traveling is often precluded by time constraints. Parks in the Southern Ontario region probably receive a higher proportion of short-term (weekend) campers than the Northern Ontario parks. However, this is by no means certain since many campers in the north may be stopping overnight en route to other parks. Unfortunately, data limitations at this time prevent any detailed breakdown regarding length of park visit and eventual destination. The parks selected ranged in size from 42 acres (Oastler) to 4333 acres (Pinery). A number of the parks selected were located on the Canadian Shield, an area generally considered more attractive than the Paleozoic areas to the south and west. Some parks were close to large urban centers and presumably would generate a different type of flow than would the parks located in more remote, wilderness-type areas. The parks used in the study were:

| Park | Size (acres) | Campsites |
|------|--------------|-----------|
| Pinery | 4333 | 1075 |
| Killbear Pt. | 2334 | 722 |
| Presqu'Ile | 2170 | 500 |
| Marten River | 1059 | 240 |
| Outlet Beach | 265 | 350 |
| Rideau River | 130 | 191 |
| Ipperwash | 109 | 268 |
| Black Lake | 76 | 200 |
| Emily | 67 | 88 |
| Oastler | 42 | 120 |

**TABLE 2**

*Method and results.* The gravity model was used in this, the initial phase of a long-range program of research, despite the previously discussed limitations of using this model. The assumptions were that camper flow is related to city population (*P*), city-park distance (*D*), and park capacity (*C*). The Ontario Department of Highways made up a questionnaire, and surveys carried out by the Department of Lands and Forests provided a sample of origin-destination data. Distances were computed in miles and park capacity was expressed as the number of campsites multiplied by the average number of campers in a party, which in this case was four. The general form of the equation was as follows:

$$Nij = K P_i^x C_j^y D_{ij}^z$$

where $Nij$ = the number of trips from city *i* to park *j*
$Pi$ = population of city *i*, in 000's
$Cj$ = park capacity
$Dij$ = park-city distance in miles
*x*, *y*, and *z* are exponent values

The Department of Highways' IBM 7040 Computer was used to calculate the exponents for population, camp capacity, and distance. The resulting equation was as follows:

$$Nij = 20.3 \, Pi^{1.11} \, Cj^{0.71} \, Dij^{-1.53} \quad \begin{array}{l}(r = 0.81) \\ (r^2 = 0.65)\end{array}$$

The t-test indicated that all of the variables were significant at the 0.025 level—distance, population, and capacity, in that order. A refinement was made in the model by the incorporation of an adjusted capacity measure (*E*). This was expressed as the product of capacity and the percent of available sites that were actually used for camping. The revised equation was:

$$Nij = 3.52 \, P_i^{1.12} \, E_j^{1.03} \, D_{ij}^{-1.45}$$
$$(r = 0.81, \, r^2 = 0.65)$$

*Analysis of results.* Attendance at parks located on the Canadian Shield was in all cases underestimated (see Table 3).[21] Suggested explanations are in terms of the greater attraction of these parks and a directional bias on the part of people from Southern Ontario. There is little doubt that the juxtaposition of forests, lakes, and rock outcrops makes this an area of high scenic quality. Furthermore, Wolfe[22] and Lucas[23] have shown that outdoor recreationists have a directional preference favoring the north.

Pinery Park, the largest park in the sample, was underestimated. This park has a reputation of being one of the most beautiful parks in the provincial park system. However, it is also possible that scale effects may be important. A large park may be able to provide more and better facilities and activities than a smaller park, resulting in higher camper attendance.

| Park | No. of Cities from Which Visitors Were: Underestimated | Overestimated | No. of Errors ≤ 20% | ≥ 50% | Median Percent Error |
|------|------|------|------|------|------|
| Marten R. | 9 | 0 | 1 | 6 | 61 |
| Killbear Pt. | 7 | 2 | 3 | 5 | 59 |
| Oastler | 9 | 1 | 2 | 7 | 55 |
| Black Lake | 5 | 2 | 0 | 4 | 53 |
| Rideau River | 6 | 3 | 0 | 6 | 69 |
| Outlet | 3 | 6 | 4 | 4 | 32 |
| Presqu'Ile | 5 | 4 | 2 | 5 | 58 |
| Emily | 4 | 4 | 4 | 3 | 27 |
| Ipperwash | 5 | 4 | 3 | 4 | 46 |
| Pinery | 7 | 3 | 1 | 5 | 49 |

**TABLE 3.** Residual and Percent Error Analysis for Sampled Parks of Southern Ontario

Note: 1. Data omitted where observed numbers of visitors to a park was less than 5.

   2. Percent error defined as

$$\frac{\text{Expected} - \text{Observed}}{\text{Observed}} \times 100$$

Parks where the number of visitors was overestimated the greatest number of times included Outlet, Presqu'Ile, Emily, and Ipperwash. Outlet and Presqu'Ile are both located on Lake Ontario to the east of the urban centers of Southern Ontario. Another detracting factor may be the extremely cold waters of Lake Ontario. Furthermore, the boundary of the Canadian Shield swings southward in this area and it is only a short trip from the Lake Ontario shore to the attractive Kawartha Lakes to the north (see Figure 1). Emily, the smallest park in the sample, is located a few miles to the south of the Canadian Shield. The availability of camping opportunities in an attractive nearby area contributes to the lower-than-expected attendance at this park. Ipperwash, even though attendance was underestimated in some cases and overestimated in others, suffers because it is close to Pinery Park.

There were more campers than expected from the small urban centers and fewer from Hamilton and Toronto, the two largest centers (see Table 4).

The result supports Hauser's theory of an inverse relationship between city size and camping propensity.[24]

## CONCLUSION

A number of conclusions, tentative though they may be, can be drawn from the preceding analysis of camper flow to a sample of Southern Ontario parks. The results do indicate possible orientations for further research. The attractiveness of a park relates to its situation. Parks located on the Canadian Shield have greater drawing power than parks located elsewhere. Site characteristics will also determine how attractive a particular park will

| City | No. of Parks Where Visitors Were: | | Percent Error | | Median Percent Error |
|------|-------------------|--------------|--------|--------|--------------|
| | Underestimated | Overestimated | ≤20% | ≥50% | |
| Toronto | 3 | 7 | 3 | 4 | 29 |
| Hamilton | 4 | 6 | 3 | 6 | 56 |
| St. Catharines | 5 | 4 | 1 | 5 | 53 |
| Kit.-Waterloo | 8 | 2 | 3 | 6 | 56 |
| Guelph | 7 | 1 | 0 | 6 | 67 |
| London | 7 | 3 | 3 | 5 | 53 |
| Windsor | 10 | 0 | 2 | 7 | 66 |
| Sarnia | 8 | 0 | 1 | 5 | 74 |
| Ottawa | 5 | 5 | 4 | 4 | 35 |
| North Bay | 3 | 1 | 0 | 2 | Omitted |

**TABLE 4.** *Residual and Percent Error Analysis for Sampled Cities of Southern Ontario*
Note: 1. Data omitted where observed number of visitors to a park was less than 5.
2. Percent error defined as

$$\frac{\text{Expected} - \text{Observed}}{\text{Observed}} \times 100$$

be. For example, a park with a long stretch of sandy beach will generally be more attractive than a park lacking a beach. Facilities, both type and number, also influence the attractiveness of a park.[25]

When two parks are located close to each other, the tendency is for one to dominate the other. For example, Ipperwash appears to suffer because of its location with respect to Pinery, and Outlet because of its nearness to Presqu'Ile. This whole question of the spacing of parks requires careful attention and will necessarily demand some consideration of intervening opportunities. An indication of the linkages between parks will be possible following the analysis of 1966 data. A random sample of provincial park visitors was taken over the entire 1966 summer season at each park in Ontario. Each vehicle became a sample vehicle for the duration of the park season and was given a yellow sticker. A questionnaire was completed each time a sample vehicle entered a park. This method had the effect of a "carbon tracer" on the park visitations of sampled vehicles.

There is evidence to indicate that park size and attractiveness are related. Attendance at Pinery Park, the largest park in the sample, was underestimated to a greater degree than any other of the parks. Research needs to be directed to this question of size. Is there an optimal park size from both the managerial standpoint as well as that of people using the park? Are small parks less attractive than large parks? If so, is it a question of inadequate facilities or are there problems of insufficient space and deficient aesthetic qualities?

The volume of camper traffic generated appears to vary with the size of city. Large cities generate proportionally fewer campers than smaller cities. This might be related to the fact that large cities have many recreational activities that are not found in smaller cities. Further refinements could be made by considering the socioeconomic structure of cities since it has been demonstrated that the probability of a person being a camper increases with income, education, and professional status.[26]

The gravity model appears to have potential for the analysis of recreational travel patterns. In this phase of the research, its use met with limited success. However, refinements can be made by the incorporation of more parks and cities, and by the introduction of additional variables. Other modes of recreational travel, for example, travel to cottages and commercial resorts, also need to be analyzed. And, lastly, there is a need to experiment with other techniques, for example, by using the intervening opportunities approach and the systems analysis approach.

However, it is not enough to understand patterns of flow or to relate camping propensity to a number of socioeconomic variables. This type of research needs to be coordinated with research which concerns itself with determining what is meant by quality in the recreational experience. Here the elements are subjective and, furthermore, the standards used to define quality invariably change. Despite the problems involved, it would seem that questions relating to quality should be paramount in the planning of future outdoor recreational activities.

What type of approach should be employed by public agencies in an attempt to preserve and create a quality environment? One approach argues that public policy, in order to improve the quality of the environment and consequently the quality of the recreational experience,

> should seek not to maximize beauty but minimize ugliness, these not being bi-polar opposites. It is easier to identify that which is ugly through the misfit and thus make the shared environment more agreeable to the many sensitive people in our midst. But if this were all to such a policy we might well have found ourselves in pursuit not of beauty, but widespread mediocrity. Therefore we must seek to provide some accessibility to all for the rare and unique experience. In this we are limited by nature and opportunity but much more so by talent and the lack of a public policy that really desires or knows how to utilize talent.[27]

The preceding ideas could be used as a framework for the planning and design of outdoor recreational activities: elimination of that which is objectionable, and reliance on the creative individuals in our society for the aesthetically satisfying.

# NOTES

[1] For a general review of gravity model concepts see David F. Bramhall, "Gravity Potential, and Spatial Interaction Models," in Walter Isard, ed., *Methods of Regional Analysis* (Cambridge, Mass.: M.I.T. Press, 1960), pp. 493–568.

[2] Donald J. Volk, "Factors Affecting Recreational Use of National Parks," paper given at the Annual Convention of the Association of American Geographers, Columbus, Ohio, 1965. See also Edward L. Ullman, Ronald R. Boyce, and Donald J. Volk, "The Meramec Basin" (St. Louis, 1961); Edward L. Ullman and Donald J. Volk, "An Operational Model for Predicting Resevoir Attendance and Benefits: Implications of a Location Approach to Water Recreation," *Papers, Michigan Academy of Science, Arts and Letters,* XLVII, 1962 (1961 Meeting), pp. 473–84.

[3] A similar method was used to analyze the effect of distance on the demand for day-use, camping, and interior use in Algonquin Park, Ontario. See Robert L. Adams, "The Demand for Wilderness Recreation in Algonquin Provincial Park," unpublished M.A. thesis, Department of Geography, Clark University, 1966.

[4] For the effect of urbanization on the degree of participation in outdoor recreational activity see: Philip M. Hauser, "Demographic and Ecological Changes as Factors in Outdoor Recreation," in *Trends in American Living and Outdoor Recreation,* U.S. Outdoor Recreation Resources Review Commission, Study Report 22 (Washington, D.C.: Government Printing Office, 1962), pp. 81–100. The relationship between socioeconomic variables and outdoor recreation is described in *National Recreation Survey,* U.S. Outdoor Recreation Resources Review Commission, Study Report 19 (Washington, D.C.: Government Printing Office, 1962). Socioeconomic characteristics of campers are described in David A. King, "Characteristics of Family Campers Using the Huron-Manistee National Forests," U.S. Forest Service Research Paper LS-19 (1965), Lake States Forest Experiment Station, St. Paul, Minnesota, 1965; Roy I. Wolfe, "Parameters of Recreational Travel in Ontario: A Progress Report," D.H.O. Report no. RBIII, paper prepared for presentation at the 46th Annual Convention of the Canadian Good Roads Association, Saskatoon Downsview, Ontario, October 1965.

[5] Volk, "Factors Affecting Recreational Use of National Parks."

[6] Lawrence Leonard Schulman, "Traffic Generation and Distribution of Weekend Recreational Trips," unpublished M.Sc. thesis (Civil Engineering), Purdue University, 1964.

[7] Adams found a break in slope between the 150- and 220-mile zones in his analysis of recreational visits to Algonquin Park, Ontario. See Adams, "The Demand for Wilderness Recreation. . . ." Similar findings were also obtained by Ullman, Boyce, and Volk. See Ullman, Boyce, and Volk, *The Meramec Basin,* particularly Vol. 3, p. 15.

[8] Schulman, "Traffic Generation and Distribution of Weekend Recreational Trips," p. 77.

[9] Charles C. Crevo, "Characteristics of Summer Weekend Recreational Travel," *Highway Research Record* 41, (1963): 51–60.

[10] The theoretical number of trips to park $A$ from zone $i$ was calculated by multiplying the total number of trips to park $A$ by the proportion of the state population in zone $i$.

[11] James Ivor Whitehead, "Road Traffic Growth and Capacity in a Holiday District (Dorset)," *Proceedings of the Institution of Civil Engineers* 31 (May, 1965): 589–608.

[12] J. C. Tanner, "Relations between Population, Distance and Traffic—Some Theoretical Considerations," *Research Note RN-2921,* Road Research Laboratory, Hammondsworth, January 1957 (unpublished).

[13] Carlton S. Van Doren, "A Recreational Travel Model for Predicting Campers at Michigan State Park's," unpublished Ph.D. thesis, Department of Geography, Michigan State University, 1965. Also refer to Jack B. Ellis and Carlton S. Van Doren, "A Comparative Evaluation of Gravity and Systems Theory Models for Statewide Recreational Traffic Flows," paper presented at the Twelfth U.S. Annual Meeting of the Regional Science Association, Philadelphia, Pennsylvania, November 12–14, 1965.

[14] Hauser, U.S. Outdoor Recreation Resources Review Commission, Study Report 22, p. 48.

[15] Wolfe, "Parameters of Recreational Travel in Ontario."

[16] Adams, "The Demand for Wilderness Recreation in Algonquin Provincial Park."

[17] Volk, "Factors Affecting Recreational Use of National Parks."

[18] For descriptions and evaluations of the intervening opportunities model see Clark, Colin, and G. H. Peters, "The Intervening Opportunities Method of Traffic Analysis," *Traffic Quarterly* 19, no. 1 (1965): 101–119; Chicago Area Transportation Study, Volume II, *Data Projections* (1960), pp. 79–86; D. K. Witheford, "Comparisons of Trip Distribution by Opportunity Model and Gravity Model," Pittsburgh Area Transportation Study (1961); Clyde F. Pyers, "Evaluation of the Intervening Opportunities Trip Distribution Model," paper presented for the 44th Annual Meeting of the Highway Research Board, Washington, D.C., 1965.

[19] Jack B. Ellis, "Analysis of Socio-Economic Systems by Physical Systems Techniques," unpublished Ph.D. thesis, Department of Electrical Engineering, Michigan State University, 1965; Ellis and Van Doren, "A Comparative Evaluation of Gravity and Systems Theory Models for Statewide Recreational Traffic Flows."

[20] Ellis and Van Doren, "A Comparative Evaluation of Gravity and Systems Theory Models for Statewide Recreational Traffic Flow," pp. 3–4. References to the electrical engineering literature include: Seshu, Sundaran, and Merrill B. Reed, *Linear Graphs and Electric Networks* (Reading, Mass., 1961); J. B. Ellis and D. N. Millstein, "A Behavior—Specific Component to System Construct for Traffic Flows," Proceedings, *Third International Symposium on Traffic Flow,* New York, June 1965.

[21] The total number of visitors to a park was used as a measure of park attendance. A highway department is interested in the number of campers visiting the parks. On the other hand, a parks department probably is more interested in the average length of stay at the parks, and consequently a measure involving camper-days would be more appropriate.

[22] Wolfe, "Parameters of Recreational Travel in Ontario," p. 5.

[23] Robert C. Lucas, "The Recreational Use of the Quetico-Superior Area," U.S. Forest Research Paper LS-8, Lake States Forest Experiment Station, St. Paul, Minnesota, 1966, p. 38.

[24] Hauser, U.S. Outdoor Recreation Resources Review Commission, Study Report 22, p. 48.

[25] A more sophisticated measure of park attraction will be possible following the evaluation of 1966 data. A detailed questionnaire sent to rangers in all of the provincial parks in Ontario will provide the necessary data.

[26] Wolfe, "Parameters of Recreational Travel in Ontario," p. 5.

[27] Robert W. Kates, "The Pursuit of Beauty in the Environment," *Landscape* 16, no. 2 (Winter, 1966–67): 25.

# 5

## VACATION HOMES IN THE NORTHEASTERN UNITED STATES: SEASONALITY IN POPULATION DISTRIBUTION

### Richard Lee Ragatz

This chapter outlines the significance of the vacation home market in shaping urban and regional development in terms of the seasonal redistribution of the population. Richard Ragatz points out that existing urban and regional theory has accounted for the distribution of population only in accordance with the permanent place of residence without considering how this distribution varies on a seasonal or semipermanent basis. Ragatz applies some of the traditional methods of analysis to this seasonal movement of the urban population in the northeastern part of the United States in order to determine the implications of changes in the economic base, demands for community services, and the general impact on regional development.

Past urban and regional theory concerning the distribution of population has concentrated on the location of permanent residence. The distribution has been described as conical, with population density dispersing gradually outward from a central point of urban agglomeration. Before the real distribution of population can be explained, however, account also must be taken of seasonal residence, which refers to part-time occupancy of a place of residence other than the primary one. One important type of seasonal occupancy is vacation housing in the hinterland. . . .[1]

Existing studies concerned with the vacation home market fall into three primary categories. The first category includes those concerned with predicting future demand, which have been completed primarily by economic consultants for private land developers and building materials producers.[2] A second category involves the analysis of demographic

Reprinted from *Annals* of The Association of American Geographers 60, no. 3 (September, 1970): 447–55, by permission of The Association of American Geographers and the author. This article has been extensively edited for this volume and the notes and figure renumbered.

The article was originally part of a doctoral dissertation in the Department of City and Regional Planning at Cornell University which was entitled, "The Vacation Home Market: An Analysis of the Spatial Distribution of Population on a Seasonal Basis." It was funded by the Appalachian Regional Commission.

characteristics of vacation home occupants. For the most part, these studies have fallen under the domain of sociologists and rural sociologists.[3] A third category, concerned with the economic costs and benefits of vacation homes to local community development patterns, includes studies by regional planners and agricultural economists.[4]

Few studies have analyzed the spatial location of vacation homes and the resultant patterns of seasonal population distribution. Some geographers and regional planners have investigated this topic, but for the most part, emphasis has been placed on a micro-region such as a specific county.[5] Only a few have investigated the regional distribution of vacation homes or placed this land use within the context of urban and regional theory.

The objective here is to suggest that a "theory of vacation residency" should be added to the existing body of urban and regional theory in order better to explain the real distribution of population on a seasonal basis. The number of people in a given locality at different times is a basic factor in regional planning and development. It is essential for sound planning to know not only where people are listed for census counts but where they require services and consume products, and patterns of vacation home occupancy should be thoroughly investigated in order to improve the planning and development processes.

A second reason why seasonal occupancy of vacation housing is important relates to economic development. The location of people affects economic activity at any given time. The occupancy of vacation housing is directly related to economic activity—especially on a regional basis in the more rural, underdeveloped areas of the country. The exodus of primary industries has caused the present plight of rural areas, and consideration of a new alternative land use that may be a substitute for obsolete land uses involves many land areas in the United States. The restoration of land values, the possibilities of recapturing sunken capital and vanishing wealth, the creation of a new economic base, and the revitalization of construction and some service industries all are related to the vacation home market.

A third reason for investigating vacation home occupancy is related to the physical environmental situation. The foremost issue is the potential health problem that could be created. This country has achieved high levels of health because large proportions of the population have been concentrated in urban areas. Environmental health controls could be imposed and medical facilities provided within short distances of a large part of the population. The penetration of thousands of vacation home families, who for the most part are accustomed to a controlled urban environment, into rural areas where sparse population density does not allow such controls and facilities, should only complicate the public health situation. Other potential problems relating to the physical environment include: (1) hazardous driving conditions on rural road systems because of probable high speeds and traffic congestion; (2) invasion of prime agricultural land by vacation homes; and (3) environmental deterioration if the development of vacation homes takes place in an uncontrolled or unattractive manner.

A final reason is social. Vacation home occupancy has implications for the integration of urban-oriented vacation home owners into the local rural community. Each sector of the population must be made aware of the other's values and goals in order to minimize potential forces of disturbance. Improved channels of communication and understanding must be developed in order to encourage harmonious relationships, with as many community decisions as possible made by mutual consent. . . .

## CURRENT EXTENT OF THE MARKET

A combination of two basic factors has provided this opportunity for vacation home ownership. The first is having sufficient income to allocate money from the household budget to a nonvital item. The second is adequate time away from the place for employment to spend this income on leisure-type activities. Without these two factors, a market for an object as costly as a house only for seasonal-recreational purposes would not exist. While these factors provide the opportunity for ownership, others provide the motive. These include equity appreciation, escape from a busy urban environment, and a chance to participate in outdoor recreation. Supplementing these motive-factors are several elements that make participation in the market easier, such as improved highway accessibility, intensive institutional advertising, and the recent availability of additional types of vacation homes and sites.

The trend toward vacation home ownership is strong. It is estimated that some three million families in the United States currently own vacation homes.[6] This is about 5 percent of the total number of families in this country. It also is estimated that somewhere between 100,000 and 200,000 new vacation homes are added annually.[7] When multiplied by the estimated average family size of owners, the figures indicate that between ten and twelve million persons occupy privately owned vacation homes sometime during the year.[8] In addition, it is estimated that another several million persons occupy rental units and also must be added to the total. Although not included in the above estimate, other types of seasonal shelter also should be considered—such as mobile homes, houseboats, and old farm houses. The average length of occupancy per vacation home tends to be around three to four months.[9] Thus, a considerable depopulation of urban areas and repopulation of rural areas occurs during different periods of the year. . . .

Roughly 2 percent of the families in the United States (about one million in absolute numbers) are seriously considering the purchase of a vacation home in the immediate future.[10] Another 4 to 5 percent are considering purchase at some indeterminable date. If all families anticipating purchase actually fulfill their intention within the next ten years, the annual number of vacation homes under construction could reach over 300,000. Of course, all of these families will not complete their plans. On the other hand, many families without present plans probably will enter the market as production and marketing techniques are improved and financing becomes more liberal. Therefore, it appears that the market could easily double within the next ten to twelve years. This means that some six to seven million vacation homes could be found in rural areas and that some twenty to twenty-five million persons could be commuting between their permanent and vacation homes.

## VACATION HOMES IN THE NORTHEAST

Vacation homes should be included in the existing body of urban and regional theory in order to predict where seasonal occupancy may become a significant phenomenon, where additional capital may be allocated for economic development in rural areas, and where local communities should prepare for the related social and economic costs and benefits. In order to determine how vacation homes are distributed in this country, data may be used from the 1960 United States Census of Housing.[11] The statistics are outdated and poorly defined, but they represent the only uniform data available on a country-wide basis.

The following analysis concentrates on the distribution of vacation homes in the thirteen states of the North Atlantic Region.[12] Besides containing many traditional vacation home areas, these states also participate directly in the market area of Gottman's Megalopolis.[13] Although some western and southern counties are rather remote from the primary metropolitan areas, their recreation and scenic amenities still attract vacation home buyers, and improved transportation systems are continually increasing their accessibility.

A simple tool for analyzing the distribution of vacation homes is the location quotient. Such quotients are obtained by dividing an area's relative share of the total number of housing units of the selected universe into its share of the total vacation homes in the universe.[14] The universe is the thirteen states in the North Atlantic Region, and the areas are the component 398 counties. Quotients can range from zero to infinity; a quotient of 1.0 means that a state has an equal share of vacation homes and total housing units. A quotient near zero means that the state has less than its expected share of vacation homes, with the reverse being true for a quotient approaching infinity. The location quotient is a problematic rather than a true ratio scale of measurement. One quotient twice the size of another does not indicate that the concentration of vacation homes is twice as much in the first area as in the second, and the quotients only give some rough approximation of the true variation between area concentrations.

The overall quotient of vacation housing for all thirteen states is 1.29, higher than for any other region in the country (see Table 1). Every one of the 398 counties in the thirteen states possesses some vacation housing, but certain counties have quotients of over 2.5, suggesting a fairly high concentration of vacation use. Maine, Vermont, and New Hampshire have the largest percentage of counties in the top quartile. Concentrations are near Lake Champlain, Lake Winnepesaukee, the Atlantic Ocean, and the remote northern sections of these states, where permanent residents are few, and hunting and fishing are excellent. Three additional areas of intense concentration are the Cape Cod region of Massachusetts, the Poconos of Pennsylvania, and the southern New Jersey shore. Other popular vacation home areas are on Chesapeake Bay, in the Catskill and Adirondack Mountains of New York, and in northern Pennsylvania.

| State | Vacation home quotient | Estimated number of vacation home units |
|---|---|---|
| Maine | 5.35 | 64,000 |
| New Hampshire | 4.56 | 33,750 |
| Vermont | 4.13 | 18,100 |
| New Jersey | 1.84 | 120,250 |
| Massachusetts | 1.57 | 86,650 |
| Rhode Island | 1.55 | 14,450 |
| New York | 1.31 | 244,000 |
| Delaware | 1.28 | 6,000 |
| Connecticut | 1.17 | 31,400 |
| Maryland | .78 | 23,700 |
| Pennsylvania | .72 | 84,250 |
| West Virginia | .71 | 13,250 |
| Virginia | .59 | 22,600 |
| | 1.29 | 762,400 |

**TABLE 1.** *Vacation Home Quotients and Estimated Number of Vacation Homes Units in Thirteen States of the North Atlantic Region, 1960*
Source: Calculated from *U.S. Census of Housing, 1960, States and Small Areas, United States Summary* (Washington: Government Printing Office, 1963), Final Report HC (1)-1, Table 3.

The quotients indicate the importance of the vacation home "industry" in areas having relatively few major industries. Although service industries in general, and recreation in particular, contribute limited amounts to a local economy, they must not be dismissed. In regions such as Appalachia and northern New England, very few alternatives to recreation and vacation homes are available. The possibility of additional dollar input contributed by vacation home owners in terms of expenditure patterns, property taxes, and construction should not be neglected in regional economic development.

Analysis of absolute numbers indicates where the greatest number of vacation homes are located, rather than merely their relative importance. The counties in the North Atlantic Region which contain .25 percent (1,900 units) or more of the total vacation homes (762,400 units) in the region represent the top quartile of total vacation homes on a county-by-county basis. The most significant difference between these two sets of data is the tighter concentration of vacation homes in counties adjacent to, or containing, a metropolitan center, and only the counties in Maine are relatively distant from major cities. Concentric rings of vacation homes are around all the cities in the northeastern part of the region, including Erie and Philadelphia, Pennsylvania; Buffalo, Rochester, Syracuse, Albany, and

New York City, New York; Boston, Massachusetts; Providence, Rhode Island; New Haven and Bridgeport, Connecticut; Newark and Jersey City, New Jersey; and Montreal and Quebec, Canada. In many cases the concentric ring encloses the city since its component county is included in the top quartile group. This is especially true for urban counties adjacent to shorelines.

It appears that proximity to market and availability of recreational facilities are major determinants in the location of vacation homes. If two areas have comparable attractions, most families probably will choose the one nearer to their place of permanent residence, thus creating a greater demand in recreational areas which are closer to urban centers. Complicating this generalization, however, are several factors for which causal relationships cannot be proven due to lack of adequate data. These factors include family income, reputation of and personal acquaintance with the area, family and friendship ties, rental versus ownership patterns, and transportation facilities. The purpose here, however, is not to formulate any complex explanations but rather to suggest a general schematic pattern of vacation home distribution.

One factor to investigate is the distance a family is willing to drive between its permanent place of residence and its vacation home. The closer together the two homes, the more convenient and usable is the vacation home. However, in close proximity to metropolitan areas it often is difficult to find suitable sites that have the desirable amenities of scenery, recreation facilities, and a low to moderate selling price. Distance traveled between the vacation home and the permanent home depends on many variables, but some tentative conclusions can be drawn from existing market surveys. Since these surveys have different universes, sample sizes, and distance intervals, it is difficult to make valid generalizations from the results. In order to provide some factual data, however, the following list is a review of major findings from some available surveys:

1. 51.9 percent of respondents in a survey of several vacation home communities stated the distance between their permanent home and vacation home was between 100 and 200 miles (160 and 320 km.);[15]
2. 66.2 percent of respondents in a utility company survey stated it was less than 100 miles (160 km.);[16]
3. 52 percent in a building supply manufacturer's survey said it was less than 100 miles (160 km.);[17]
4. 47 percent of vacation home owners in a recreation-oriented county in New York State said it was less than 100 miles (160 km.).[18]

In summary, it appears that if permitted a choice, by far the greatest number of people would prefer a vacation home within 100 to 150 miles (160 to 240 km.) of their permanent home, a convenient distance for short weekend trips. It is unrealistic to conclude, however, that an area will not feel the penetration of vacation homes if it is farther than 100 to 150 miles (160 to 240 km.) from a major city. If sufficient amenities exist, people certainly will travel a considerable distance as evidenced by the significant recreation industries in Maine, Florida, and Colorado. The vast majority of families probably travel to their vacation home by automobile, however, and areas within easy weekend driving time from population concentrations appear most amenable for the vacation home market.

This suggested distance of 100 to 150 miles (160 to 240 km.) will increase as transportation facilities are improved and driving time to previously remote areas is lowered. The distance also will increase as land in closer proximity to urban areas is depleted or increases significantly in value. The combination of these two factors eventually will create a demand for vacation home sites in areas considerably more distant than 100 to 150 miles (160 to 240 km.) from major cities.

## SCHEMATIC DISTRIBUTION OF VACATION HOMES

Some general conclusions may be made in regard to the distribution of vacation homes in this country. A lack of well defined and reliable data negate the process of hypothesis testing, and the objective here only is to suggest a distribution pattern in broad, schematic terms. Although vacation homes are scattered throughout the country, the majority appear to be concentrated within 100 to 150 miles (160 to 240 km.) of major urban centers. Their distribution can be described roughly as a volcanic cone. (see Figure 1). The vertex of the cone is nonexistent due to the location of the central city and the immediately surrounding suburbs. At some point beyond the central core is a transition zone where permanent homes in suburbia and exurbia are interspersed with vacation homes. Most vacation homes probably are located in the succeeding rings outward. Density continues to decline outward to a point about 150 miles (240 km.) from the central city, where it becomes very low because the distance is beyond feasible weekend driving time. Within the individual rings the units tend to gravitate toward nuclei of various types of recreation, with the degree of gravitation depending upon such attractions as water, mountains, availability of outdoor sports, scenery, and low land cost. Another major factor in the degree of concentration is accessibility from permanent place of residence.

Thus, the nation has two series of population cones. One reflects permanent residence, with its primary peak at the central city, and a gradient sloping outward and downward. Interspersed throughout this sloping gradient are outlying cities, towns, hamlets, and rural farm and nonfarm populations of the hinterland. A second cone, of vacation homes, is volcanic in shape. Specific peaks of this cone represent vacation home areas having recreational attractions and close proximity to the city. The two cones frequently intersect as vacation homes and permanent homes become mixed in outlying areas. This whole schematic distribution takes on a pulsating appearance during different seasons of the year as families leave their permanent residence to occupy their vacation home in the hinterland. During the summer the major central city peak slumps and the minor peaks of vacation home concentrations rise. This appearance usually will be reversed during the winter except in areas suited to winter sports.

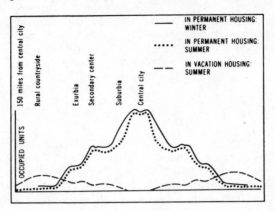

**FIGURE 1.** *Schematic Distribution of Population, by Seasons, in Permanent and Vacation Housing Units*

## SUMMARY

This discussion suggests that existing urban and regional theory is incomplete because it only considers the distribution of population in its permanent place of residence. The current and projected market for seasonal-recreational housing is of such magnitude that this theory must also consider the interaction of persons between their permanent home in the urban center and vacation home in the hinterland. This paper has provided limited empirical evidence of the actual distribution of vacation homes in the hope that more sophisticated research will be undertaken. Such research will be useful for all regional planners and economic developers who are concerned with population distribution and its related activities.

Some interesting implications concern the seasonal distribution of population. Although related to more than vacation-home occupancy as defined in this paper, Jones suggested some possible effects of multiple home ownership:[19]

> We will be faced, as never before, with the half empty city. At the present time, we can experience this phenomenon; for example, in Philadelphia on any Sunday morning in July, or conversely in Atlantic City on any Wednesday in January. We shall have to develop new methods for estimating the service needs at any moment and forecasting their fluctuations throughout the year. This will affect all kinds of urban services from schools, to water systems, to police and fire protection, to sewage disposal capacity, to traffic and transportation flows.

Jones thus envisioned a fluctuating population in urban centers with related changes in demand on public services, and he went on to say:[20]

> A further phenomenon will occur, I believe, that will upset even more our abilities to cope with the service needs of the population. At the present time, we take care of service needs to a large extent by assuming that the population occupies their domiciles, and providing services to these domiciles. However, it is becoming increasingly true, and by the 21st century will have developed to staggering proportions, that a substantial percentage of the population is out of range of normal services at any given time because it is away from home.

This discussion emphasizes the importance of comprehensive and coordinated planning on a broad, regional basis, because vacation home occupancy is as relevant to urban areas as to rural ones. In the past, students of regional activity have used rent and gravity concepts to predict services required, expenditure patterns, and other human activities. Too frequently, however, these concepts provide an incomplete surrogate for the actual number of people to be served. In order for regional planners and developers to provide facilities more intelligently, the existing body of explanatory urban and regional theory must be expanded to include the seasonal occupancy of vacation housing in the hinterland.

## NOTES

[1] Vacation housing is defined as permanently located single-family housing used on a private-personal basis for seasonal outdoor recreation. The occupants must have some other primary place of residence, and the vacation home must have been originally constructed for the purpose of leisure-time activities.

[2] For example, see J. S. Chin, "A Statistical Study of Second-Home Owners," unpublished study conducted for Weyerhaeuser Company, Department of Economics, University of Washington, 1966; *Vacation Home Consumer Study for Western Wood Products Association* (Portland, Oreg.: McCann-Erickson, 1966); and *Survey of Vacation Home Purchasers* (Baltimore: Sidney Hollander, 1965).

[3] For example, see R. L. Carroll, "A Social Analysis of Southold Town, Long Island," Department of Rural Sociology, Cornell University, 1965; and W. Thompson, "The Urban Fringe: First Thoughts on Sociological Perspectives," Department of Sociology, Cornell University, 1961.

[4] For example, see Chautauqua County Planning Board and Department of Planning, *Second Homes and Their Impact on the Economy of Chautauqua County* (Mayville, N.Y.: Chautauqua County Planning Board and Department of Planning, 1966); I. V. Fine and E. E. Werner, "Private Cottages in Wisconsin," Bureau of Business Research and Service, School of Commerce, University of Wisconsin, 1960; and R. Snyder, "Seasonal Recreation Properties in Minnesota," Department of Agricultural Economics, University of Minnesota, 1967.

[5] For example, see I. V. Fine and R. E. Tuttle, "Private Seasonal Housing in Wisconsin," State of Wisconsin Department of Resource Development, 1966; W. W. Graham, "Cottage Development in Rural Areas," Department of Geography, Carleton University, Ottawa, Ontario, 1967; and R. I. Wolfe, "Summer Cottages in Ontario," Department of Geography, University of Toronto, 1950.

[6] This estimate was derived from an unpublished nation-wide survey by the American Telephone and Telegraph Company, "Survey of 9,231 Bell System Telephone Users," American Telephone and Telegraph Company, New York, 1965.

[7] This estimate was derived from results of various surveys, articles, and discussions with suppliers of the vacation home market.

[8] Results from the American Telephone and Telegraph Company survey in 1965 showed that the average size of vacation home families was 3.7 members; the estimated average size of all American families in that year was 3.4 members.

[9] For example, see: Carroll, "A Social Analysis of Southold Town"; Chautauqua County Planning Board and Department of Planning, *Second Homes and Their Impact*; and Stanmar, Inc., "Market Analysis of Vacation Home Potential in the Boston Area," unpublished study conducted by the company, Sudbury, Mass., 1962.

[10] American Telephone and Telegraph Company, "Survey."

[11] The number of vacation homes was determined from the 1960 Census of Housing by adding the categories "Other Seasonal Vacant Units" to "Units Held for Occasional Use" and subtracting those "Vacant for Migratory Workers." Total housing units included both vacant and occupied units.

[12] The North Atlantic Region includes the states of Maine, New Hampshire, Vermont, Massachusetts, Rhode Island, Connecticut, New York, New Jersey, Pennsylvania, Delaware, Maryland, Virginia, and West Virginia.

[13] J. Gottmann, *Megalopolis* (New York: The Twentieth Century Fund, 1961).

[14] The vacation home quotient for counties is defined as:

$$V_i/C_i \div V_t/C_t$$

where $V_i$ = number of vacation homes in individual county.

  $C_i$ = total number of housing units in individual county.

  $V_t$ = number of vacation homes in the 398 counties.

  $C_t$ = total number of housing units in the 398 counties.

[15] Unpublished survey conducted by the author, 1966.

[16] American Telephone and Telegraph Company, "Survey."

[17] Stanly Works, "Survey of Vacation Home Plan Consumers," unpublished study conducted by the company, New Britain, Conn.

[18] Chautauqua County Planning Board and Department of Planning, *Second Homes and Their Impact*.

[19] B. G. Jones, "Land Uses in the United States in the Year 2000," *Man's Environment in the Twenty-First Century*, Publication no. 105 (Chapel Hill: University of North Carolina Department of Environmental Sciences and Engineering, School of Public Health, 1965), p. 231.

[20] Jones, "Land Uses in the United States in the Year 2000," p. 231.

# SPATIAL BEHAVIOR IN RECREATIONAL BOATING

**Barry Lentnek**
**Carlton S. Van Doren**
**James R. Trail**

This chapter by Barry Lentnek, Carlton Van Doren, and James Trail is similar to many of the studies dealing with recreational travel in that it generates as many questions as it answers. This fascinating examination of boaters' travel behavior in the state of Ohio reveals interesting differences between sailors and fishermen, for example. An unlimited number of questions are generated as well: Is fishing a discrete activity ill-suited to multiple purpose areas? Do sailors enjoy relatively crowded conditions? What are the acreage requirements for different kinds of boating activity?

This study is significant because it provides a method or an approach that could be effectively used for the investigation of any outdoor recreational activity in any location.

## INTRODUCTION

The growing interest in outdoor recreation, coupled with increasing population, has overtaxed many public facilities and focused attention on the supply of outdoor recreational resources. The first nationwide study of outdoor recreation resources, conducted by the Outdoor Recreation Resource Review Commission (ORRRC), recognized that water is a primary recreation resource.[1] Boating is a popular water-based recreation activity—33,900,000 individuals participated in boating other than canoeing and sailing in 1965.[2] It has increased rapidly in popularity throughout the country,[3] with the highest rates of participation in the North Central region.[4] This article examines some spatial aspects of recreational boating in Ohio.

Watercraft can be used for a variety of recreational activities. The most important are: pleasure cruising, fishing, water skiing, sailing, and canoeing. Considerable skill and practice are often required to engage in these

Reprinted from the *Journal of Leisure Research* 1, no. 2 (Spring, 1969): 103–24, by permission of the National Recreation and Park Association and the authors. This article has been edited for this volume and the notes and figures renumbered.

activities and many individuals focus on one boating activity as their primary recreational objective. Boaters who specialize in one activity are termed "activity-specialized." The primary hypothesis of this study is that activity-specialized boaters differ markedly in varying activity specializations and differ from non-specialized boaters in their lake selection process. The boater's decision process has a definite space dimension, thus affecting spatial movements and behavior.[5] It is concluded that, in Ohio, activity-specialized boaters tend to choose the nearest lake that can be used for their activity—as evidenced by concentrations of other, similarly specialized boaters. Non-specialized boaters tend to travel longer distances in seeking water bodies remote from the metropolitan areas. Non-specialized boaters also tend to spend more time at their destination. Presumably, they are seeking a more "natural" (non-commercialized) environment offering a wide variety of outdoor activities in addition to the water resource itself. . . .

## THE OHIO RECREATIONAL BOATING SURVEY

The present study is a consideration of the effect of the locations of water bodies upon the rate of participation for boating and its subtypes. A spatial analysis of boaters' trips to publicly owned lakes was the first of a three-phase analysis based on data collected during the summer of 1966 in the Ohio Recreational Boating Survey (ORBS).[6] The overall objective of Phase One was to analyze the spatial behavior of boaters.[7]

Phase Two of the study will include an analysis of the social characteristics of boaters as related to their choices of lakes and boating activities.

Phase Three of the survey is directly concerned with the environment of the lakes in terms of how boaters perceive and react to variation in the quality of the resources for boating. Although the data have been arbitrarily divided into three phases, the ultimate goal is to combine these findings into a meaningful interpretation of the spatial interconnections of recreational boating in the study area. It is hoped that by combining site and situational themes the study may lead to new insights which will aid in the allocation and management of water resources for boating purposes.

The survey included interviews at 14 inland lakes and one access point on Lake Erie. Inasmuch as natural lakes are severely limited in number in Ohio, almost all pleasure boating occurs on man-made reservoirs, Lake Erie, or the larger rivers. The survey included lakes within or near the southwest-northeast urban belt in Ohio. Lakes were selected to maximize variation in acreage (ranging from 364 to 5,800 acres), motor horsepower regulations (from six horsepower to unlimited horsepower),[8] and location relative to population concentrations (within two hours driving time). A majority of the state's registered watercraft[9] are in urban centers.

Interviews were conducted on weekends from June 29 to September 11, 1966. With few exceptions interviewing teams of two or more were sent to two lakes per weekend. A total of 906 boating groups were interviewed during the summer, with a majority of groups contacted at public boat launching sites and campgrounds. Excluded by this procedure were boat and sailing clubs as well as boaters owning private homes. In general, the survey was directed toward the mobile boater transporting a boat by trailer.

The Muskingum Watershed Conservancy District supplied boats to the investigators at Atwood, Tappan, and Leesville Reservoirs in order to obtain 35 interviews on the water surface from occupants of boats. Every effort was made to obtain a representative cross-section of the boating population when sampling for interview purposes at the lakes. Since it was almost impossible to control the sample when conducting interviews at the lakes, the sample was random but not systemically designed for measures of reliability. Nonetheless, we believe that the sample taken during the summer of 1966 was broadly representative of that year's boating population.[10]

There are segments of the general boating public which can be distinguished by their participation in various subactivities and also by different trip patterns associated with these activities. Boaters are analogous to shoppers in that consumers of retail goods initially order their choice of a shopping center according to their trip objectives and the number and type of products offered at the alternative centers.[11] Boaters who have an activity objective in mind are seeking a specific type of experience. The boater's trip purpose, then, can be expected to affect movement in space in terms of trip length, direction, and length of stay at a lake. The activities commonly associated with boating behavior in the study are: sailing, water skiing, pleasure cruising, and fishing. In addition, there is a recognizable group of boaters preferring to engage in a number of these activities on one outing without particular emphasis placed upon any one activity. These boaters usually tend to blend boating with other land-based activities such as picnicking and overnight camping.

A formal definition of boater's activity specialization is adopted on a purely heuristic basis. A boater is classified as activity-specialized when he spends more than 60 percent of his boating time during a given season at one activity, e.g., fishing. Approximately two-thirds of the boaters interviewed indicated they were activity-specialized.

Lakes may be classified by a similar procedure. A lake is considered to be activity-specialized when more than one-half of the boaters interviewed at that lake were found to have the same activity specialization. For example, a lake is classified as specializing in fishing when more than 50 percent of the interviewed boaters at that lake spent more than 60 percent of all of their boating time fishing.

The relative specialization of lakes is depicted in Figure 1. The axes of the equilateral triangle are scaled in percentages of all activity-specialized boaters. Non-specialized boaters are not included in the calculations. As a result, the triangle has its limitations as a lake-classification device.

Classification of lakes separate from that of boaters is not tautological because it is logically possible for lakes to attract equal numbers of differently specialized boaters. (See, for example, Rocky Fork in Figure 2.)

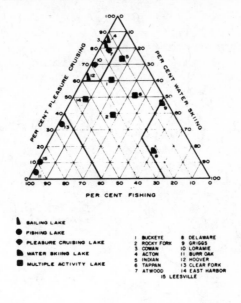

**FIGURE 1.** *Lake Activity Classification Triangle*

In fact, it is obvious upon visiting the lakes that boaters specializing in the same activity tend to cluster at particular lakes. This clustering tendency may be tested statistically by performing a chi-square analysis of the data based on the hypothesis that all specialized boaters attend only lakes which are similarly specialized. Hypothetical and observed distributions are presented in Table 1. Since the computed chi-square is approximately 13 while tabled $X^2$ at 9 degrees of freedom is 17, there is no significant difference between the hypothesized and observed distributions at the 95 percent level of confidence. We may conclude that specialized boaters tend to cluster at particular lakes.

It appears from inspection of Figure 2 that lakes which specialize in sailing and water skiing are closest to the southwest-northeast metropolitan corridor. Lakes which are farthest away from the metropolitan corridor are identified with either fishing or multipurpose boating activities. Pleasure-cruising lakes generally are found at intermediate distances from the urban centers.

The dominance of the metropolitan areas as origins of boaters is clear from Figure 3. The figure shows the average length of boating trips in terms of travel time (estimated to the nearest 15 minutes) for each of eight compass directions by the length of the vectors. The importance of the metropolitan boater at any of the lakes is indicated by the short vectors of lakes near metropolitan centers and longer vectors for lakes that are more remote (e.g., Burr Oak in the southeast and East Harbor in the north). If the volume of boaters by direction is analyzed graphically (Figure 4), it is seen

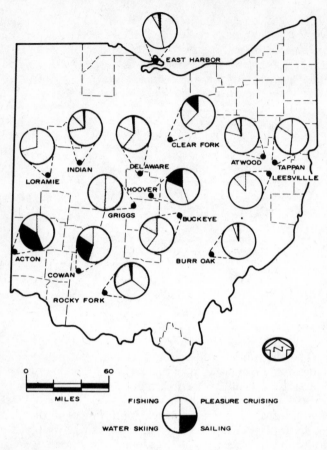

SUSAN ANGELON

**FIGURE 2.** *Activity Specialization by Lake*

that few boaters are traveling long distances, and the metropolitan centers as an origin for most boaters is again emphasized.

In order to facilitate a more precise understanding of the spatial behavior of the boaters than is afforded by the use of cartographic analysis alone, additional origin-destination metrics were utilized. Based on the reasonable assumption that travel time is more likely to influence boaters' choices of destinations than physical distance, the first step was to calculate the average rate of speed of the boaters to each lake. The questionnaires provided information concerning the amount of time spent in transit from each boater's home to the lake at which he was interviewed. In addition, the location of his home was ascertained. Using detailed maps, the airline distance from each boater's home to the lake at which he was interviewed was calculated (there was a 99 percent correlation between airline and highway distances for all boaters in the sample). Average time distances were divided into average airline distances (in miles) to yield estimates of the rate of speed characteristic of the average boater at each lake. "Time zones" were created by multiplying the average number of miles traveled per minute by 15. The zones are in the form of concentric circles and so are based on the assumptions that average speed does not depend upon the direction of travel to a particular lake and that travel frictions are uniform. The distance between the zone boundaries (a constant number of miles for each zone away from one lake) corresponds on the average to 15 minutes of travel time. Naturally, the spacing in miles between these isochrones varies between lakes. The method of data arrangements permits the calculation of frequency distributions of specialized boaters away from all 15 lakes. The number of sailors with origins located between 0 and 15 minutes away from the lakes was counted and summed for all successive time zones. Frequency counts were also performed for water skiers, pleasure cruisers, fishermen, and boaters who did not specialize in any one activity. The frequency distributions were converted to proportions of the total number of boaters in each activity group and the proportions were cumulated.

| Boaters Classified by Activity Specialization | Lakes Classified by Activity Specialization | | | |
|---|---|---|---|---|
| | Sailing | Water Skiing | Fishing | Pleasure Cruising |
| Sailing | 52 | 1 | 10 | 0 |
| | (84) | (0) | (0) | (0) |
| Water Skiing | 0 | 32 | 0 | 0 |
| | (0) | (51) | (0) | (0) |
| Fishing | 21 | 7 | 51 | 18 |
| | (0) | (0) | (68) | (0) |
| Pleasure Cruising | 11 | 11 | 7 | 60 |
| | (0) | (0) | (0) | (86) |

**TABLE 1.** *Observed and Predicted Correspondence Between Activity-Oriented Boaters and Lakes**
* Predicted values are in parentheses.

Kolmogorov-Smirnov tests were conducted of the hypothesis that the activity groups were drawn from different populations. Thus, the cumulative proportions of boaters grouped by activity and coming from increasing time-distances away from the lakes were compared. The results of the statistical tests of these comparisons are found in Table 2 and the conclusions may be summarized as follows:

1. The distribution of sailors and water skiers over space does not differ significantly. The same is true for fishermen and non-specialized boaters.
2. The spatial distribution of sailors differs significantly from that of

fishermen and non-specialized boaters. The spatial distribution of water skiers differs significantly from that of fishermen and non-specialized boaters.

3. While the spatial distribution of pleasure cruisers does differ significantly from that of sailors, it does not vary significantly from the spatial distribution of the other three groups.

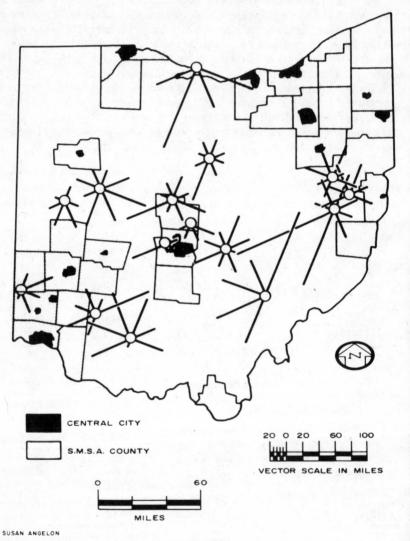

CENTRAL CITY

S.M.S.A. COUNTY

20  0  20      60      100

VECTOR SCALE IN MILES

0                    60

MILES

SUSAN ANGELON

**FIGURE 3.** *Average Length of Trip by Direction*

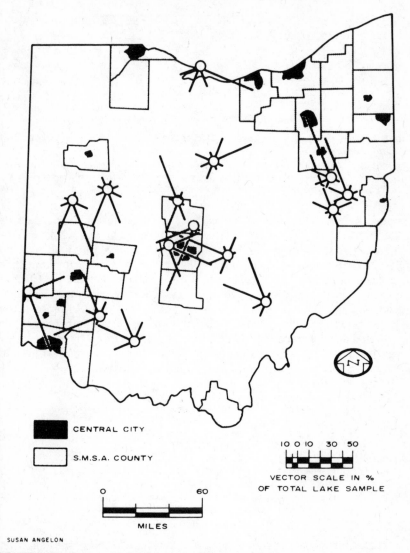

CENTRAL CITY

S.M.S.A. COUNTY

10 0 10   30   50

VECTOR SCALE IN %
OF TOTAL LAKE SAMPLE

0                    60

MILES

SUSAN ANGELON

**FIGURE 4.** *Proportion of Lake Sample by Direction of Origin*

Having established that there are two patterns of spatial behavior which statistically differ from one another, and a third group whose frequency distribution in space is intermediate between the first two, the next question concerns the relative distances traveled by the activity groups. In order to generalize the findings of the study as much as possible, a distance index was constructed. Boaters generally visit between one and three lakes during a given season, with very few visiting more than three. The distance index was derived by summing the product of the airline

| | Water Skiers | Pleasure Cruisers | Fishermen | Non-specialized Boaters |
|---|---|---|---|---|
| Sailors | .160 | .204 | .294 | .285 |
| | (.190) | (.160) | (.163) | (.152) |
| Water Skiers | | .161 | .180 | .185 |
| | | (.163) | (.163) | (.150) |
| Pleasure | | | .114 | .106 |
| Cruisers | | | (.107) | (.122) |
| Fishermen | | | | .054 |
| | | | | (.122) |

**TABLE 2.** *Kolmogorov-Smirnov Tests of Differences Between the Spatial Distributions of Activity Groups\**

\* Pairs of activity groups whose cumulative frequency distributions differ significantly at the 95 percent level of confidence as underlined. Numbers in parentheses refer to critical values of $K_D$ at the 95 percent level of confidence and were computed as $1.36\sqrt{n_1 + n_2/n_1\, n_2}$.

distance between the boater and each of the first three lakes which he visited and the proportion of total boating time spent at each lake. This summed product is an indication of the distance traveled by boaters to all different destinations during a given boating season. Visits to more than three lakes were considered as visits to the third lake which had the effect of increasing the proportion of time spent at the third lake. The bias introduced into the data by this device is quite small. Table 3 presents the average distance index for each activity group. The numbers may be interpreted as a measure of the average propensity to travel by each activity group relative to the other groups. Note the similarities between sailors and water skiers, and fishermen and non-specialized boaters.

| Activity Groups | Number of Boaters | Mean Distance Index | Variance in Distance Index |
|---|---|---|---|
| Sailors | 81 | 25.6 | 14.5 |
| Water Skiers | 72 | 27.9 | 21.1 |
| Pleasure Cruisers | 143 | 33.1 | 21.8 |
| Fishermen | 139 | 36.8 | 32.7 |
| Non-specialists | 186 | 37.6 | 24.8 |
| All Boaters | 621 | 33.5 | 25.0 |

**TABLE 3.** *Mean Distance Traveled by Activity-Specialized Groups*

Heretofore, boaters were classified according to activity specialization or trip purpose. It appears, however, from inspection of Table 3 that there are essentially three categories of trip lengths associated with the five categories of trip purposes. Boaters traveling short distances (mean distance index less than 30) are visiting lakes which are on the fringe of metropolitan centers (see Figure 3). Conversely, boaters traveling long distances (mean distance index of 35 or more) are visiting lakes which are remote from metropolitan centers. It is convenient to spatially classify sailors and water skiers as attending "metropolitan fringe" lakes. Similarly, the destinations of fishermen and non-specialized boaters are predominately "metropolitan remote" lakes. For want of a better term, pleasure cruisers are classified as being intermediate in their spatial behavior between the two more extreme categories. The resulting statistics for these spatially classified groups are presented in Table 4. Thus, the propensities of the boaters to travel as indexed above vary in direct proportion to the proximity of the lakes to metropolitan areas.

| Locational Classification | Number of Boaters | Mean Distance Index | Variance in Distance Index |
|---|---|---|---|
| Metropolitan Fringe | 153 | 26.7 | 17.6 |
| Intermediate | 143 | 33.1 | 21.8 |
| Metropolitan Remote | 325 | 36.9 | 28.2 |

**TABLE 4.** *Mean Distances Traveled by Locationally Classified Groups*

Concerning the discussion of the relationship of distance traveled to activity specialization, a hypothesis may be advanced that there is a direct relationship between the length of a trip undertaken and the amount of time which boaters spend at the site. If this is true, then we would expect that sailors and water skiers spend the least amount of time at the lakes, and fishermen and non-specialists the most. That this is the case may be seen by inspecting Table 5.

| Activity Groups | Number of Boaters | Mean | Variance |
|---|---|---|---|
| Sailors | 81 | 5.2 | 2.0 |
| Water Skiers | 72 | 17.4 | 35.3 |
| Pleasure Cruisers | 143 | 39.7 | 73.8 |
| Fishermen | 139 | 45.5 | 77.3 |
| Non-specialists | 186 | 34.5 | 62.0 |
| All Boaters | 621 | 32.2 | 57.0 |

**TABLE 5.** *Mean Time Spent at Lakes by Activity Groups (In Hours Per Trip)*

The amount of time spent in transit is apparently a function of the amount of time spent at the site. Beyond this, however, little can be said at this point concerning the relationship between the time spent at the site and activity preferences.

The tendency for activity groups to differ in terms of spatial behavior may be estimated directly by fitting a distance decay function to the spatial distributions. The crude frequencies of activity-specialized boaters at different time-distances from all lakes were utilized. While several different functions may be used to estimate the rate of decline for participation with increasing distance, the negative exponential function, $f = ae^{-ab}$ where $f =$ the frequency of boaters' origins and $d =$ time-distances measured in units of time zones, gives an adequate fit to the data.[12] Table 6 presents the parameters of the decay functions and Kolmogorov-Smirnov tests of "goodness" of fit between the estimated and observed frequencies (the functions are also shown in Figure 5). As expected, sailors and water skiers show the highest rates of decline, fishermen and non-specialized boaters the lowest, and pleasure cruisers fall in an intermediate position. (Estimates of the functions are also presented for groups aggregated by orientation to metropolitan centers.)

| Activity Groups | Parameters of Function | | Kolmogorov-Smirnov Tests* | |
|---|---|---|---|---|
| | "a" | "b" | Observed | Tabled |
| Sailors | 56.8 | 0.40 | .047 | .727 |
| Water Skiers | 32.5 | 0.28 | .048 | .555 |
| Pleasure Cruisers | 61.0 | 0.25 | .036 | .555 |
| Fishermen | 33.8 | 0.18 | .138 | .410 |
| Non-specialists | 10.3 | 0.14 | .228 | .364 |
| Metropolitan Orientation of Activity Groups | | | | |
| Metropolitan Fringe | 91.0 | 0.37 | .043 | .555 |
| Intermediate | 61.0 | 0.25 | .228 | .364 |
| Metropolitan Remote | 54.6 | 0.17 | .183 | .364 |

**TABLE 6.** *Estimated Parameters of the Distance Decay Functions by Activity Groups*
* Tabled values of the Kolmogorov-Smirov tests are at the 95 percent level of confidence.

Given the differences in the distance functions relative to activity goals of the boaters and the fact that boaters with similar activity goals tend to cluster at the same lakes, it follows that there should also be variations in the distance functions by lake destinations which correspond to the lakes' activity specializations. To allow for variation in the population distribution about each lake, the crude frequencies over time zones were converted to rates of participation by dividing the frequency count in each zone by the population residing in that zone. Thus Table 7 presents the parameters of the function: $f^* = ae^{-bx}$ where $f^* =$ the rate of participation per million inhabitants and $e =$ the natural base of logarithms. Several conclusions may be drawn from analysis of Table 7.

1. There is considerable variation in the decline rate of the boaters' participation rate at lakes.
2. While participation declines with increasing distance for all lakes,

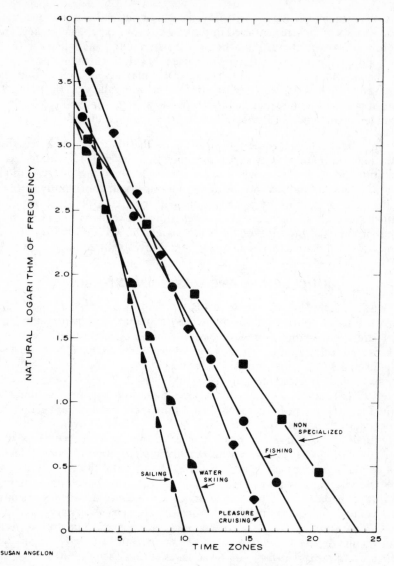

SUSAN ANGELON

**FIGURE 5.** *Distance Decay Functions by Activity Specialization*

the rate of decline for the last few lakes listed is so small that it could conceivably be zero upon repeated sampling.

    3. Of the top seven of the 15 lakes studied, five specialize in either sailing or water skiing. None of the lakes which specialize in either sailing or water skiing had a decline rate in the rate of participation below the average for all lakes. Conversely, all three lakes which specialized in fishing had decay rates below the average for all lakes. In agreement with all

previous results reported in this study, pleasure-cruising lakes demonstrated decay rates which were scattered in ranking between the fourth highest and the lowest lakes in the listing. The only purely multiple-activity lake (East Harbor on Lake Erie) had the lowest decay rate in the listing.

4. All decay functions fit the data distributions very well in that the observed values of $K_D$ were well below the critical values of $K_D$ at the 95 percent level of confidence. Thus, there is a high probability that the predicted distributions do not differ from the observed distributions.

In conclusion, these relationships suggest that there is a rank ordering to the association of activity specialization with the slopes of distance decay functions. Naturally, the specific parameters will show regional variation. The pertinent question is: do the activity groups rank consistently in their decline rate in the rate of participation with increasing distance over the United States? If so, there are many interesting implications to be drawn in terms of a spatial ordering of the service areas for recreational resources. The answer, of course, depends upon further investigation.

## CONCLUSIONS AND UNRESOLVED ISSUES

Evidence gathered in this survey leads the authors to conclude that there are five distinct boating groups defined by activity specialization and that there are three spatially oriented groups characterized by different propensities to travel. Sailors and water skiers tend to have the shortest time-distances, pleasure cruisers somewhat longer, and fishermen and non-specialized boaters the longest of all. These different propensities to travel are associated with different slopes of a negative exponential function of the form $f = ae^{-bd}$. Larger amounts of time spent traveling are generally associated with longer periods of time spent at the lakes. Given that nearly three-quarters of surveyed boaters live in metropolitan centers, this association of spatial behavior with activity specialization of boaters leads to a spatially ordered utilization of lakes according to the activity use of lakes. Because boaters may (and often do) engage in almost all the activities at most of the lakes, they have an almost free choice of destinations. Thus, it is assumed that spatial behavior of activity-specialized boaters results in the specialization of lakes. The exceptions to this statement are the four lakes which are devoted *entirely* to either fishing (Burr Oak and Leesville) or sailing (Acton and Cowan). At these lakes, the laws prohibit the use of motors with more than 10 horsepower and, thus, such activities as water skiing are effectively ruled out.

If we assume, as Clawson and Knetsch have,[13] that distance may be regarded as a variable cost to be paid by recreationists in visiting public facilities, then the decay functions may be regarded as consumption functions. Since boaters in any one metropolitan center have a choice of destinations at which they could boat (i.e., substitution of destinations is possible), demand curves could be derived from the consumption functions. The slope of a demand curve when both the quantity and price axes are in

| Name of Lake | Size of Sample | Activity Specialization | Parameters of Function "a" | "b" | Kolmolgorov-Smirnov Tests* Observed | Tabled |
|---|---|---|---|---|---|---|
| Hoover | 36 | Sailing | 5.43 | 0.83 | .044 | .960 |
| Delaware | 61 | Water Skiing | 6.88 | 0.80 | .042 | .680 |
| Griggs | 48 | Water Skiing | 5.56 | 0.70 | .078 | .785 |
| Buckeye | 96 | Pleasure Cruising - Multiple Activity | 5.99 | 0.57 | .030 | .608 |
| Atwood | 79 | Pleasure Cruising | 6.17 | 0.56 | .046 | .608 |
| Acton | 62 | Sailing | 5.56 | 0.52 | .017 | .785 |
| Cowan | 66 | Sailing | 5.28 | 0.48 | .014 | .785 |
| Tappan | 50 | Multiple Activity | 4.91 | 0.41 | .085 | .580 |
| Rocky Fork | 128 | Multiple Activity | 5.65 | 0.37 | .038 | .467 |
| All Lakes | 621 | | 5.01 | 0.33 | .129 | .467 |
| Clear Fork | 38 | Fishing | 4.85 | 0.33 | .203 | .467 |
| Indian | 73 | Pleasure Cruising - Multiple Activity | | | | |
| Loramie | 36 | Pleasure Cruising | 4.31 | 0.32 | .149 | .555 |
| Leesville | 58 | Fishing | 4.50 | 0.30 | .260 | .467 |
| Burr Oak | 26 | Fishing | 1.00 | 0.29 | .153 | .608 |
| East Harbor | 49 | Multiple Activity | 3.59 | 0.21 | .072 | .467 |
| | | | 2.73 | 0.11 | .090 | .467 |

**TABLE 7.** *Distance Decay Functions and Activity Specializations of ORBS Lakes*

* Tabled values of $K_D$ were computed at the 95 percent level of confidence by:
$1.36\sqrt{n_1 + n_2/n_1 n_2}$.

83

logarithmic scales is called the "price elasticity of demand" which may be formally defined as a percentage change in the quantity demanded with a percent change in price. Regarding the rate of participation as a measure of the quantity demanded (after some manipulation) and distance as an index of transport cost (i.e., variable price), we may derive from the decay function relationship an index of the "spatial elasticity of demand." Calling this a spatial demand relationship is justified because it is clear that the independent variable being used is distance.

It is obvious from the results of this study that there is considerable variation in the spatial elasticities of demand between activity groups. This fact may be of great significance in estimating the relative benefit to be derived from lakes specializing in different activities. However, further discussion of the estimation procedures lies outside the scope of this article.

These empirical findings imply the existence of a definite spatial structure to the activity specializations of the 15 surveyed lakes. Not known is the extent to which this structure is related to supply factors such as varying horsepower restrictions at different lakes, or to the existence of incompatible activities (for example, the presence of large numbers of water skiers may discourage the use of that lake by fishermen), or to spatial variation in the qualities of the lakescape and facilities desired by activity specialists. It may be that the tendency of activity specialists to cluster in space and the propensities of these groups to travel different distances account for most of the present geographic pattern. It is recognized that other factors, besides distance, are inherent in this study. The design of the study—a limited number of lakes plus some uncontrolled extraneous variables—may be very influential factors.

As Wingo has recommended, a useful conceptualization of "the space economy of leisure activities" [14] should begin with spatial distributions of the recreational participants and of the facilities. We recognize that the data presented and the conclusions set forth in this article are only a part of the entire leisure outdoor recreation system. Nothing has been stated concerning the social, economic, demographic, or perceptual characteristics of the boating groups nor has any detailed evaluation been made of the boat activity opportunities and resources at the various lakes. The goal is a conceptualization of an analytical system, based on empirical evidence in one region which aids in understanding recreational behavior. The utility of such a system depends upon similar investigations in other regions which test the model. Hopefully, continued research will provide a basis for rationally planned recreational facilities.

# NOTES

[1] U.S. Outdoor Recreation Resources Review Commission, *Outdoor Recreation for America: A Report to the President and to the Congress* (Washington, D.C.: U.S. Government Printing Office, 1962), p. 173.

[2] U.S. Bureau of Outdoor Recreation, *Outdoor Recreation Trends* (Washington, D.C., U.S. Government Printing Office, 1967), p. 23.

[3] The National Association of Engine and Boat Manufacturers and the Outdoor Boating Club of America estimated the number of recreational boats in use in 1956 as 6,686,000. In 1966 the estimate from *Boating 1966—A Statistical Report on America's Top Family Sport* was 8,074,000.

[4] U.S. Outdoor Recreation Resources Review Commission, *National Recreation Survey*, Study Report 19 (Washington, D.C.: U.S. Government Printing Office, 1962), p. 24.

[5] For an excellent example demonstrating that decision behavior varies in space among a population see Julian Wolpert, "The Decision Process in a Spatial Context," *Annals* of the Association of American Geographers 54, no. 4 (1964): 537–58.

[6] *Michigan Outdoor Recreation Demand Study*, Vol. 2, Technical Report No. 6 (Lansing: Michigan Department of Commerce, State Resources Planning Program, 1966), pp. 10.1–10.38. The Ohio Recreation Boating Survey was sponsored by the Natural Resources Institute, The Ohio State University, Charles Dambach, Director. The senior editors of this article were Co-Directors of the study. Hereafter, the Survey will be referred to as "ORBS" for convenience.

[7] There are three major parts to the questionnaire used in the survey: (1) a one and one-half page list of short questions relating to the origin, travel time, frequency of boating trips, age composition and size of boating parties, and background characteristics of the head of the boating party; (2) four questions calling for verbatim responses by the head of the boating party concerning the reasons for his choice of a lake and the quality of the boating environment; and (3) a set of questions requesting a response indicated along a scale with five intervals. The end points of this scale represented extreme opinions (e.g., the quality of the launching ramps is: very poor to very good, with five intervals marked along a line). Only data from the first section of the questionnaire is used in this study.

[8] Specifically, five lakes had horsepower limitations from 0–10, two from 11–25, one with 65, and seven with no limitations. However, one of the latter group, Lake Loramie, has an enforced speed limit. In terms of lake size, one was less than 500 acres, nine between 501 and 2,000 acres, four between 2,001 and 4,000 acres, and one, Indian Lake, 5,800 acres. The acreage for the Lake Erie site at East Harbor is limited to the area enclosed by the harbor jetty, 850 acres. The selection of lakes in addition to providing for combinations between lake size and horsepower, was in part dictated by boating use. Some small lakes, less than 500 acres, with low horsepower restrictions, did not have enough useage to allow the expenditure of interviewing time.

[9] See the *1965 Ohio Boat Registrations*, Books 1–3 (Columbus: Division of Watercraft, Ohio Department of Natural Resources, 1966). Included are the registrant's name, mailing address, type of boat, length, and water area of principal boat use. As of December 31, 1965, Ohio had 154,741 registered watercraft.

[10] This belief appears to be substantiated by comparing certain key characteristics of the survey sample with other data. For example, 72 percent of the sampled boaters lived in Standard Metropolitan Statistical Areas (S.M.S.A.) compared with 73 percent of Ohio's population. The *National Recreation Survey* found that 70 percent of their sampled boaters in the North Central States came from S.M.S.A.'s. The boats used by the surveyed boaters were 14.5 feet in length, while the national average length of new boats sold is 15.4 feet (data obtained from the Outboard Boating Club of America—see Note 3). The engines used by the sampled boaters averaged 27 horsepower, while the national average of new motors sold in 1966 was 30 horsepower. Furthermore, published data indicate that the average size of boat and motor has increased steadily over the past decade; consequently the size of the average boat and motor *held* by the surveyed boaters ought to be somewhat smaller than the national average of new equipment sold in 1966.

[11] For example, see David L. Huff, "A Topographical Model of Consumer Space Preferences," *Papers and Proceedings of the Regional Science Association* 6 (1960): 159–73; or David L. Huff, "A Probabilistic Analysis of Shopping Center Trade Areas," *Land Economics* 39 (February, 1963): 81.

[12] For a detailed discussion of a negative exponential decline in interaction with distance see Brian J. L. Berry, James W. Simmons, and Robert J. Tennant, "Urban Population Densities: Structure and Change," *Geographical Review* 53 (July, 1963): 389–405. Additional discussion of fitting mathematical functions to the relation between distance and the frequency of contact or movement can be found in Richard L. Morrill and Forrest R. Pitts, "Marriage, Migration, and Means Information," *Annals* of the Association of American Geographers 57 (June, 1967): 401–22. Reference should also be made to transportation and urban planning literature: for example, Walter Y. Oi and Paul W. Shuldiner, *An Analysis of Urban Travel Demands*, The Transportation Center, Northwestern University (Evanston: Northwestern University Press, 1962); J. Douglas Carroll, Jr., "Spatial Interaction and the Urban-Metropolitan Regional Description," *Papers and Proceedings of the Regional Science Association* 1 (1965): D - 1–14; and "Land Use and Traffic Models," A Progress Report in a Special Issue of the *Journal of the American Institute of Planners* 25, no. 2 (May, 1959).

[13] Marion Clawson and Jack L. Knetsch, *Economics of Outdoor Recreation* (Baltimore: Johns Hopkins Press, 1966).

[14] Lowdon Wingo, Jr., "Recreation and Urban Development: A Policy Perspective," *Annals of the American Academy of Political and Social Science* 352 (March, 1964): 135.

# FURTHER READING

## Surveys of the Patterns of Recreational Resource Use

Cesario, F. J., Jr., "Operations Research in Outdoor Recreation," *Journal of Leisure Research* 1, no. 1 (Winter, 1969): 33–51.

Wolfe, R. I., *A Theory of Recreational Highway Traffic*, Report no. RR128 (Ontario: Department of Highways, 1967).

## Concepts and Methods Related to the Analysis of Patterns of Recreational Resource Use

Boggs, G. D., and R. McDaniel, *Characteristics of Commercial Resorts and Recreational Travel Patterns in Southern Ontario*, Report no. RR133 (Ontario: Department of Highways, 1968).

Burby, R. J., III, "A Quantitative Analysis of Factors Influencing Residential Location in Reservoir Recreation Areas," *Journal of Leisure Research* 3, no. 2 (Spring, 1971): 69–80.

Crevo, C., "Characteristics of Summer Weekend Recreational Travel," *Highway Research Record* 41 (1963): 51–60.

Ellis, J. B., *A Systems Model for Recreational Travel in Ontario: A Progress Report*, Report no. RR126 (Ontario: Department of Highways, 1967).

Ellis, J. B., and C. S. Van Doren, "A Comparative Evaluation of Gravity and System Theory Models for Statewide Traffic Flows," *Journal of Regional Science* 6, no. 2 (1966): 57–70.

James, G. A., et al., "Origin of Visitors to Developed Recreational Sites on National Forests," *Journal of Leisure Research* 4, no. 2 (Spring, 1972): 108–18.

Johnston, W. E., and G. H. Elsner, "Variability in Use Among Ski Areas: A Statistical Study of the California Market Region," *Journal of Leisure Research* 4, no. 1 (Winter, 1972): 43–49.

Lewis, J. E., "An Analysis of the Spatial Distribution and Location of Ski Resorts in Southern Ontario," unpublished M.A. thesis, Waterloo Lutheran University, Waterloo, Ontario, 1967.

Owens, G., "Outdoor Recreation: Participation, Characteristics of Users, Distance Travelled, and Expenditures," Report by the Ohio State University Departments of Agricultural Economics and Rural Sociology, 1967.

Tombaugh, L. W., "Factors Influencing Home Locations," *Journal of Leisure Research* 2, no. 1 (Winter, 1970): 54–63.

Ullman, E. L., et al., *The Meramec Basin: Water and Economic Development*, 3 vols., Report of the Meramec Basin Corporation (St. Louis: Washington University Press, 1961).

Wennergren, E. B., and H. H. Fullerton, "Estimating Quality and Location Values of Recreational Resources," *Journal of Leisure Research* 4, no. 3 (Summer, 1972): 170–83.

Wolfe, R. I., "Summer Cottagers in Ontario," *Economic Geography* 27, no. 1 (January, 1951): 10–32.

# Part Three
## BEHAVIORAL ASPECTS
## OF RECREATION

## PREFACE

Important developments in the study and understanding of the uses of leisure time are developing. Initially these were represented by a number of studies that looked at patterns of recreational land use. "User surveys" came into vogue and basic social information was gathered about people using recreational facilities. This type of study culminated in the National Recreation Survey which was done as part of the Outdoor Recreation Resources Review Commission (ORRRC). That Survey attempted to find out what kinds of people participated in what forms of recreational activity. The when, where, and how often of these activities were determined as well. Projections were generated in an attempt to gauge recreational space needs to the year 2000. These needs are integral considerations in the final recommendations of the ORRRC and their impact can be seen in the Commission's land classification method.

Coinciding with the ORRRC Survey, a number of studies were beginning to probe the somewhat more subjective and difficult behavioral questions of recreational land use. What are the psychological, physiological, and social needs that can be satisfied by recreation and how can we identify and accommodate people's values and attitudes? To what extent does participation represent demand, what are the barriers to greater participation, how satisfying is the recreational experience, what are the constraints on satisfaction, how substitutable is one kind of recreational space for another, and can particular landscape tastes be identified and accommodated in the managerial and planning process? Of what is an amenity or attractive landscape composed and how can we measure its real value?

Public participation has emerged as a parallel and important concern. The concern is not only one of how public needs and values can be identified, but also how can such values be accommodated in the planning process?

The overall objective of Part Three is threefold: (1) to provide a greater understanding of the behavioral dimension of recreation; (2) to introduce some basic behavioral techniques and their application; and (3) to provide an introduction to how such traditionally "soft" information as human values can be collected and presented in a form that will have utility in the planning process.

# 7

# TOWARD A BEHAVIORAL INTERPRETATION OF RECREATIONAL ENGAGEMENTS, WITH IMPLICATIONS FOR PLANNING

**B. L. Driver**
**S. Ross Tocher**

This chapter by B. L. Driver and S. Ross Tocher assists the recreationist, who wishes to embark on behavioral investigations in recreation, by providing him with a most effective conceptual framework for his studies. The importance and nature of such considerations as motivation, satisfaction, and need are discussed. Recreation is viewed as an "experience," and the nature of that experience is carefully examined.

The purpose of this paper is to present a conceptual framework within which the conventional activity approach to recreation planning is supplemented by a behavioral interpretation of recreation. Framework is used within the context of a logical and cohesive structure within which tests can be made to evaluate the phenomena of recreation. As with all concepts, the following are neither true nor false; they are only more or less useful.

## RECREATION DEFINED

"What is recreation, outdoor or indoor?" This is a question not infrequently asked of recreation planners or by them.

Webster defines recreation as "a refreshment of strength and spirits after toil; diversion or a mode of diversion; play." Webster's definition is rather complete, intuitively acceptable, and semantically useful for purposes of communication. It includes the notions of nonwork activity, replenishment, change from the routine, pleasure, and all the other ingredients commonly attributed to recreation. But how useful is the definition to recreation planners? Obviously, it has general usefulness, but it offers few, if any, specific guidelines for planning and investment scheduling. What criteria does it provide for recommending action? Can we plan for pleasure or for the refreshment of spirits? If so, how do we project the

Reprinted from B. L. Driver, ed., *Elements of Outdoor Recreation Planning* (Ann Arbor: University Microfilms, 1970), pp. 9–29, by permission of The University of Michigan and the authors.

demand? What "spirit-refreshing" facilities do we provide? It is difficult to imagine that agency budgets will include line items for such things as 500 units of play!

Perhaps the definitional problem is not as great as suggested. Private and public recreation agencies have established guidelines for action. Further, they have realistically and pragmatically interpreted their important individual responsibilities. Nevertheless, problems associated with defining recreation have helped cause recreation planners to view recreation as *participation in activities* which, seemingly, are recreational to the participant. Through this approach, fishing becomes recreation, swimming becomes recreation, exercising becomes recreation, and so on.

The activity approach has many advantages, such as the ease of identifying who participates in what activity, when, where, and for how long. However, it suffers disadvantages because it does not make explicit the need to consider other relevant questions: Why is the recreationist participating in the activity?[1] What other activities might have been selected if the opportunities existed? What satisfactions or rewards are received from the activity? How can the quality of the experience be enhanced? In other words, the activity approach frequently assumes that supply defines preferences (and sometimes that supply will generate demand), but it does not question what latent preferences are not being met. It causes recreation planners to focus on supply and give too little attention to demand, which is frequently appraised in terms of past consumption. In summary and somewhat contradictorily, the activity approach is rather passive. This is especially true when projections of demand (participation) are made based on past types and rates of participation.

Even though the activity approach has many practical advantages, is it the only way to conceive of recreation? Perhaps it would be useful to view recreation not as an activity but instead as a psycho-physiological experience measured in terms of recreational responses and/or a mode or process of responses. Under this behavioral approach, recreation will consist of more than participation in an activity.[2]

To develop the proposed behavioral approach, we will make and explain five postulates about recreation.[3] These non-mutually exclusive postulates are:

1. Recreation is an experience that results from recreational engagements.

2. Recreational engagements require a commitment by the recreationist.

3. Recreational engagements are self-rewarding: the engagement finds pleasure in and of itself, and recreation is the experience.

4. Recreational engagements require personal and free choice on the part of the recreationist.

5. Recreational engagements occur during non-obligated time.[4]

The first postulate states what recreation is. The remaining four serve as descriptors or criteria to differentiate recreational behavior from other forms of human behavior. For this differentiation, *all* of the last four descriptors must be applicable if the action or event (response) is to be considered recreational.

The postulates are arranged in a numerical order of increasing specificity. Number one is a rather generic descriptor with applications to a wider array of human behavior than is number five. The key words are nonobligated time, personal choice, and rewarding (not punishing) engagements. Notice the word engagement, rather than activity, is used to incorporate better the psychological dimensions. We might be mentally engaged only.

At the risk of causing confusion we will point out that recreation stands in opposition to work if work is defined as occurring during obligated time and/or is not, in and of itself, (positively) rewarding. For many people, "work" (as commonly defined), is recreational. It is recreational if these people are not obligated to "work" and if the "work" is, in and of itself, rewarding.

Each of these descriptors will now be briefly expanded, explained, and related to recreation planning.

## RECREATION IS AN EXPERIENCE

**Introduction:**

There are analytical and conceptual advantages in viewing recreation behaviorally. Psychologists define behavior as any observable action (response) of a person or thing (Morgan and King, 1965). Also, it is commonly accepted that most human behavior is goal-directed or goal-guided and that *a person's responses are instrumental in obtaining some goal-object or need satisfaction.*[5] Thus, although we are not always aware of the goal-objects being pursued, it is relatively safe to say that most of what we do is done in the pursuit of a goal-object. These behavioral pursuits, which are observable as instrumental responses, are underlaid by motivations to obtain the goal-object; that is, to consummate or to receive gratification for the need leading to the goal. We can now state that participation in recreational engagements (activities, if the reader prefers) are instrumental in experiencing recreation. Further, it is being postulated that humans are motivated to recreate, that there are psychological and physiological forces, motives, drives, etc., which cause the recreationists to pursue the recreational goal-object(s) and to experience recreation. Implicitly, it is being suggested that motives to recreate can be identified. Let us expand the first descriptor and postulate that recreation is an experience that exists to *the extent to which* the needs or desires to recreate are gratified. It is the experience of attaining special recreational goal-objects. The level of the experience is a function of the goal-state of the recreationist—his condition or situation with respect to attaining the goal-object.

Laing (1967) explains the basic concept being developed in simple language:

> We see other people's behavior, but not their experience. . . .
> Experience is man's invisibility to man. . . . Experience as invisibility of man to man is at the same time more evident than anything. *Only* experience is evident. . . .
> If, however, experience is evidence, how can one ever study the experience *of the other?* For the experience *of the other* is not evident to me, or it is not and never can be an experience of mine. . . .
> . . . I wish to define a person in a twofold way; in terms of experience, as a center or orientation of the objective universe; and in terms of behavior as the origins of action. Personal experience transforms a given field into a field of intention and action; only through action can our experience be transformed. . . .
> People may be observed to sleep, eat, walk, talk, etc., in relatively predictable ways. We must not be content with observation *of this kind alone.* Observation of behavior must be extended by inference to attributions about experience. . . .
> In a science of persons, I shall state as axiomatic that: behavior is a function of experience, and both experience and behavior are always in relation to *someone* or *something other than self.*

Records of participation in recreational activities are simply recorded observations of behavior. But, "We must not be content with observations of this kind alone. Observations of behavior must be extended by inference to attributions about experience. . . ." Actually, we need inferences about recreational experiences supported by data.

Before we attempt to identify some specific motivations to recreate, we will raise a few basic questions: From where do these motivations to recreate come? How do they arise, and why do they take the directions they do? These are difficult questions to which an oversimplified answer will be given. They come primarily from learning based on past experience. To elaborate, the two basic sources of human behavior are instinct and learning. Instinctive behavior stems from inherited characteristics that cause us to perform, respond, or act in a certain manner. Learning, the second source of behavior, is defined as a *relatively permanent change* in behavior that is the *result of past experience or practice of the individual* (Morgan and King, 1965). It is now commonly accepted that most human behavior is learned behavior. Even those behavioral patterns which are generally considered to be underlaid by instinct, such as sexual drives or motivations to eat (prompted by hunger pains), are overshadowed by man's sophistication in learning. Taboos on sexual behavior, eating for self-love or for the demonstration of affluence, and the scheduling of meals at a convenient time are examples. That learning and skill development are important aspects of recreational behavior is conventional recreation wisdom. Changes in tastes and preferences for different recreational engagements must be explained by learning. It is also important in the following discussion of specific motivations to recreate.

## Motivations to Recreate

To begin this discussion of specific motivations to recreate, imagine that recreation occupies a bipolar behavioral continuum with needs to escape temporarily or to disengage passively situated at one pole and motivations to engage actively listed at the other pole. Further, imagine that the extent to which either of the polar goal-states is realized is measured in terms of the types and amount of information received externally or generated internally during the recreational experience. Information is used here as a measure of the ability of an individual to make decisions and to discriminate meaningfully among different values, with these additional degrees of freedom being gained either from the external (sensory) stimuli received or the internal inferential and reflective cognitive processes enacted during the engagement.

The motivation to escape—to disengage, re-engage, or engage randomly—would then underlie the *re*creational aspects of recreation. Rather loosely, it can be said that such motivations constitute drives or priming forces which "push" the recreationist from a rather structured (nonrandom) life space he wishes to avoid *temporarily* into a recreational life space in which he anticipates he can *re*plenish his adaptive energies. For example, he might be escaping an information overload situation and desire a change in stimuli (information) orientation solely for restorative purposes. At the other pole, the motivations to engage actively would underlie the creative aspects of re*creation*. More positive or "pulling" forces attract the recreationist to learn and gain *new* information rather than to escape to change his external informational environments.

The notion of informational environments being both external and internal to the person was presented to point out that the information received must somehow be processed. This processing, at least in part, requires that the new information be related to information that has been received during prior perceptual (learning) activity. This associative process is an ongoing cognitive activity of information categorization and storage (Bruner, 1957). These associations help us to develop our mental images (representations or maps of ourselves and our external world). The representations are not dependent on just the environmentally monitored data our perceptors feed to our brain. They are formed and changed in a complex, not well understood, and interactive process of reception, association, classification, categorization, reflection, and prediction. Thus, the internal environment is important, and each recreationist will process and appraise the information from his engagement according to his individual cognitive style and for his own purposes.

The above bipolar conceptualization is perhaps useful. However, it is too simplistic and provides limited knowledge for functional planning. Let us develop a slightly different conceptualization of human behavior, so we can leave the bipolar scheme and view recreation as a response to a multitude of motivating forces which may exist independently or in some combination simultaneously. To do this we will use Gutman's (1967) and Maslow's (1954) hierarchies of human behavioral responses.

95

Gutman differentiated human responses into six classes defined by the complexity of the behavior. The classes, which are not mutually exclusive, are:

1. vegetative
2. reflexive
3. conditioned
4. learned
5. problem solving
6. creative

Vegetative behavior refers to basic physiological behavior, such as the intake of food and excretion of wastes. Reflexive behavior is a relatively rapid and consistent unlearned response to a stimulus, ordinarily not conscious or subject to voluntary control, lasting only so long as the stimulus is present. An example would be the doctor's tap of a hammer on the knee and the well-known response. A conditioned response is produced by a conditioned stimulus after learning. The best example is Pavlov's dog that salivates with no food present when hearing a bell (the conditioned stimulus) if the bell has previously been paired with the presentation of food for some period of time. Learned behavior is as defined before. In addition to conditioned learning, it would include instrumental and perceptual learning. Problem-solving is an even more complex type of learned behavior. It occurs when a situation exists which constitutes an obstacle to need gratification and requires cognitive processes of the individual to arrive at a solution. According to Gutman, creative behavior is the most complex form of human behavior. He defines it as any activity by which man imposes a *new order* upon his environment, frequently his mental environment. It is an organizing activity. More specifically, it is the original act by which that new order or organization is first *conceived* and given expression.

Gutman's schema complements Maslow's hierarchy of man's "lower to higher" needs. Maslow's listing includes physiological needs, safety needs, belongingness and love needs, esteem needs, and the need for self-actualization. Maslow argues that as the lower needs are satisfied, we seek gratification of the next higher need in the hierarchy.

Gutman's and Maslow's ideas are useful in developing a behavioral interpretation of recreation. Both make explicit the multidimensional aspects of behavior. Maslow's conceptualization helps explain increasing demands for luxury items and recreational experiences in an economy that is quite rapidly removing constraints on gratification of lower level needs. Both hierarchies, along with judgment, permit us to postulate that in recreational pursuits, we find interesting opportunities to engage in the most complex and "highest" forms of human behavior—learning, problem solving, creativity, and self-actualization.[6] Especially relevant to recreation planning is the possibility that these types of behavior might be useful in defining functions of such planning. To follow this thought, let us leave our bipolar continuum, add to our list of motivations to recreate, relate these motivations to different types of behavior, and make inferences about how recreation planning can either help constrain or facilitate the realization of the goal-objects toward which the motivations lead.

What are some other possible (and at this stage of theory development, speculative) motivations to recreate? Desires that one's children may experience certain recreational and/or learning situations can be considered a motivation. Parents and others, such as close friends, may feel motivated to recreate to share those experiences with loved ones. Or people may recreate to *affiliate* themselves with a group. The motivation in this case could be to maintain a social identity or a source of esteem.

Skill development would appear to be another important motivation to recreate. For such engagements, the amount of satisfaction (however scaled) of the recreationist should be positively correlated with the extent to which he felt he was able to apply or develop the relevant skill(s). Such satisfaction can possibly be interpreted in terms of *needs to achieve,* which appear to be important human needs (McClelland, 1961).

The *pursuit of status,* especially the collection of status symbols (such as trophies, rocks, or even photographs), seems to motivate many people into engagements which they find recreational.

Research in psychology suggests that individuals are motivated to recreate in order to satisfy *exploratory needs,* which would contain elements of problem-solving (Berlyne, 1960). Or the exploratory behavior may primarily serve a *creative function,* the rewards of which are the realization that we have established a new order in our environment.

Is the conceptualization thus far relevant to recreation planning? It should be for several reasons. Much is read in our literature about the need to provide a wide array of real opportunities for personal choice. Hopefully, the conceptualization contributes to a better understanding of why different opportunities are pursued and why the array is important. Possibly more relevant is the insight provided about the relationships between motivations, opportunities for engagement, and drive consummation, or need gratification. To illustrate, opportunities to escape, to explore, or to collect status symbols, all imply environmental arrangements which differ one from the other. Or the opportunities to gain status might differ from those to create. For example, does not Old Faithful Inn in Yellowstone Park primarily, but not totally, serve the function of providing opportunities to gain status? To be sure, it is an architectural curiosity and has many historical values. But the question still remains, should scarce funds be allocated through public recreation agencies for the attainment of status in a unique area if other opportunities, possibly of higher value, are foregone in the process? The problem is one of determining and ranking the mix of opportunities to be provided.

Several other comments relevant to recreation planning can now be made. First, much behavior is related to the simultaneous pursuit of several goal-objects. These may be complementary and mutually supportive, or competitive and introduce conflict. Thus, we can find learning (a possible goal-object) and recreation happening together and frequently impossible to differentiate. Or we can find the recreationist, especially the tourist, rushing as he recreates.

The planner should recommend the enhancement of opportunities for supplemental or complementary engagements, such as the provision of interpretative and other informational facilities. He should aim to help reduce points of conflict, such as recommending the provision of certain services (lodging, food, etc.). The mix will vary for different types of engagements (i.e., for different motivations to recreate and for different recreational goal-objects being pursued). Second, it might be useful for the recreation planner to view different classes of uses as having different "goal-packages." The goal-packages of an elderly person could differ significantly from those of a teenager.

### The Recreation Experience Continuum:

It was stated that the recreational planner has impact on recreational experiences through his influence on the provision of opportunities to pursue recreational goal-objects. But he can also affect the experiences in other ways. To elaborate this statement, let us view the recreationist as receiving value (utility) from the experience—from goal-object attainment. The magnitude of this utility is determined by several interacting factors. The most important ones are the antecedent conditions, which give rise to and determine the strength(s) of the need(s) to recreate; the attractiveness of the goal-object(s); and the nature and consequences of the intervening variables which the recreationist encounters during his pursuit of the goal-object.

To make more explicit how the recreation planner can effect these values, let us elaborate these sources in tabular form. See Figure 1.

The antecedent conditions are those which give rise to motivations to recreate. They are not mutually exclusive and can be considered as priming forces which lead to pursuits of the goal-objects. Environmental stimuli are the conditions or things to which an individual is exposed (e.g., to which he is sensitive) in his ordinary life-space(s). These stimuli are varied and would include among others those measured by variables like density, environmental pollutants, pressures of the job, ethnic "place," and status incongruity. Physiological drives are self-explanatory and refer to such conditions as the need for exercise. They can find their source either in heredity or learning. Hereditary factors also are self-explanatory and refer to conditions, such as differences in neurophysiological makeup or in body structure, which could change the ability of the individual to engage in certain activities, such as strenuous activities. Prior learning has been discussed before. Particularly relevant is the fact that prior learning determines the relative attractiveness of the goal-object—the level of utility expected to be realized from goal-object obtainment. Maturity is here used to mean stability of behavioral characteristics reflected in the differences in latitudes of variation between children and the elderly (Bloom, 1965). The elderly have rather stable and fixed behavioral patterns and less flexibility

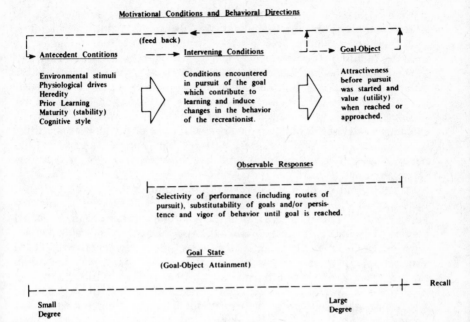

### Motivational Conditions and Behavioral Directions

(feed back)

**Antecedent Contitions** — — — → **Intervening Conditions** — — → **Goal-Object**

| Environmental stimuli Physiological drives Heredity Prior Learning Maturity (stability) Cognitive style | Conditions encountered in pursuit of the goal which contribute to learning and induce changes in the behavior of the recreationist. | Attractiveness before pursuit was started and value (utility) when reached or approached. |

### Observable Responses

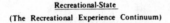

Selectivity of performance (including routes of pursuit), substitutability of goals and/or persistence and vigor of behavior until goal is reached.

### Goal State
(Goal-Object Attainment)

Recall

Small Degree  Large Degree

### Recreational-State
(The Recreational Experience Continuum)

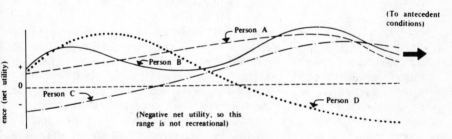

(To antecedent conditions)

Person A

Person B

Person C

Person D

ence (net utility)

+

0

−

(Negative net utility, so this range is not recreational)

**FIGURE 1.** *Schematic Presentation of Recreation Behavior*

for *basic* changes in these characteristics. Cognitive style refers to the different approaches various individuals will take in a problem situation. The intervening variables are those which the recreationist encounters enroute to his goal-object. They can cause changes in expectations of accomplishing the goal, and through feedback and learning, changes in the antecedent conditions for subsequent and concurrent motivational states. The observable consequences serve as measures of behavioral responses. They are appraised in terms of selectivity of performance (such as the activities engaged in and how engaged), the vigor of the response, the persistence in the pursuit of the goal (how long engaged and with what persistence and intensity, etc.), and the substitutability of goal-objects (changes in activity, etc.).

Attainment of the goal-object will consummate the drive for a given motivational state. An example would be reaching the top of a mountain being climbed. The attractiveness of the goal-object relates to the expected value to be received from attaining it. Expected values and actual utility received might differ significantly in either a positive or negative direction. For example, if there is a low level of anticipation, but a very rewarding on-site experience, the difference is positive. Similarly, if the on-site experience is lower than anticipated, the difference will be negative. In either case, the utility from the experience becomes a component of the antecedent conditions for subsequent behavior. Net utility (utility minus disutility) is received from either approaching or attaining the goal-object. It is conceptually possible that net utility might be at its peak before the drive is consummated. For example, we might find the anticipation of and preparation for a fishing trip more rewarding than facing the elements at the stream.

One aspect of the recreational behavioral continuum is not clear in the tabular schema. This is the element of recall, memory, or reminiscence. As we see it, this form of recreational engagement may take one or more of three forms. First, it can best be considered as a distinct recreational pursuit with its goal-object(s), at least in part, being reminiscence. This would be the case when we show our trophies or slides to friends. In these situations, the recreational goal-object would be associated with other, and socially determined, goal-objects. Second, the memories may put us on a new recreational continuum in a slightly different way. They may enter as antecedent conditions (not goal-objects) which prompt us in the pursuit of another goal-object similar to the one which gave us the satisfactory memories. Alternatively, the memories might be unsatisfactory and reduce our motivations to engage similarly again. Or the memories might crop up as intervening variables to strengthen or weaken the strength of a drive-state. In both of these two forms or modes of recall, we are on a new continuum if the four differentiating descriptors can be applied. The third form of recall requires that the recreational-behavioral continuum be extended past goal-object attainment as indicated by the dashed line at the bottom of the table. In this case, the recall need not be associated with a new goal-object and is usually a spontaneous engagement to which the separate application of the four differentiating descriptors have little meaning. It would seem that elements of all three of these forms usually exist—they strongly emphasize the educational or learning aspects of recreational behavior.

Based on the above statements, it can be seen that there is a difference between a goal-object, a goal-state, and a recreational-state. The goal-object (the trophy, skill development or application, a different environment, etc.) is that with which the recreationist relates to determine the direction and to gauge the progress of his pursuit. His changing perceptions of its relative value affect the strength, persistence, and consistency of responses emitted. These perceptions are determined by the nature of the reinforcement (positive or negative) he receives enroute. Attainment of the goal-object dissipates the drive for that particular motivational-state and some other drive takes over.

The goal-state refers to where the recreationist finds himself at any point in time with respect to goal-object attainment. There are a variety of possible goal-states extending from anticipation (defined in terms of the antecedent conditions) to recall.

The recreational-state is the state or level of the experience. As defined early in the paper, this experience exists to the extent to which the needs or desires to recreate are gratified. Thus, *recreation itself is a state of mind.* This explains why it is so easy for us to engage in certain forms of recreation by doing nothing more than thinking. The level of the experience is determined by many variables which are influenced by factors both under the control of the recreationist and not under his control. Therefore, although recreation is highly personal, it can be significantly affected by the actions of others. Being highly personal, the level of the recreational experience will vary from person to person even though they might be subjected to the same external conditions. Further, the level of the experience can vary from goal-state to goal-state. Some people may "peak" during anticipation, others at the point of goal-object attainment, and others during recall. Or the level of the experience may vary at essentially the same goal-states for the same person during different but essentially the same type of engagements.

It is realized that this conceptualization, especially the "dynamics" of the recreational experience continuum at the bottom of Figure 1, is an oversimplification of several aspects of human behavior as it is currently understood. Problems associated with the pursuits of subgoals and the complex and more dynamic nature of reinforcement-responses emitted have not been adequately considered. For example, the importance of feedback has not been covered sufficiently. Also, the notion of net utility, at any point in time, does an injustice to the cumulative effects of memory on the level of the experience at that point in time. Although these additional dimensions are important, we feel that for the purposes of this paper they cannot and should not be considered. They would require much time and space to elaborate, would make the structure unreasonably complex and would, thereby, increase the probability of misunderstanding. The structure is reasonably consistent with existing theory and, as an introductory conceptualization, should be both meaningful and applicable as it is presented.

### Relevance to Recreation Planning:

What roles do, or can, the recreation planner play in enhancing the experience of the recreationist? There are many situational contexts within which the planner directly or indirectly enters the "experience continuum" of the recreationists. He enters at the *antecedent condition level* in several ways. Studies of user responses show that recreationists generally have at least partial information about the nature of the experience expected. Frequently this information comes either from prior on-site experiences of the recreationist or of his friends. The recreation planner also strongly influences other decision makers responsible for the design and provision of facilities, for educational programs, and so forth. Thus, they indirectly affect the amount of information conveyed and received, and concomitantly, the expectations of the potential users of these landscapes and facilities. Further, if outdoor recreation planners could work more closely with other environmental planners in the creation and/or maintenance of more *harmonious and compatible everyday* life spaces and in the development of such programs as environmental education, these interactions might alter antecedent conditions in a manner which is favorable both to the planners and to the recreationists. Perhaps we would then create and maintain environments which are more liveable and from which certain people would not need to escape temporarily to the degree postulated. Recreation for these citizens, especially those in the inner cities, would not be offered as a monofunctional bandaid but instead as part of an integrated multifunctional program. If this is too Utopian we should at least attempt to provide readily available opportunities for meeting basic recreation needs—opportunities within or near those environmental settings which have superordinate influence on the antecedent conditions.

In addition to the recreation planners' effects on the *antecedent conditions,* many examples can be given of how the recreation planner and developer *intervene* during the recreationists' goal pursuits. For example, the type of on-site information provided affects the extent to which a goal can be realized. So do the type and arrangement of facilities; the restrictions, such as rules and regulations; and the learning environment within which the recreationist is "placed" by the designer. Each of these are significantly influenced by recommendations of the planners. As a specific example, what recommendations should the planner make with respect to the emerging programs which are developing to bus city children to the parks? Should recommendations be made that programs be established to provide learning or orientation sessions prior to the journey to the park, at the park, on the bus back to the city or all three? Or, as another specific example, does the planner always recognize the constraints he might be indirectly imposing on certain age groups, especially the elderly? His studies of use rates should disclose that many of our trails are too steep or otherwise inaccessible to our older adults. These constraints are significant intervening variables.

The above discussion of recreation as an experience includes the fundamental elements of the conceptualization. The remaining discussion of the other four descriptors is geared primarily toward differentiating recreational behavior from other types of human responses.

## RECREATION REQUIRES A COMMITMENT

Our proposition that recreation behavior is goal-directed implies that psychological commitments are present. We pointed out earlier that they may be at the subconscious level. Most of them, however, appear to be more overt.

It is difficult to give an explicit definition of commitment. The one offered is that commitment is an assignment of energy, time, and other personal resources, including money. An assignment means a decision and, as with all decision situations, this implies a course or even a program of action. Energy, as used here, includes both psychic and physical energy. Psychic energy means a personal identity or association with a cause, object, or event, such as one's identity with a team in the World Series. Physical energy is self-explanatory and is related to an assignment of time. Time means personal cost, either in real or opportunity terms. For example, the time allocated to recreation could be allocated to the acquisition of additional income. The commitment will vary by type of activity engaged in, will relate to the goal-objects being pursued, and will be reflected in the expenditures made on equipment, the level of skill development, and other factors. The recreationist can be committed as an active participant or as a spectator. It is difficult to be more explicit because there are gradations in intensities and/or magnitudes of commitments.

The notion of commitment has some interesting implications for recreation analyses. For example, would comparative degrees of commitment provide rough measures of the ordinal values placed on different recreational experiences? Do commitments to weekend engagements differ from those for vacations? Are commitments to "disengagement" (to temporary escape) different from those to active engagement, and do responses vary accordingly? Are commitments to wilderness engagements stronger than those to swimming locally? Can the recreation planner expect the wilderness user to expend more energy than the user of a national recreation area? Can he expect the user to walk some distance for certain services? Do some users find the quality of their experience to be increased if they expend a little additional energy? If so, how willing are they to do so? Also, are there identifiable constraints (information, income, etc.) which need to be removed before certain commitments can be made?

## RECREATIONAL ENGAGEMENTS ARE SELF-REWARDING

Two criteria are offered in this descriptor. First, the gratifications received from attainment of recreational goal-objects are of such a nature that these objects are pursued for their own sake and not primarily for their effects on or contributions to the attainment of other goal-objects. Contrasted with work, which is pursued for income to be used to meet other goals, *recreation is an end in itself.* Second, recreational experiences are rewarding, not punishing. The experiences have net positive values: utility exceeds disutility. Together the criteria state that recreational engagements find utility in and of themselves. This does not mean that we *cannot* recreate with secondary payoffs in mind. It only means that we *need* not do so, if we are recreating as defined.

## RECREATION INVOLVES PERSONAL AND FREE CHOICE

This descriptor is closely related to the one above and should be relatively self-explanatory. Several brief comments are: it is difficult to conceive of recreational engagements as *self*-rewarding if not made as a free choice, and recreational activities might best present the opportunity for man to be free. By our definition, engaging in recreational pursuits (especially with respect to obligations of time) is the only opportunity for many people to be completely free, if pure or complete freedom is defined as existing when an individual's action reflects his personal intentions, and his intentions are self-determined (Hampshire, 1965). Obviously, the problem of determinism enters, and man as a social entity with all his roles, expectations, identities, and ambiguities is seldom—if ever—free to determine personally his intentions. As with commitments, there is a gradation or continuum of freedom going from complete constraint to pure freedom. It is suggested that recreation lies at the end of the continuum where constraints are minimal and opportunities for spontaneity are the greatest.

Again, the implied question is whether environmental designs are constraining or facilitating. Implied in the descriptors are these three criteria of importance to recreation planners: (1) that an array of *opportunities exists* from which to make a choice, (2) that the individual is *free* and able *to choose,* and (3) that he is *free* and able *to do.* There is a difference between available and real opportunities. Many individuals can *choose* to do something, but their plan of action associated with this commitment and decision cannot be implemented because the individuals are somehow constrained from following through on their choice. These constraints could exist because of low income levels, racial discrimination, information deficiences, or other factors which make available opportunities unreal.

## RECREATION OCCURS DURING NON-OBLIGATED TIME

It is difficult to define the word obligation. The task becomes even more difficult when the temporal dimension is added—when obligated time is being defined. Oblige stems from the Latin meaning "to bind," which gives one a feeling for the concept of obligated time. Another way to explain the concept is that obligated time refers to time spent during which the allocation is accompanied by a sense of urgency. We are temporally obligated to the extent which we are not free now and in the future to do something other than that which we are doing. The problem of definition is made difficult because we experience gradations in the degree to which we feel obligated with respect to time. We do because we vary in our commitments to those things which bind us temporally. These things in turn require different amounts and scheduling of time. Some are highly structured and require relatively large blocks of time while others permit more discretionary scheduling in small blocks. For example, we feel a greater temporal obligation to our work and to our school activities than we do to our household chores (such as painting the house). There is a greater sense of *urgency* with fewer opportunities for discretionary scheduling. Further, we feel less obligated to certain social commitments and to engagements in nonplay type of recreation such as a hobby activity. Finally, we feel less and perhaps no temporal obligations, in true play type activities in which there are fewer rigid structures, greater personal freedom of choice, and few (or no) feelings of being time-bound. The point is that during recreational engagements we feel a reduced obligation or no sense of obligation, urgency or boundness, with respect to time. All parents have experienced this "unconsciousness of time" of children playing before dinner—"will they never learn to get to the table on time?" Based on a limited sample, these feelings of the parents are not as intense (or even present) when they too are playing, such as on a camping trip.

It was stated that time allocated to recreation is unobligated. This allocation can occur during time which is allotted to means and ends other than recreation but is not being fully used for these other ends and means. Examples could be reflecting on a happy event while driving, enjoying the roadside amenities while enroute to work, or mentally developing a hobby while performing a routine work task. However, in most cases the time during which recreation is pursued would appear to be time allocated to recreation.

Much information is needed on personal time budgets before many prescriptive statements can be made about the significance of this descriptor to recreation planning. However, it can safely be said that in our society time is a resource, perhaps a unique resource, and should be considered as such in planning studies.

In most planning reports time is considered to be an independent variable and is generally quantified in terms of the length of the work-week, the work-day, or the vacation. If we really desire ours to be a leisure society defined in terms of creative and self-fulfilling uses of nonwork time (and all the psychological and sociological implications associated with the possible demise of the Protestant Ethic), should we as planners not give serious consideration to viewing time allocated to recreational engagements as a dependent variable? By viewing time as an independent variable, we tend to accept the idea that recreation is a *residual* rather than the important social input it is. Recreation planners have much to learn about the facilitating and constraining effects of uses and psychological perceptions of time on recreational behavior and about the effects of this behavior on general welfare.

It appears that a structuring of time is necessary before recreation takes on social significance. This structuring, which became more discernible after the Industrial Revolution, makes words like nonobligated, leisure, and discretionary time more meaningful. Recreation planners must question their role in resolving any social problems being created by increasing "structured" leisure time. Viewing leisure time as a residual hardly seems like the best approach. Perhaps we should encourage more social rewards for leisure behavior to balance those for work.

At first commitments and allocations of time seem to be one and the same. But this is not the case. Allocations of time can help define the extent of a commitment, but we can be committed to a goal without feeling "time bound" while pursuing it. Both of these dimensions (postulates) offer interesting possibilities for gaining a better understanding of what recreation is.

## CONCLUSION

Certain implications of the behavioral interpretation of recreation planning have been considered above. At this stage of the development of the "science of recreation," recreation planners will adopt those approaches which are useful in getting the job done. Hopefully, the behavioral interpretation will be a useful supplement to the conventional activity approach. Perhaps the primary usefulness is the raising of specific questions in a slightly different manner within a different comparative structure. Perhaps we can now find a little more meaning in such frequently asked questions as, "Are we providing appropriate opportunities to recreate?" The question can now be reworded to ask, "Are we providing those recreational opportunities which will elicit those responses in the user that are most instrumental in satisfactorily meeting his needs and desires?" These responses (the engagements in activities), the needs of the recreationist (reflected in his goal-objects), and his satisfaction (the level of the experience) can all be associated within the conceptual structure presented. Admittedly, we need greater objectivity and better quantification, but progress is being made in that area too. Perhaps someday we will have a general theory of recreation behavior.

## RECREATION BEHAVIOR AND RECREATION DEMAND

Another possible way in which the conceptualization might be useful to recreation planning is that it requires us to go beyond the four conventional causal factors of demand (mobility, leisure time, population, and income). What are the positive (and negative) forces (the antecedent conditions) which shape our needs and desires? What causes and gives vigor and direction to our motivations to recreate?

Ours has been called the age of anxiety. If true, could this be a causal factor in rapidly increasing demand for recreation? Also, is this demand of a type that will best be met through the provision of particular types of opportunities, say for jogging? If an increasing number of people are recreating as a form of stress mediation or reduction (as there is strong evidence to support), are we providing appropriate opportunities for the venting of the frustrations and anxieties which accompany high stress levels? Perhaps we should have punching bags, more do-it-yourself wood piles, or other modes of creative destruction in our parks and recreation areas.

The authors are convinced that many of our recreational engagements are underlaid in large part (and others to a lesser degree) by our desires to escape temporarily—to disengage, to leave the structured and the nonrandom. These recreationists are "pushed" from their everyday life-space, by that life-space, at least temporarily, into a restorative ecological behavioral setting—into an environment that is less demanding, into one that is remedial and one that is in many ways, more predictable and less threatening. •

Studies of user attitudes, especially reasons for recreating, support the argument that disengagement from the routine is an important reason for engagement in certain forms of outdoor recreation. The high frequencies of answers like "tranquility," "peace and quiet," "leave the city," and so on, suggest that escape is an important motivation and that replenishment of adaptive energies is an important goal.

Researchers in physiological and psychological stress (actually the two cannot be separated because of complex feedback mechanisms, especially endocrinal activity) [7] agree that the human organism, (including his "psyche"), seeks diversion, escape, locomotion, isolation, disengagement (the terms vary from writer to writer) as modes of coping with stress, frustration, or other threats to the biological or psychological integrity of the individual.[8] Although it is tenuous to postulate relations between recreation as a form of stress mediation and reductions in conflict, hostility, and aggression, the existence of such relationships is just as difficult to disprove.

The frequently heard argument that recreation, generically conceived, is *not necessary* for mental health is misleading. What is mental health? It is appraised differently by each individual. It is not an absolute and appears to have few definitive requirements before complete breakdown. Are sexual relations (one of our most important forms of recreation) *necessary* for "mental health"? Probably not, but most adults find such relations satisfying, plan to continue to engage in them, and would be somewhat disturbed if they were told they could not. The point is that many people find certain forms of outdoor recreation to be personally satisfying and useful to them for normal functioning. This is mental-health-reason enough without giving too much conern to the spillovers to society (which in the judgment of the authors are, at the margin, frequently equal to or greater than the external effects of other forms of social capital, including education and national defense). We are not advocating that the recreationists should not ever pay to engage. Rather, we are saying that before specific recommendations can be made we need to consider which types of recreation needs are being met. Opportunities for temporary escape, which we conjecture have marginal utility curves with non-negative slopes, would logically provide more spinoff benefits to society than would opportunities for skill development, the maintenance of a self-image, or the collection of status symbols.

## RECREATION PLANNERS AS INNOVATORS

Another question being raised is: are recreation planners weather vanes of current styles of life, social conditions, and tastes, or are they reflectors of past conditions? Using only the activity approach recreation planning must, by necessity, be based on past responses, which unfortunately might not satisfy current or future needs or tastes. The reader might ask "Is it being suggested that the recreation planner become an innovator as well as a provider?" The answer offered is, "Are the risks really much different?" Certainly we can afford the risks of recommending more experimentation and innovation in design and management. If the *primary* task of the recreation planner is to plan to provide an appropriate array of real choice opportunities, should we not know more about the latent demands not being supplied? Are the opportunities provided as rewarding as would be alternative opportunities, and how can those opportunities which are provided lead to more rewarding experiences? Lastly, with regard to the function of recreation planners, are we concerned with large blocks or with marginal (incremental) units of utility? It would seem that, in a relatively affluent society, our concern is increasingly being devoted to enhancing welfare in small bits rather than in a lump-sum manner. If so, the questions being raised have even greater relevance.

Based on the previous comments, it is submitted that the demand for or supply of recreation, as defined in this paper, can never be predicted or projected. Can we project the demand for love, the supply of hostility, the future magnitude of society's greed or happiness? It is realized that we need measures of the extent to which recreational goals are being satisfied, but are we using the most appropriate measures? Certainly surrogates, such as rates of use (including numbers of visitors and visitor days), willingness to pay, resource supply and capacity, and other conventional measures must be used. But these measures tell us little about the output of recreation systems. We have better measures of the productivity of other social service systems like health and education. Few of us would accept counts of users of schools and hospitals as sufficient indicators of the effectiveness of investments in these facilities.

We make estimates of short-run participation in selected recreational *activities,* and these are too frequently taken as demand projections. But should we not attempt to measure also the meanings that people attach to their recreational experiences? Should we not know what types of constraints are being imposed on the application or development of user skills, and will participation rates give us the answer? Since most human behavior is learned behavior, can we as planners in our data acquisition gather any information on what is desired to be learned, explored, or escaped into, what status symbols are collected, why, and with what personal and social benefits?

## RECREATION AS A SOCIAL SERVICE

Finally, it is suggested that through a behavioral approach to recreation, the provision of recreation services will be more appropriately viewed as a social service system or subsystem (like education and health services), which provides *important and necessary inputs* to the total social system. These inputs can help *maintain the integrity* or homostasis and/or *promote the growth and development* of individual members of society.

The inputs to any system consist of matter, energy, and information— with matter being defined as anything having mass, such as picnic tables, energy being defined as the ability to do work, and information, in general systems theory, being defined as messages, signals, or symbols containing meaning which enhance the operants of the system to discriminate and to make decisions. It would seem a fruitful area of inquiry for recreation planners to attempt to appraise the informational value of recreation. The authors are convinced that the degree to which an experience is recreational or not is *best* reflected in the information transformations which occur from the time the user "enters" any recreation system to the time he "leaves" such a system. It is doubtful if he ever really enters and leaves, but the conceptualization is useful. What is being suggested is that the recreationist, with all his learned behavioral patterns, including his norms, values, and expectations, enters a recreation system and during the throughput process of the system's operation experiences information changes.

These information transformations occur when the participant inter-acts with other components of the recreation system, such as the producers or suppliers, other participants, the facilities, and the landscape, within this different ecological behavioral setting. The transformations could be of a learning nature and enhance the ability of the recreationist to discriminate. They may be of a buffering type and enhance his adaptive capacities through a change in stimuli orientation (such as would be the case when there is a motivation to escape temporarily information overload). It is contended that these changes in the information of the participant *best* measure the extent to which his experience is recreational or not.

Admittedly, there are important energy transformations which occur in many highly active forms of recreation. Part of the experience from these engagements is feeling better physiologically. But the feeling is still based on information processing, either strictly in a physiological sense or including cognition. Accompanying the relaxed physiological state, fol-lowing the burning up of excessive hormones and other biochemical constituents, is our knowledge that we feel better. The conceptualization does not permit that exercising in and of itself is recreation. Rather, exercise is a response which is instrumental to experiencing a recreational state.

In conclusion, it is suggested that the above conceptualization helps make more apparent the types of information necessary for successful recreation planning. Admittedly, much of this information is difficult to obtain, but current progress is encouraging.

Finally, it is hoped that the discussion in this paper has helped establish a psychological set in the mind of the reader which he will find useful in the on-gong process of pursuing a better understanding of recreation phenomena—a goal-pursuit that is not always recreational!

## NOTES

[1] Recreationist in this paper refers to the person seeking a recreational experience and not to the recreation planner, developer, or administrator as the word is sometimes used.

[2] Several authors have pointed out these broader implications of recreation, but they have all tended to emphasize activities in their analyses and discussions. Cf. Neumeyer and Neumeyer (1958) and Clawson and Knetsch (1966).

[3] Elements of the ideas expressed in these postulates are found in several works. Cf. Larrabee and Meyersohn (1958) and Huizinga (1966).

[4] These criteria can be combined to define recreation as a human experience which finds its source in voluntary engagements which are motivated by the inherent satisfactions derived therefrom and which occur during non-obligated time. This definition is similar to the one adopted by Gray (1961).

[5] The exceptions to goal-directed behavior would be expressive behavior, such as the way we carry ourselves when we walk.

[6] As an aside, the authors would advocate that the *ultimate* objective of recreation planning is to promote self-actualization. But we have a way to go before even the more simple forms of recreational behavior are readily and easily experienced. This is especially true for the poor and for certain minority groups.

[7] See Christian and Davis (1964).

[8] See Biddle and Thomas (1966); Festinger (1958); Lazarus (1966); Mayer and Van Gelder (1963); Selye (1956); and Speilberger (1966).

## REFERENCES

Atkinson, J. W. 1968. *An introduction to motivation.* Princeton, N. J.: Van Nostrand.

Berlyne, D. E. 1960. *Conflict, arousal and curiosity.* New York: McGraw-Hill.

Biddle, B. J., and J. Thomas, eds. 1966. *Role theory: Concepts and research.* New York: Wiley.

Bloom, B. S. 1965. *Stability and change in human characteristics.* New York: Wiley.

Bruner, J. S. 1957. On perceptual readiness. *Psychological Review* 64: 123–52.

Clawson, M., and J. Knetsch. 1966. *Economics of outdoor recreation.* Baltimore: Johns Hopkins Press.

Christian, J. J., and D. E. Davis. 1964. Endocrines, behavior and population. *Science* 146: 1550–60.

Festinger, L. 1958. The motivating effects of cognitive dissonance. In G. Lindsley, ed. *Assessment of human motives.* New York: Grove Press.

Gray, D. E. 1961. Identification of user-groups in forest recreation and determination of the chracteristics of such groups. Unpublished Ph.D. dissertation, School of Public Administration, University of California.

Gutman, H. 1967. "The biological roots of creativity." In R. Mooney and T. Razik, eds. *Explorations in creativity.* New York: Harper and Row.

Hampshire, S. 1965. *Freedom of the individual.* New York: Harper and Row.

Huizinga, J. 1966. *Homo ludens: A study of the play element of culture.* Boston: Beacon.

Laing, R. D. 1967. *The politics of experience.* New York: Random House.

Larrabee, E., and R. Meyersohn, eds. 1958. *Mass leisure.* Glencoe, Ill.: Free Press.

Lazarus, R. S. 1966. *Psychological stress and the coping process.* New York: McGraw-Hill.

Maslow, A. H. 1954. *Motivation and personality.* New York: Harper and Row.

Mayer, W., and R. Van Gelder, eds. 1963. *Physiological mammalogy,* vol. 1. New York: Academic Press.

McClelland, D. C. 1961. *The achieving society.* New York: Van Nostrand.

Morgan, C. T., and R. A. King. 1966. *Introduction to psychology.* New York: McGraw-Hill.

Neumeyer, M. H., and E. S. Neumeyer. 1958. *Leisure and recreation.* New York: Ronald Press.

Selye, H. 1956. *The stress of life.* New York: McGraw-Hill.

Speilberger, C. D. 1966. *Anxiety and behavior.* New York: Academic Press.

# 8

# THE AVERAGE CAMPER WHO DOESN'T EXIST
## Elwood L. Shafer, Jr.

In recent years the North American camper has been assaulted by an army of questionnaire-laden recruits from the many agencies concerned with the provision of outdoor recreational space.

More often than not these studies have been ill-conceived, poorly administered, and badly analyzed. But Elwood Shafer's study is a good example of an "on-site" survey. Not only does this study provide interesting results, but the approach taken should be of great value to anyone contemplating a survey of recreationists.

If the reader contemplates using the approach suggested by Shafer, he would be well advised to refer to the original unedited version.

In survey studies of campers, you can no more lump together data for different campgrounds than you can mate widgeons and wombats. Campers differ not only from campground to campground, but also at the same campground from month to month. . . .

If you study campers by sampling at random at several campgrounds, you may find that your data describe an "average" camper who simply does not exist. Such information is not good enough for recreation planners who need reliable information for making decisions.

A study was made in 1964 in northeastern New York State to determine if personal-interview data differ significantly among five campgrounds and three summer months. Campgrounds, months, or their interaction significantly affected the results of all 17 questions used in 1,140 interviews. . . .

## STUDY DESIGN

The five parks used were Fish Creek, Hearthstone Point, Rogers Rock, Rollins Pond, and Green Lakes. The parks differed considerably in physical site characteristics (see Table 1).

Reprinted from U.S. Forest Research Paper NE-142 (1969), pp. 1–27, by permission of the United States Department of Agriculture, Forest Service, Northeastern Forest Experiment Station and the author. This article has been edited for this volume; additional tables are contained in the original article that describe the data and the analytical procedures in more detail.

| Characteristics[1] | Fish Creek | Hearthstone Point | Rogers Rock | Rollins Pond | Green Lakes |
|---|---|---|---|---|---|
| Campsites ........ Number ... | 379 | 246 | 301 | 257 | 202 |
| Average distance between campsites .......... feet... | 58 | 45 | 64 | 84 | 45 |
| Average slope of campground .... percent .... | 2 | 13 | 12 | 18 | 4 |
| Average density of vegetative screening between campsites[2] ...... percent .. | 18 | 13 | 39 | 50 | 5 |
| Average overstory density of all tree species[3] ........ percent .. | 68 | 88 | 75 | 88 | 35 |
| Average distance between a campsite and lake ... feet.. | 18 | 578 | 272 | 148 | 2,680 |
| Lake available for motorboats ....... acres ... | 5,638 | 28,200 | 28,200 | 422 | 0 |
| Additional lake available by canoe portage ..... acres... | 2,015 | 0 | 0 | 2,015 | 0 |

**TABLE 1.** *Physical Site-Characteristics of Parks Used for Camper Survey, 1964*

[1] Average values computed from measurements taken at 10 randomly selected campsites at each park. Other data obtained from the files of the New York State Conservation Department and the Central New York State Park Commission.

[2] As measured according to procedures described by Nord and Magill (2).

[3] As measured according to procedures described by Strickler (7).

June, July, and August were used as three sampling periods. Climate, social, economic, and psychological factors were associated with different summer months. For example, water and air temperatures, number of insects, school vacations, and fishing success are associated with different periods of the summer. Total effect of any one factor does not begin and end exactly within each month. Nonetheless, a summer month represents a fairly uniform condition for many of the factors that affect camper behavior.

Personal interviews were conducted during three months at Fish Creek and Hearthstone, and at all five parks during July. The questionnaire that was used is described in another study (Shafer and Hamilton, 1967). Approximately every fourth camping party that registered at each park was personally interviewed, for a total of 1,140 interviews.

The other campers were used in a secondary phase of this study that compared personal interview results with results from three other user survey techniques (Shafer and Hamilton, 1967).

Throughout the sampling procedures, completed questionnaires within each month-pack category were assigned systematically each day to one of two replications. For example, if 24 camping parties were interviewed in one day at Fish Creek in June, every other interview was assigned to replication one, and the other 12 were assigned to replication two.

The total number of interviews within each park-month replication varied from 36 to 94.

## ANALYSIS

Each answer category for a question was analyzed separately. Analysis of variance (model I, fixed effects) was used to detect nonrandom differences among two parks and three months, and among five parks during July (Snedecor, 1959). Orthogonal comparisons (Walker and Lev, 1953) were used to compare results for June versus the average combined results for July and August; and also July versus August results. The Scheffé test (Scheffé, 1959) was used to make all ten possible two-way comparisons between parks in July.

It was necessary to transform the data before analysis because the variances were not uniform at different times and places. For certain questions, the number of people in each answer category was expressed as a percent of total response to the question, and then was transformed (Snedecor, 1959) to arcs in $\sqrt{\text{percent} + 1}$ for analysis.

Answers to other questions involved a camping party's cost $(X_j)$ of the trip or camping equipment. The transformed value analyzed within each park-month replicate, with sample size $N_i$, was

$$\sum_{j=1}^{N_i} \log (X_j + 1).$$

In these cases the analysis followed the procedure described by Snedecor (1959) for a two-factorial experiment with disproportionate subclass numbers.

Irregular camper registration and departure patterns made it impossible to obtain an equal number of observations in all treatment combinations without biasing the results. Furthermore, different length-of-stay patterns among months and parks made it impossible to obtain *proportional* subclass samples. For example, the ratio between sample sizes for Fish Creek and Hearthstone was not equal throughout the three summer months:

$$101:73 \neq 131:172 \neq 89:183$$

### Type of Camping Party

Over 90 percent of all parties interviewed at the five campgrounds were single families or groups of families. Approximately two-thirds of these families had children under 12 years of age and roughly one-third to one-half of the families had children between 12 and 18 years old. However, at this point the similarity among campers ends.

### Type of Visit

The percent of campers on vacation at Fish Creek and Hearthstone followed different patterns throughout the summer, and thus caused a significant park-month interaction. For example, vacationing campers at Hearthstone increased from 56 percent in June to around 82 to 84 percent in July and August. An opposite trend occurred at Fish Creek where 85 to

89 percent of the campers were on vacation in June and July, but this dropped to 79 percent in August. In July, slightly more than two-thirds of the camping parties at Green Lakes were on vacation. This differed significantly from the 89 and 88 percent at Fish Creek and Rollins Pond respectively (see Figure 1).

A significant park-month interaction also occurred with those campers who used the parks for a weekend excursion (see Figure 1).

Furthermore, Fish Creek and Hearthstone were used as stopover points significantly more often in August than during the rest of the summer. And almost 10 percent of the campers at Green Lakes were stopovers in July; however, this difference from the other parks may be because Green Lakes is only a 10-minute drive from an interstate throughway.

An interesting pattern was found at Green Lakes, where 16 percent of the family respondents camped while the father commuted daily to work in the nearby Syracuse metropolitan area (see Figure 1).

## Length of Stay

Length-of-stay distributions were placed into four categories:

1. The *transient* camper who stayed one night.
2. The *short-stay* camper who camped two to four nights.
3. The *one-week* camper who stayed approximately one week—five to seven nights.
4. The *two-week* camper who camped eight to fourteen nights.

The proportion of short-stay campers at Fish Creek and Hearthstone differed significantly among months. For each of the other length-of-stay categories there either was a park-month interaction; or parks and/or months differed significantly.

Throughout the summer, Fish Creek had a greater proportion of two-week campers than Hearthstone, whereas Hearthstone consistently had a greater proportion of one-week campers (see Figure 2).

Rollins Pond, the most heavily wooded and most secluded campground of the five, had the greatest proportion of two-week campers (45 percent). Hearthstone, with the least primitive surroundings of all the campgrounds, had the smallest proportion of two-week campers (20 percent). At all parks, the two-week camper accounted for an equal or greater amount of total days of campsite use than the transient or short-stay camper.

The multimodal length-of-stay patterns (see Figure 2) at most parks show why it is not meaningful to use average length of stay per camping party, or a count of total number of campers, as an indication of use intensity. Rather, total number of user-days ($U$) throughout a season is more realistic. Where $d_i$ is the length-of-stay for each of $n$ total camping parties,

$$U = \sum_{i=1}^{n} d_i$$

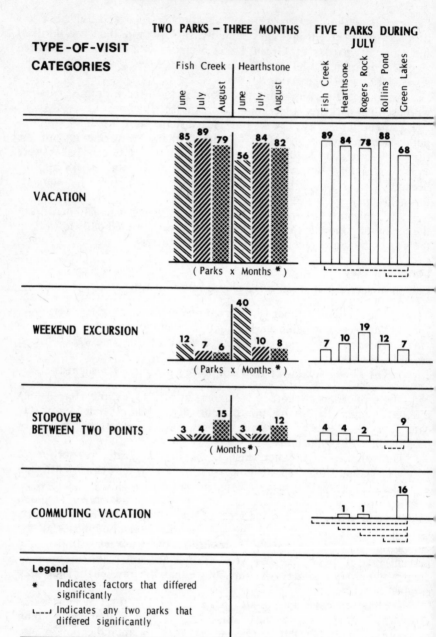

**FIGURE 1.** *Type-of-Visit Patterns.* Bars indicate percentage of camping parties in each category.

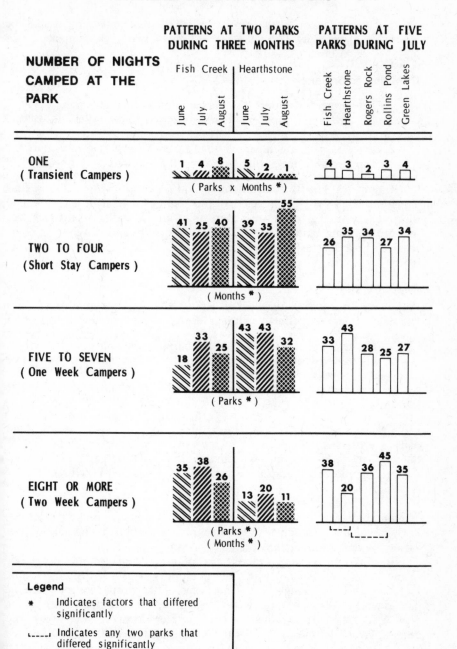

FIGURE 2. *Length-of-Stay Patterns.* Bars indicate percentage of camping parties in each category.

For *U* to reflect the shape of the length-of-stay pattern, it may be necessary to multiply *U* by the proportion of two-week campers. Other types of weighting are also possible.

## Camping Experience

1. The *neophyte* camper who was camping for the first time.
2. The *fledgling* camper who was gaining camping experience over a two- to five-year period.
3. The *experienced* camper who had camped for six to ten years.
4. The *veteran* camper who had camped for more than ten years.

Campers at Hearthstone differed from Fish Creek in three of these four categories. In July, Hearthstone had the greatest number of neophyte and the smallest number of veteran campers of all five parks. Fish Creek had just the opposite pattern (see Figure 3). Neophyte and fledgling campers seem to like Hearthstone because it is surrounded by suburban conveniences and tourist attractions.

## Repeat Visits

Preference for a park is reflected, at least partially, in the number of times one camps there. An effective classification for this type of behavior was:

1. The *initial* visitor who visited the park for the first time.
2. The *repeat* visitor who returned to the campground for two to five consecutive or intermittent years.
3. The *continuous* visitor who returned for six or more consecutive or intermittent years.

Campers at Fish Creek were distributed about evenly across all three of these categories. Significantly unlike this pattern, 66.5 to 80 percent of the campers at Hearthstone were initial visitors. Other parks in July also differed significantly within these various categories (see Figure 4).

## Other Camping Areas Used

The number of different campgrounds that individual camping parties use throughout their camping experience provides some indication of the variety of campgrounds they prefer.

Results of my inquiry about use of other campgrounds depended mainly on where, but not when, the question was asked. Fish Creek and Hearthstone differed significantly in terms of the proportion of camping parties who used six or more, two to five, and no other campgrounds within New York State during their camping career. Many of the five parks differed greatly within the latter category during July (see Figure 5).

## Factors that Influenced the Visit

Between 92 and 100 percent of the respondents gave at least one reason for visiting the campground where they were interviewed. Reasons mentioned

THE AVERAGE CAMPER WHO DOESN'T EXIST

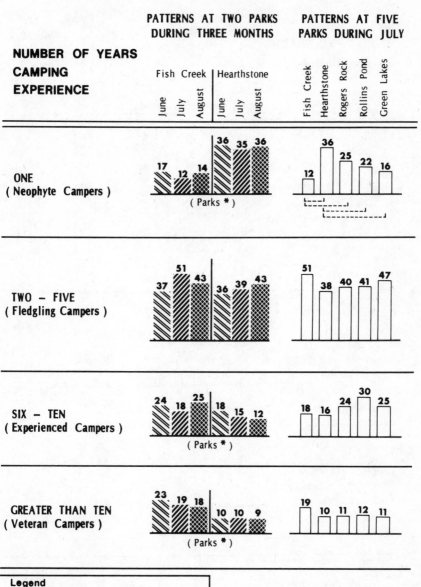

**FIGURE 3.** *Camping-Experience Patterns.* Bars indicate percentage of camping parties in each category.

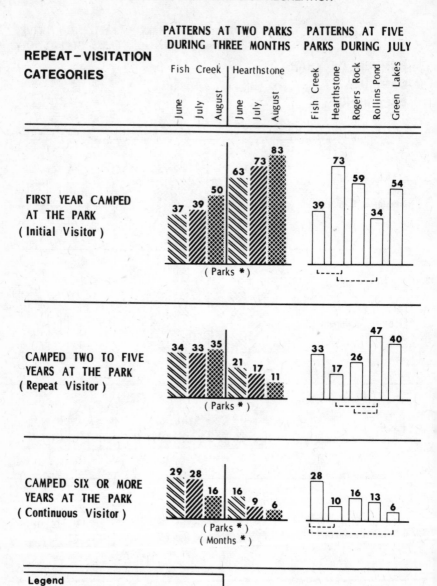

**FIGURE 4.** *Repeat-Visitation Patterns.* Bars indicate percentage of camping parties in each category.

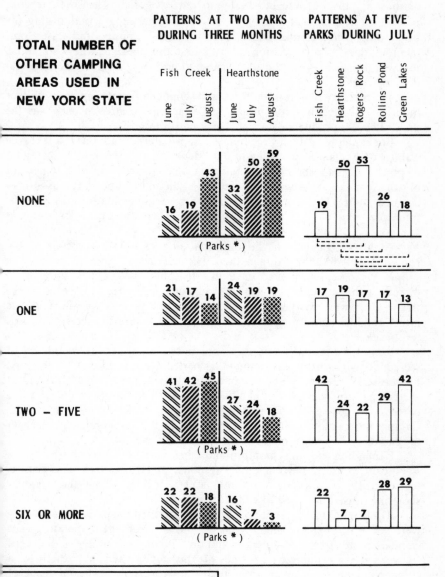

**FIGURE 5.** *Total Number of Camping Areas that Camping Parties have Used in New York State, Other than the Park in which the Survey was Conducted.* Bars indicate percentage of camping parties in each category.

as most important were grouped into ten categories. The seven reasons mentioned by 5 percent or more of the camping parties at a park during any one month were: campsite nearness to water, swimming and water-sport facilities, landscape variation surrounding the park, nearness to home, tourist attractions near the park, campground design, and recommendations by friends.

The primary reason usually differed significantly between parks and/or months. Usually, the predominant physical feature at each park was the major item that influenced a significant proportion of visits.

For example, at Fish Creek most campsites are located near a lake (see Table 1). So it is not surprising to find (depending on the month) that 46 to 59 percent of the respondents at this park, as compared with 1 to 16 percent at other parks, said nearness to water was the most important reason they camped there. This reason, together with recommendations by friends, influenced the *initial* visit to Fish Creek. Thereafter, campers returned annually because the campsites are near the lake.

At Green Lakes, on the outskirts of Syracuse, 37 percent of the respondents said they camped there because it was close to home. The proportion of campers who gave this reason at Green Lakes increased directly with the number of years they had camped there. At the other parks this reason was mentioned only by 1 to 14 percent of the campers interviewed, except during June at Hearthstone, where 28 percent gave this response.

Rollins Pond campground is composed of a heavily wooded and secluded environment, unlike the other parks investigated (see Table 1). At this park, 32 percent of the respondents camped there because they liked the campground design and campsite layout. In comparison, only 1 to 12 percent of the campers at the other four parks gave this reason. Campground design influenced attendance at Rollins Pond, regardless of the number of years respondents had camped there.

Depending on the month, landscape variability accounted for a significant 21 to 32 percent of the response at Hearthstone. This park is surrounded by mountainous terrain and is located along the irregular shoreline of island-studded Lake George.

A substantial 22 percent of July campers visited the parks because they were recommended by friends. Thus we find a rub-off effect operating once campers return to their residences and describe their experiences to others. Clawson (1959) inferred a trend of this type when he described a recollection phase of an outdoor recreation experience. The influence of friends ceases to be important after the initial visit.

Swimming and other water-sports facilities influenced 8 percent of the respondents to visit each park. However, swimming facilities are an important part of campground *design* at Fish Creek and Rollins Pond, where campers can swim and launch their boats a few feet from their campsites. The overall swimming facilities, other than the developed beaches at these two campgrounds, probably were included in the two major reasons for camping there—nearness to water and campground design.

In another study of *observed* use-intensities at Adirondack campgrounds, we found that measurements of the lake, swimming beach, and campground design can be used to mathematically describe use-intensity at a campground (Shafer and Thompson, 1968). These complementary results indicate that respondents in our study provided reliable and valid reasons for choosing a particular park.

Only a few camping parties mentioned that the type and amount of trees and shrubs in the park were important to the visit. However, respondents may have considered vegetation as part of the dominant physical features of the landscape.

In summary, there are several factors that influence a person to camp at a specific park. How close it is to home is most important in some instances. Next, aesthetic features and nearness to water at the campground seem to be the prime factors. Finally, the decision to camp at a place for the first time can be most influenced by the comments of others who previously visited the area.

## VARIATION IN ECONOMIC CHARACTERISTICS

### Equipment Used

The proportion of campers who used tents, collapsible trailers, and house trailers was the same at Fish Creek and Hearthstone throughout the summer (see Figure 6).

Tents were used by 63 percent of all the campers interviewed; 50 percent of these campers had bought their tents within the previous 5 years. Twenty-one percent of the respondents had house trailers and 16 percent had collapsible trailers. Most house and collapsible trailers were purchased within the previous 5 years, and this reflects a trend toward more comfortable and more convenient camping equipment (see Figure 6).

Use of higher-priced camping equipment was significantly related to an individual's camping experience. Only 10 percent of the neophyte-campers (first-year campers), but more than 40 percent of the veteran-camper group (11 or more years camping experience) had house trailers (see Figure 7).

### Cost of Equipment

A significant park-month interaction, in terms of average *total* cost of equipment per camping party, occurred at Fish Creek and Hearthstone and four of the two-way comparisons among five parks differed significantly during July.

At the beginning of the camping season in June, the average total cost of equipment used at Fish Creek and Hearthstone was almost $1,000. During the high-intensity-use months of July and August, total equipment costs at Fish Creek remained close to $1,000, but equipment costs were 30 to 50 percent lower at Hearthstone.

123

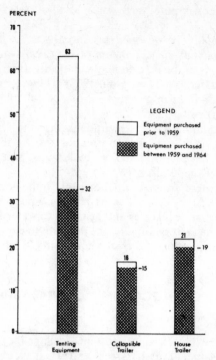

**FIGURE 6.** *Equipment Used by Campers.* Bars indicate the percentage of camping parties having each type of equipment.

The average cost of any one item covered a wide range of values, depending on where and when the data were obtained.

Park-month interactions were significant for five of the six items analyzed. Average cost of different equipment items also fluctuated significantly among the five parks in July.

The average cost of house trailers at Fish Creek ranged from $1,600 to around $1,900. This was 10 to 40 percent higher than the average cost of trailers used at Hearthstone. One explanation for these differences is that most campers at Fish Creek had more camping experience (see Figure 3) and probably were more strongly committed to camping than campers at Hearthstone. Therefore, we would expect most campers at Fish Creek to have more expensive equipment.

Depending on the sampling location and period, average tenting-equipment costs ranged from $97 to $142, collapsible trailer costs varied from $483 to $727, and miscellaneous equipment costs ranged between $78 and $148.

The average cost of boats used at Hearthstone varied between $637 and $837. This was 30 to 60 percent higher than boats used at Fish Creek.

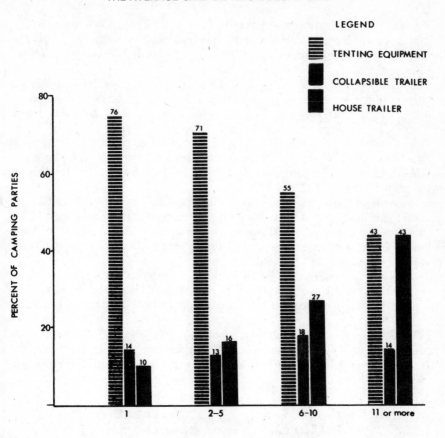

**FIGURE 7.** *Relation between Camping Experience and Equipment-Ownership Patterns.* Bars indicate percentage of camping parties in each category.

However, we might expect to find more expensive boats at Hearthstone because there is five times more lake area than at Fish Creek (see Table 1).

## Cost of Camping Trip

During their visit, campers spent an average of $49 to $70 per party. Summer months significantly influenced the average total on-site expenditure per camping party at Fish Creek and Hearthstone. Between June and July, total average on-site costs rose 26 percent at Hearthstone, and 15 percent at Fish Creek. Also, for this same data, there were significant differences among the five parks in July.

Expenditure patterns were extremely variable between parks when the average total on-site cost was segmented into its five major components: food, entertainment, camping fees, gas and oil, and other miscellaneous expenses. Average money spent for lodging outside the campground was negligible.

Throughout the summer season, average camping-fee expenditures per camping party ranged between $7 and $13. As might be expected, average cost for camping fees and food followed approximately the same trend; from a low in June to a high in July, followed by a drop in August. These trends are related directly to the fluctuations in length-of-stay patterns at the parks (see Figure 2). At Fish Creek, average food costs were the major on-site expenditure, ranging from $29 to $38 while those at Hearthstone averaged between $22 and $30.

At both parks, money spent for entertainment rose from June through July, and this was the only thing that campers at Hearthstone spent more for—as much as 150 to 300 percent—than those at Fish Creek. Entertainment costs at Hearthstone undoubtedly were associated with the many tourist attractions in the Lake George area.

Significant differences between many of the parks during July, in terms of average on-site costs, provided further indications of the wide range of values that can be encountered, depending on where the data are gathered.

## Income

Income distributions fluctuated significantly among months but were the same between parks. Ranges in income levels reported during the summer were as follows:

| Income Class (dollars) | Percent of camping parties |
|---|---|
| 0 to 3,999 | 1 to 3 |
| 4,000 to 6,999 | 19 to 27 |
| 7,000 to 9,999 | 37 to 46 |
| 10,000 or more | 27 to 34 |

About two-thirds to three-quarters of the respondents reported incomes of $7,000 or more.

## VARIATION IN PREFERENCE FOR CAMPGROUND DESIGN

### Number and Spacing of Campsites

Campground size did not seem to concern the respondents. The majority of campers at all parks sampled either were satisfied with the present campground size; or its size was not important to them. Thus expansion of present facilities may be satisfactory to most users.

Depending on the individual park, average distance between campsites was 45 to 84 feet (see Table 1). Most campers (66 to 85 percent) felt that present campsite spacing was satisfactory, but another 14 to 28 percent preferred campsites twice as far apart as they are now.

## Vegetative Screening

On-site conditions at individual parks seemed to influence preferences for vegetative screening. At Fish Creek, where there was an 18-percent screening density (see Table 1), 43 percent of the campers in July desired sparse screening between campsites. In July at Rollins Pond, where there was a 50-percent screening density, none of the respondents chose the sparse-vegetation category.

Most people (85 percent) preferred either partial or very sparse screening between campsites. At most of the parks, understory vegetation density was sparse (see Table 1). Campers—except those at Rollins Pond, the most primitive area—were not too concerned with the amount of understory vegetation available. In fact, the lack of screening in many cases presented the opportunity for campers to display camping and boating equipment. This in turn, may have afforded some degree of social prestige.

## Nearness to Lake

On the average, 77 percent of the respondents at Fish Creek wanted to camp as close to the lake as possible, but only an average of 35 percent of the campers at Hearthstone wanted this (see Figure 8). But again, on-site conditions seemed to influence questionnaire response. At Fish Creek, the average distance from a campsite to the lake was 18 feet, while at Hearthstone it was 578 feet (see Table 1). At the other extreme, Rollins Pond, where most campsites were almost completely screened from the lake by natural vegetation, and were located an average distance of 148 feet from the lake, 72 percent of the respondents wanted lakeshore vegetation either partially or completely undisturbed by campsites (see Figure 8).

## DISCUSSION

The months and parks studied do not represent random selections from a larger population. Therefore our results are restricted to the conditions investigated. However, in future surveys that deal with other summer seasons and campgrounds we can expect to find similar variation in the characteristics and preferences of the camping public.

In one phase of this study, survey data differed significantly 35 percent of the time between two parks, 24 percent of the time among three months, and 12 percent of the time in park-month interactions. In another phrase, survey data differed significantly 38 percent of the time among five parks in July.

Therefore, if you plan to survey campers, you should stratify your sample beforehand by monthly intervals and similar campgrounds. Specifically, campgrounds within a strata should be approximately the same in

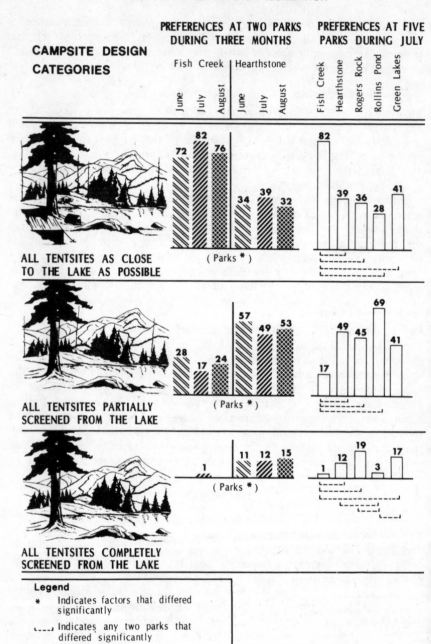

**FIGURE 8.** *Preference for Campground Design.* Bars indicate percentage of camping parties in each category.

terms of: number of campsites, campground design, lake acreage available for boating, surrounding landscape, number of tourist attractions near the campground, and distance from population centers.

Otherwise, if you survey several campgrounds at random throughout a summer, your results will describe a nonexistent *average* camper who eventually can cause more management problems than your study intends to solve.

At present, one should relate management decisions and use-predictions to the physical and social environments that surround *individual* parks.

The same type of variation found among campers in this study probably exists also among fishermen, hunters, skiers, and other types of recreationists who use a wide variety of environments for their sport.

## REFERENCES

Clawson, M. 1959. The crisis in outdoor recreation—Part 2. *American Forests* 65 (4): 28–35, 61–62.

Nord, E. C., and A. W. Magill. 1963. A device for gaging campground screening cover. *Journal of Forestry* 61: 450–51.

Sheffé, H. 1959. *The analysis of variance.* New York: Wiley.

Shafer, E. L., Jr., and J. F. Hamilton, Jr. 1967. A comparison of four survey techniques used in outdoor recreation surveys. U.S. Forest Service Research Paper NE-86. N.E. Forest Experiment Station, Upper Darby, Pa.

Shafer, E. L., Jr., and R. C. Thompson. 1968. Models that describe use of Adirondack campgrounds. *Forest Science* 14: 383–91.

Snedecor, G. W. 1959. *Statistical Methods.* 5th ed. Ames: Iowa State College Press.

Strickler, G. S. 1959. Use of the densiometer to estimate density of forest canopy on permanent sample plots. U.S. Forest Service Pacific Northwest Forest and Range Experiment Station Research Note 180.

Walker, H. M., and J. Lev. 1953. *Statistical inference.* New York: Holt.

# OBSERVATION AS A TECHNIQUE FOR RECREATION RESEARCH
**William R. Burch, Jr.**

To date practically all recreational surveys have involved the use of questionnaires. William Burch suggests a useful but much neglected technique—simple observation.

This study introduces the reader to methods that can be used to systematically observe recreational behavior. Although the example that Burch provides is yet another campground, the techniques he introduces could be used in a great variety of settings. The student should ask himself: How could this method be adapted for the study of residential backyards, city parks, or children's playgrounds?

This kind of technique, properly employed, will greatly enhance behavioral studies in recreation.

## INTRODUCTION

The recreation researcher interested in human behavior may often find that the nature of his problem or outside restraints may inhibit his use of standard interview and questionnaire techniques. Or he may find it useful to have a supplemental check upon whether there is a discrepancy between what people say and what they actually do. In such cases, the researcher may find that observational techniques as developed in the social sciences can provide useful data.

Further, many of the problems in recreation research require the recording of behavior simultaneously with its spontaneous occurrence; yet interviews and questionnaires are inadequate for such a task. As Jahoda, Deutsch, and Cook[1] suggest:

> All too many research techniques depend entirely on retrospective or anticipatory reports on human behavior by the subjects of study; in such cases reports are, as a rule, made in a reflective mood, in which the respondent is somewhat detached from the stresses and strains which influence what he does or says in the ordinary course of events, while he may be influenced by other factors which are peculiar to the research

Reprinted from U.S. Forest Research Paper (August, 1964), pp. 1–19, by permission of the United States Department of Agriculture, Forest Service, Pacific Northwest Forest and Range Experiment Station and the author. Notes have been renumbered and the bibliography deleted.

situation. The degree to which one can predict behavior from interview and test data is limited. In contrast, observational techniques yield data that pertain directly to typical behavior situations. Where the social scientist has reason to believe that such factors as recall or detachment may significantly distort the nature of his evidence as he needs it for a specific research purpose, he will always prefer observational methods.

The important key to this statement is the emphasis that one's research problem should dictate one's method, not the obverse.

This paper accepts their argument and attempts to explore where observational techniques may be usefully applied in forest recreation research. First, some limitations of the technique are indicated; then, some representative problem areas where observational techniques might be usefully applied are presented. These general issues are then illustrated with specific examples from a preliminary field test of two observational schedules.

## SYSTEMATIC OBSERVATION—SOME LIMITATIONS AND SOME PROSPECTIVE RESEARCH PROBLEM AREAS

It should be clarified at the outset that, when I am talking about observation as a research technique, I am not referring to casual, everyday awareness (though this in itself has strong empirical reality—to cease to observe and respond to the interpretation of these observations is to cease to function). A more appropriate model is the naturalist's method, such as Adolph Murie's study of the McKinley wolf, where a specific problem structures the kinds of observations collected and the kinds which are residual. An even more relevant case is the observer who attempts to calibrate mechanical counters of recreation visits. This observer sits at an access point near the counter and records vehicles entering, number of occupants in the vehicle, and so forth. He ignores other items of interest, such as the occupants' wealth, beauty, and psychological motivation, in order to systematically discover how many visits are being made to a given recreation area. Such observation, then, differs from everyday observation in that it is systematically structured by a specific theoretical or practical problem.

In this report, I mean by the act of observing "to see or sense, especially through directed, careful, analytic attention." The noun "observation" will refer to "an act of recognizing and noting some fact or occurrence." I will add to the word "observation" the qualifier "systematic," which shall mean "marked by or manifesting system, method, or orderly procedure; following or observing a plan." Thus, for our purpose, "systematic observation" is a planned procedure for noting certain facts or occurrences of human behavior. However, regardless as to how systematic our observations may be, they, as do other research techniques, have certain limitations.[2]

## Limitations of the Observation Technique

To take first things first, the researcher must be aware of the unique hazards in the reliability and validity of data collected by observation. How can we be certain that what the observer says is so? How consistent will the observations of independent observers be with one another? As these questions have a long history of discussion, our main need here is to but indicate their relevance for the use of observation in recreation research.

Major checks upon observer reliability and validity would be mechanical recorders, such as motion picture cameras, still cameras, and tape recorders, research by other scientists, and the common sense impressions of field officers. The opportunities for falsification of data are no greater in observation than in the interview or laboratory situation. The unethical researcher can manufacture data wherever he is, and tangible instruments are no guarantee against this person. It is the continuing dialog of any science which discredits his falsified data and makes his research career of short duration. If the above checks on validity—mechanical recorders, retesting by independent observers, and common sense insights—seem unsatisfactory and not absolute enough insurance, then we must shift our attack to the bases of scientific faith rather than the specific technique under review.

In the two observation schedules presented in this report, reliability and validity are somewhat aided by the very grossness of the categories used. It is generally evident what a person's sex or relative age is (say between child and adult), and it is fairly simple to determine when someone is cooking or playing a game. That is, we have a fairly consistent denotative vocabulary for handling such phenomena. However, the more one's research problem calls for subtle refinements (for example, such theoretical abstractions as motivation, transference, status anxiety, and so on), the more one increases the probability of inconsistency in interpretation and recording of observations.

Now we come to a third limitation of the technique—the investigator is often limited to descriptive statements rather than causal statements. The researcher is held to "what is" questions rather than "how come" questions. He can say such and such did happen; he is unable, with any degree of certainty, to say what brought it about. This limitation to description is not an entirely unhappy situation; cultural anthropologists have seemed to manage such limitations, and with the introduction of experimental variables, causal statements may be possible. To date, much of recreation research has been caught in the problem of defining what its problems are and describing the phenomenon to be studied. The resource manager often has more interest in description than in causality, because his major problem is to know what *is there,* so that he may act accordingly. Further, all science must begin by describing the natural history of the objects under study and by providing definitive classification of these objects. This must precede the theories concerning how these objects came to be and what they will look like or how they will behave in the future.[3] Therefore, it is in the problem areas requiring descriptive analysis that observation techniques have an important role to play.

## Representative Research Areas Where Observation Techniques Might Be Usefully Applied

The following pages indicate some of those potential research problem areas where observation would seem the natural research technique. I have also listed some specific clue questions in certain areas of recreation research interest. These areas and questions are presented for their heuristic rather than their definitive value.

*Ecological patterns of recreational use.* In this area, we are concerned with understanding the totality of relations between human actors and the recreational environments. Future research in this area might consider some of the following questions: What is the spatial distribution of user types? How does placement influence patterns of interaction? Where do people prefer to camp? What are the attributes of the most favored sites? What social factors are associated with this preference? Is there significant variation between different user groups?

The findings may allow the design of campgrounds to structure behavior or to meet the different demands of various user groups.

*Activity patterns of recreationists.* In this area, we are concerned with understanding and predicting what people do in recreation areas. Future research might consider some of the following questions: What are the representative forms, types, and kinds of activities of forest recreationists? Do certain activities tend to predominate in a given area and to be self-selective of clientele? What activities are characteristically those of one sex? What activities are age graded? For which activities is sex more important than age? For which activities is age more important than sex? What is the influence of family life cycle, social status, and so on, on participation in a particular activity? As we have more women and more children using the forests for recreation, will a corresponding adjustment in provided facilities be required?

These activities and the groups associated with them may give an indication of the output values of a recreational area. Optimum yield, therefore, may be achieved by matching the user group to the desired area.

*Interaction patterns of recreationists.* In this area, we are concerned with the influence social relations in forest areas have upon recreation uses and satisfactions. Future research in this area might consider some of the following questions: What are the natures and types of social systems prevailing in campgrounds? What are the factors associated with variability in these social systems? Do the actions of campers indicate a desire for solitude and privacy or sociability and visibility in the forest environment? What factors account for the discovered variance (if any)? Does a particular social climate prevail in a campground? What is it? What factors are associated with this?

Findings would indicate the kinds of variation needed in terms of size, placement, and distance of separation of campsites to meet the variations of taste—both minority and majority. This knowledge would aid campground designers to determine whether they are doing the best job in meeting present, future, minority, and majority tastes in their forest camps. The findings would also have relevance for social control problems.

*Patterns of social control in the recreation environment.* In this area, we would be concerned with understanding the means for protecting the recreationists from unduly harming themselves or the recreation area. Future research might consider some of the following questions: How are accommodation, competition, and social control organized in a fluid social system relatively free of legitimated authority and assigned status (in leisure periods, one is freed of normal everyday restraints)? Is there established a system of informal norms, or do the members of the camping social system come from a relatively homogeneous population and thus are already socialized into and subscribe to a common system of norms?

Patterns of response and adjustments used in one context may tend to be transferred to new and altered conditions unless the new conditions come equipped with roles and their normative indicators. Does the urban dweller shift his patterns of behavior in the city to the forest situation? Is the rural dweller a more adaptive forest user? Or does the conditioning to impersonal symbols provide the urban dweller with better adaptive equipment?

Example: In the urban environment, various specialists serve as brokers to integrate the actions of hundreds of individuals. The broker of disputes between strangers is a representative of the State. The broker between waste makers and waste disposal is the trash collector. These regularized and natural procedures allow smooth adjustment to maintain the delicate urban equilibrium. Further, the urban dweller is accustomed to responding to impersonal "do's" and "don'ts"—such as traffic signals. The logic of such symbols is not seen as an affront to his individuality. In the rural area, the adjustments are made without specialized brokers and impersonal symbols. Challenges to the rural order are seen as personal challenges to the rural dweller's well being; in this sense, he is often less amenable to impersonal controls.

Thus, with the decline of rural backgrounds in the general population will there be more intense expectations or urban-type services and controls in forest recreation environments? Or is there a code of the forests, transmitted from camper generation to camper generation and camper to camper, which transcends one's residential background? Could the increasing demand for comfort over discomfort, as symbolized by increasing use of trailers in the forests, signal the trend of packaged comfort brought to the forests to emulate the urban amenities?

These examples indicate but a few of the recreation research problem areas where observation techniques are applicable. Clearly, there is a wide range of practical and theoretical problems well suited to observation studies. The following section will present more specific guides as to the conduct of such studies.

## OBSERVATION SCHEDULES AS A MEANS OF SYSTEMATIZING OBSERVATIONS IN THE RECREATION ENVIRONMENT

The preceding section has indicated some of the general limitations of observation techniques and some research areas where such techniques can bring order out of the seeming inconsistencies of recreational behavior. This section will illustrate the preceding discussion by examining two specific observation schedules which were developed prior to field test.[4] One schedule allowed the recording of role segregation and allocation in the forest campground situation; the other allowed the recording of sociometric patterns.

As in any focused observation, neither of these was intended to capture the full variety of human behavior in the forest environment. These schedules did seem to have combined the advantage of interview (easy replication) with the advantage of observation (objective data that pertain directly to typical behavior situations). The two schedules will be discussed individually to clarify their puposes, instructions for use, and the possible utility of the findings.

### The Role Segregation-Allocation Schedule

The role segregation-allocation schedule was simply a means of seeing which activities are more characteristic of men or women, of children or adults, and which are shared. If consistency is discovered, it seems legitimate to infer that a given activity is deemed by a group as an appropriate activity for some persons and an inappropriate activity for others. In short, some of the norms of the user group are being defined.[5]

One aim in much current recreation research has been the discovery of the central activity interests of the user group. In interviews and questionnaires, this has been derived from questions such as: What was the main purpose of your visit? What were the main activities of your group while visiting here? I am uncertain as to the investigator's aim, other than meeting the statistical demands of administrators, in seeking such information. Such information could have little analytic purpose, as these responses are rarely combined with other factors such as age, sex, length of stay, etc. (if reported, they are generally phrased as percentages—such a percent fished, camped, or had general enjoyment). Such information might be useful in interpreting the long-run trends and present demands if they were combined with other relevant factors to permit analysis of possible relationships.

However, the interview or questionnaire technique often unduly biases the response: (1) It is often dependent upon the response of the male head of a family which is often a very poor estimate of his wife's and children's main enjoyment of the forests; (2) it is often dependent upon varying recall abilities of the respondents, with all the inherent memory lapses and distortions of such recall; (3) it demands a simple response when a more complex response may be the more accurate one; (4) there is the problem of consistency of connotation in the phrases of one's question, with differing vocabularies and meanings among different social classes; (5) one tends to receive a socially acceptable response which may not be the fact at all—we usually do not have categories for dreaming, loafing, drinking, or illicit sex relations (all of which may very well be central reasons for choosing one area over another);[6] and (6) it has the inherent assumption that the respondent always knows what he is about, that he is a rational being—a tenuous assumption at best. Many times people with the best of intentions say they did something or will do something when, in fact, what they do mitigates the accomplishment of such intended action.

The role segregation-allocation schedule attempts to overcome some of these biases by: (1) considering all members of a group as equally important; (2) discovering the actual range of recreational activities at a given recreation site; (3) recording what is actually done by the users; (4) allowing the discovery of the relative importance of different activities to different user groups; (5) relating the activities to differing age and sex groups; and (6) allowing the accounting of potential variance in activity interests and rewards (e.g., the same male who goes fishing with an all-male party one week and then goes fishing with his family next week will have substantivally different activity interests, rewards, and behavior patterns as he shifts groups, though the camp setting remains the same).

The details as to the means of preparing for observation and selecting sections of the recreation area for observation will be discussed below. The present instructions refer to the actual recording on the schedule; therefore, the reader should refer to Schedule 1 while reading these instructions.

The observer simply places a mark where the appropriate row and column intersect. For example: if he observes four males fishing and there are two who appear to be between the ages of 13 and 20 and two adults (20 or over), he would follow the row "fishing" across the "all male" column and place four marks. He would then continue across the row to the "13–20" column where he would place two marks and then he would place two marks in the adult column. He would do this for all activities observed within his observation sector.

Obviously these row categories can be altered by more refinement or more gross categories as the researcher's problem demands. The camp maintenance, food preparation, and sociability rows are a means of discovering the division of labor which exists in the forest camping situation. Though these represent work rather than play, they are significant parts of the experience; and, perhaps, the opportunity to work in the camp situation may be as important as the opportunity to play.

The schedule includes changes which seemed necessary after the preliminary field test. Undoubtedly other researchers will need to make further revisions.

Findings from a study of this nature should aid the resource manager to: determine and plan for the central activity interests of his clients; design his recreational facilities to encourage or dissuade certain kinds of use; understand the relationship between kinds of clients and kinds of activities

(Revised)

Campground _____
Date _____
Time _____
Sector _____

### Role Segregation-Allocation Schedule

| Activity | Group Sex Composition | | | | | Age | | | | |
| | All Male | All Female | Mixed M | F | | Child 1-13 | Teen 13-20 | Adult 20 & over | Mixed C(1-20) | A |
|---|---|---|---|---|---|---|---|---|---|---|
| Games (specify) | | | | | | | | | | |
| 1. | | | | | | | | | | |
| 2. | | | | | | | | | | |
| 3. | | | | | | | | | | |
| 4. | | | | | | | | | | |
| Fishing | | | | | | | | | | |
| Water skiing | | | | | | | | | | |
| Other (specify) | | | | | | | | | | |
| 1. Walking | | | | | | | | | | |
| 2. Boating | | | | | | | | | | |
| 3. Reading | | | | | | | | | | |
| 4. Sunbathing | | | | | | | | | | |
| 5. Rock throwing | | | | | | | | | | |
| 6. Wood chopping | | | | | | | | | | |
| 7. Meditation | | | | | | | | | | |
| 8. | | | | | | | | | | |
| Camp Maintenance (specify) | | | | | | | | | | |
| 1. | | | | | | | | | | |
| 2. | | | | | | | | | | |
| 3. | | | | | | | | | | |
| Food Preparation | | | | | | | | | | |
| Sociability | | | | | | | | | | |
| Inter-unit | | | | | | | | | | |
| Intra-unit | | | | | | | | | | |

Notes:

**SCHEDULE 1**

137

and thereby anticipate present and future demands on the site; finally, it is a beginning toward understanding what the experience means to the user.

## The Sociometric Schedule

The sociometric schedule is simply a means of measuring the amount and patterns of interunit sociability.[7] The schedule indicates all social exchanges between units regardless of who initiates the interaction. It attempts to answer the questions: How important a part of the camping experience is the opportunity for sociability, and is there variation between classes of users? As such, it provides an index for comparison with other campgrounds having similar or different user characteristics. The findings can also be placed on a map to indicate characteristic campsite patterns of interaction or zones of sociability and thus offer a means for detecting within-campground variation. Through the use of intensity-measured lines and arrows on the map, the researcher can isolate direction and focal points of sociability within a particular campground. As such, the aim of the sociometric schedule is no different than observing the growth rate of plants on fertilized plots and those on unfertilized plots. The focus is upon the particular phenomenon—growth rate or sociability rate—which the researcher is interested in to the exclusion of quality of content which would require different measures.

While reading these instructions for the use of the sociometric schedule, the reader should refer to Schedule 2. The observer selects his observation area and assigns numbers to the campsites within his view. When interunit interaction occurs, he places a mark in the cell where the engaged units intersect. For example: A person in unit 1 may ask a question of someone in unit 2. A mark is placed where units 1 and 2 intersect and for every such event thereafter until the observation period is completed. Thus, in the course of observation, unit 1 may have two contacts with unit 2, four contacts with unit 3, and one with 5, while unit 4 has no contacts with any unit. This information is placed upon the map at the conclusion of the observation period. At the end of the study period, we should have graphic indicators of degree and intensity of interaction prevailing in campgrounds and those units which seem to engender the most social contacts during the observation periods.

The research problem may require recording of duration of the interaction, inference about the content of the interaction, or listing of sex and age factors of the interactants. The observation schedule here presented is merely a tentative base which, again, can be as flexible as the researcher's imagination.

When combined with other factors, the data collected may have considerable utility in detecting user demands on the resource in addition to implications for possible control of behavior. For example, one campground with an extensive and diffuse amount of sociability would require a different control system than another campground which consistently evidenced tightly isolated patterns of sociability. In the former, one would need to utilize the existing framework for control; in the latter, the many isolated and discrete units could be controlled in something akin to a divide-and-conquer fashion. Isolated discrete units not in communication with one another are easier to control than well-knit groups, whether they be stockholders or campers (a form of public stockholding), as there is little opportunity for reinforcement by others in opposing the authority.

SOCIOMETRIC SCHEDULE

Campground _____ Date _____ Time: From _____ To _____

| Unit Code No. | 1 | 2 | 3 | 4 | 5 | 6 | 7 | 8 | 9 | 10 | 11 | 12 | 13 | |
|---|---|---|---|---|---|---|---|---|---|---|---|---|---|---|
| 1 | ⧅ | | | | | | | | | | | | | 1 |
| 2 | | ⧅ | | | | | | | | | | | | 2 |
| 3 | | | ⧅ | | | | | | | | | | | 3 |
| 4 | | | | ⧅ | | | | | | | | | | 4 |
| 5 | | | | | ⧅ | | | | | | | | | 5 |
| 6- | | | | | | ⧅ | | | | | | | | 6 |
| 7 | | | | | | | ⧅ | | | | | | | 7 |
| 8 | | | | | | | | ⧅ | | | | | | 8 |
| 9 | | | | | | | | | ⧅ | | | | | 9 |
| 10 | | | | | | | | | | ⧅ | | | | 10 |
| 11 | | | | | | | | | | | ⧅ | | | 11 |
| 12 | | | | | | | | | | | | ⧅ | | 12 |
| 13 | | | | | | | | | | | | | ⧅ | 13 |
| | 1 | 2 | 3 | 4 | 5 | 6 | 7 | 8 | 9 | 10 | 11 | 12 | 13 | |

**SCHEDULE 2**

The utility of the findings for indicating user demands upon the resource is illustrated in Table 1. Suppose this case were discovered in areas where various activities tend to predominate.

This knowledge would allow the resource manager a rational basis for making decisions concerning campground layout and problems of social control. If he determined that a recreation site was best adapted to water skiing, he could provide a camp layout which would tend to attract this kind of user and repel other kinds of users, while at the same time accommodating to the user's special needs. In similar fashion, he could evaluate the necessity of providing or not providing enforcement personnel for a given campground.

|  | Principal activity of the area | | | |
|---|---|---|---|---|
| | Water skiing | Fishing | Nature study | Other |
| Level of interunit sociability: | | | | |
| High | X | -- | -- | -- |
| Medium | -- | X | -- | X |
| Low | -- | -- | X | -- |

**TABLE 1**

The next section discusses a preliminary field test made of the above schedules. The specific problems of sample selection, cost, and time limits, and so on, are, of course, decisions to be made by the individual researcher.

## A Preliminary Field Test of an Adaptation of the Technique

It was planned that a variety of forest campground types would be sampled to provide as wide a range of recreational environments as possible. The damp fir forests of the western slopes of the Oregon Cascades and the drier pine forests of the eastern slopes; lakes, meadows, and stream locations; primitive camps to the most highly developed; those camps of easy access and those of difficult vehicle access—all types were to be sampled. To achieve this environmental variation, campgrounds in 3 National Forests were selected—3 camps in the Winema National Forest with a total of 82 family units; 13 camps in the Willamette National Forest with a total of 104 family units; 18 camps in the Deschutes National Forest with a total of 138 family units.

Two 10-day auto routes were established which would cover the above camps at differing days and times. As these camps came in sequence along the prescribed route, there was no way of predicting use at the time contacted; therefore, a means of selection or rejection of a camp for observation purposes was developed. If a camp had one-third or better of its officially announced family units occupied, it was studied. If it was to be studied, the camp was roughly mapped on graph paper, and the entire camp was divided into equal sectors. One of these occupied sectors was chosen for observation by flipping a coin.[8] This sector stood as a sample of the entire camp. The length of observation time of this sector was determined by multiplying the number of occupied units in the entire campground by 15 minutes.

I believed that the composite of observations would cover the range of potential behavior patterns. Further, the utility of observation techniques could be better tested by including a wide range and number of camps rather than concentrating on one or two. I believed that this would also allow some control over possible selective bias due to environmental variables.

The route and observation time ran from 9 a.m. to 6 p.m. with evening observation (after 7:30 p.m.) at the camp where the researcher camped that evening. To eliminate possible bias, the observer traveled by private auto and dressed as a camper. He occupied a campsite with his family, and to all intents and purposes was a camper. This provided the opportunity for extensive conversation and discussion around key questions with fellow campers. However, there was no set schedule of questions and no attempt at formal interviewing. The role of the researcher was that of a participant-observer.

Upon the observer's arrival at the selected campground, the following was the order of work:

1. Checked occupancy proportion.
2. If enough cases warranted observation, then
    a. constructed a map of the camp layout, principal topographic features, and so on (see Field Map below)
    b. recorded auto licences[9]
    c. recorded weather conditions
    d. divided the map into equal sections and randomly selected sample study area.

When the computed observation time was up, the researcher moved to the next camp in the route sequence.

As Robert Burns noted long ago, the best laid plans go astray; recreation research is as much or more subject to such happenings. Of the 20 days planned for observation, only 9 days of observation were possible due to other unpredictable research demands. It had been planned to sample representative camps on both the western and eastern slopes of the Cascades. Due to rain and cold weather on the west slopes, only one camp had a sufficient number of campers; thus, for all practical purposes, the technique was tested only on the east slopes. It did seem, however, that central activity rather than geographical variation would better account for any behavioral variation discovered. That is, it seemed that a camp which is

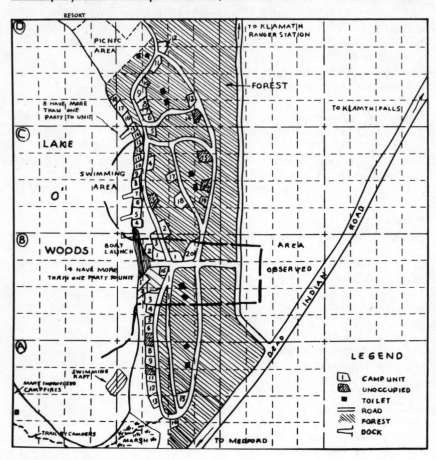

Rainbow Camp, Lake o' Woods
WINEMA NATIONAL FOREST
Aug. 14, 1962   9:30 a.m. - 2:30 p.m. —   6 p.m. - 10:00 p.m.
Aug. 13, 1962   6:00 p.m. - 10:00 p.m.

**FIELD SHEET MAP**

primarily a family fishing camp or water skiing camp would exhibit similar patterns wherever they are found, all other factors such as difficulty of access, and so on, being held constant.

Of the 41 campgrounds on the route schedule, only 15 were systematically observed; 22 were eliminated as having too few or no campers, 3 were eliminated as road conditions were so bad it appeared that the attempt to get to the camp would be a waste of travel time, and 1 was eliminated as the road was blocked by snow. A total of 38 hours and 35 minutes was spent in systematic observation, excluding travel time.

## Suggestions for Future Research Using Observation Schedules

Specific suggestions for improvement, based on this preliminary test, are as follows:

1. Findings could be coded on IBM cards at the end of each observation period. The observation schedules, as presented in this report, were developed after the field test, eliminating earlier problems encountered and allowing ease and accuracy in use.

2. The researcher could concentrate on a single representative type of campground, rather than attempt to cover an entire forest. The general sample of camps in an administrative unit is useful in identifying the campgrounds which attract a similar type of user. However, after this is done the additional travel often does not yield optimum return.

3. It is important that the researcher keep a detailed, current, and accurate field journal. Nothing is insignificant. This is a prime source of interpretation as well as a source of clues for future research.

4. One should have alternative sites as a hedge against unfavorable weather; one should also have a plan whereby one can return conveniently to areas missed.

5. Auto license numbers are most important. They are one way of following up leads requiring further information. Also, by having the camper's address, the researcher can prepare maps indicating the sources of clientele for various campgrounds. This allows an indication of the campground's radius of attraction—whether it is national or local; the distance traveled to representative camps is also an indication of the relative attractiveness of specific recreation sites within an administrative area.

6. The advance preparation of campground field maps prior to collecting observational data would save considerable time. By duplicating these maps in advance, one can simply mark the desired information without the problem of mapmaking and information gathering being part of the same process. The only maps which will be useful are those which the researcher himself has prepared in the field. The official blueprints, if any, of campgrounds will not include the many changes made, some informally by the users, since the camp was built. Relative placement of features is more important than cartographic precision on these maps.

7. There is the problem that on some weekends, the observer will be unable to find a proper place in the more crowded and popular camps to collect his data. In this case, he is wise to forego strict reliance on the observation schedules. Similar information can be gathered by moving slowly and deliberately through the campground. By talking to and observing campers, he can collect concrete data such as size of group, number of units with multiple occupancy, license numbers, a general impression of the kinds of activities followed, and the sex-age compositions of these activity groups. Obviously, this more random procedure is not preferred; however, crowded campgrounds do occur and the researcher should be prepared to capitalize on such eventualities.

The field test did suggest the possibility of combining techniques to gather the most data in the most efficient manner. A combination of short interview and observation could provide one means. Interviewing with the form in sight is possible in certain cases; however, this will often tend to bias the observation phase. It would be preferable for the interviewer-observer to have in mind the basic questions to ask the interviewee and then record the responses later. This would allow recording in a standard form any basic data which seemed necessary, e.g., occupation of household head. This combination of interview and observation would also allow the observer to check the accuracy of the respondents' verbal reports of behavior.

There is little problem in approaching campers and talking with them—most will talk 30 minutes or more covering a wide range of topics—personal to general—with little hesitation. There are many ways to establish contact with the user and thereby receive unbiased attitudes toward the administering agency and its program. Any relevant remark is an excuse for a means of entrance—how is fishing? Are there any other campsites near here? That's an interesting piece of equipment, where did you get it? Once this legitimate tie has been established, then any relevant question is in order, such as: Where are you from? How many are in your group? How long will you stay? What do you think of the camp? What is there to do? What do you like about camping? And so on.

In sum, the foregoing suggests that the observer may wish to concentrate on as many aspects of the following as possible:

*Map* units, occupied and unoccupied; indicate whether trailer or tent, etc., number of persons occupying the unit, whether one or more groups are occupying the same site, the patterns of contact, and the important topographical and social features.

*Talk* to campers about changes they would like made, their length of stay in the campground, number of times they have been camping this season, number of years in this same camp, their likes and dislikes, and so on.

*Record* what the campers do, who does it, and how often; the age and sex composition of groups; the amount and kind of interunit interaction; the patterns of work and play activity; the observer's tentative interpretations and suggestions.

## CONCLUSION

This report has offered an exploration of the utility of observational techniques for forest recreation research. It has offered some suggestions for systematizing such observations through the use of schedules. A preliminary field test of two such schedules has illustrated one means for systematizing such observations, indicated potential problems which may occur in the field situation, and suggested some ways of overcoming these problems. The report has indicated some problem areas in forest recreation research where the technique might provide useful answers to the theoretical problems of researchers and the practical problems of land administrators. The reader was cautioned that, as with all techniques, quality of observation is dependent upon the quality of the investigator. ·

# NOTES

[1] Marie Jahoda, Morton Deutsch, and Stuart W. Cook, *Research Methods in Social Relations* (New York: Dryden, 1951).

[2] More extensive discussions of the general problems associated with observation in social science research can be found in the references cited at the end of this report.

[3] Another problem of causal statements in social science is the inability to subject the causal findings to a pragmatic test—we do not and cannot build social machines as others build mechanical devices. The theory of rocketry as a venerable history; however, until technology and society permitted its costs, there was little pragmatic test of the theory on the scale presently found in the U.S.A. and U.S.S.R. At present, the social scientist is unable to test his theories with such ideal constructions—we have not, for example, launched any models of delinquency prevention, though there are a number of logically sound theories with supporting research findings.

[4] A schedule is defined as a "written or printed formal list . . . a written plan or proposal for future procedure." In our case, it is a formal listing of items to be recorded as they are observed to occur.

[5] As such, the schedule could be subtitled "Central Activity Interests of Various Classes of Forest Campers" if such gives greater clarity as to what we are about.

[6] Obviously, much of this behavior is not "readily observable." My point is that the skilled participant-observer is more likely to uncover the frequency of these actions than are the interview or questionnaire techniques.

[7] By "unit" I mean the designated Forest Service family camp unit; obviously, the use of unit can be as varied as the researcher's imagination.

[8] If the researcher is studying large campgrounds, he will, of course, need to divide the area into more than two equal sectors, and other means will be required for randomly selecting the observation sector. Such techniques are discussed in most elementary statistics textbooks.

[9] Auto licenses were recorded for two reasons: (a) to gain an indication of the ratio of out-State to in-State users; (b) to get names and addresses of users for possible followup research—such as a charting of distance traveled by campers, an indication of consumer demand.

# 10

# AMENITY RESOURCES FOR URBAN LIVING

**Arthur A. Atkisson**
**Ira M. Robinson**

This chapter by Arthur A. Atkisson and Ira M. Robinson is a particularly appropriate ending to Part Three for the following reasons: (1) it encapsulates a great many thoughts and techniques relevant not only to recreational space but to the whole area of environmental amenity values; (2) it focuses primarily on the urban landscape—a landscape in which a good deal of recreational research should be concentrated; (3) it suggests how behavioral data and information can be used in the planning process and how such information can be related to the more traditional considerations used in municipal decision-making.

As more and more people cluster into urban regions, what happens to the natural environment increasingly becomes a matter for public policy interest. Much of this interest is centered on the idea of "amenity resources"; although the concept of these highly valued resources remains vague. With growth in population, income, and leisure, pressures on such amenity resources can increase precipitously. Under such circumstances, the "management" of amenities becomes quite complex and can be extremely costly. Clarification of the concept of amenities and a better understanding of what might be called the amenity management process can contribute to public policy in this area.

It is helpful in this respect to conceive of the urban environment as a system with certain inputs and outputs and a set of conversion processes. Thus, if the outputs somehow fall short of our expectations, it becomes evident that we must look both at the quantity and quality of the inputs and at the processes by which they are being transformed, utilized, and related to the end states desired of the system. It also becomes clear that we must define the outputs we desire and the functions they are to perform.

It has been argued that such a coldly calculating approach to the design of systems which so deeply touch the quality of man's life does violence to man's very spirit and to the values of human freedom which

Reprinted from Harvey S. Perloff, ed., *The Quality of the Urban Environment* (Washington, D.C.: Resources for the Future, Inc., 1969), pp. 179–201, by permission of Resources for the Future, Inc. and the authors. This article has been extensively edited for this volume and the notes renumbered.

underpin our society. To this, former Secretary of Defense McNamara has replied: "To undermanage reality is not to keep it free. It is simply to let some force other than reason shape reality. That force may be unbridled emotion; it may be greed; it may be aggressiveness; it may be hatred; it may be ignorance; it may be inertia; it may be anything other than reason." [1]

In this paper we suggest that responses to amenities make up one of the outputs derived from man's environmental system; that these outputs can be "managed"; and that decisional criteria and management systems can be developed to accomplish this task in a rational and socially responsible manner. . . .

## AMENITY RESPONSE SYSTEM

Some basic concepts from psychology are useful here. We are told that all that man learns throughout his lifetime is dependent on the effective operation of his five senses. As he moves from situation to situation he carries with him the cumulative experience derived from the operation of his five senses in other and earlier situations. Influenced by that experience, he reacts to the environmental stimuli which occur in each situation to which he is exposed. The perceived reaction of an adult to the environmental stimuli occurring at any point in time and space can therefore be viewed as a result of the operation of his senses in that circumstance as modified by his cumulative lifetime experience.

In a typical stimulus-response model, the five senses are shown as providing for human reception of environmental stimuli and as being responsible for the consequent experience of human sensations. Based on the sensitivity of the individual to the quality, intensity, extensity, and duration of the sensations evoked by the stimulus, the human organism experiences certain feelings which lead to the establishment of an *affective value* for the experience. Feelings involve such states as unpleasantness, pleasantness, tension, relaxation, excitement, or quiet. Of these, the feelings of unpleasantness and pleasantness characterize the "hedonic tone," or degree of satisfaction obtained from the subjective experience, and are the basis for establishment of affective value.

The affective value of sensations derived from a variety of stimuli have been measured through a number of techniques, including: (1) the scaler method, in which the observer judges the affective value of a stimulus on a subjective scale, extending from very unpleasant through indifferent to very pleasant, and usually involving five or more steps; (2) the serial method, in which the observer establishes the rank order to a set of stimuli with respect to affective value; and (3) the paired comparison method, in which the observer judges the relative pleasantness of all possible paired combinations of a set of stimuli. The frequency with which a stimulus is preferred when paired successively with all others is considered a measure of its affective value.

Over time, the individual's feelings about particular sensations lead to the formation of *attitudes, motives*, and *habits*. Every attitude has an object as its focus and involves a feeling about that object. An attitude may therefore be defined as "a readiness to become motivated with respect to an object." [2]

Motives, drives, and attitudes involve some human valuing process by which appreciation or interest is expressed toward the quality of an object or phenomenon within the individual's sensory field, or which can somehow be related to that field. Value theorists suggest that *value* and the *feeling of value* are the same thing. Whether expressed in the economic marketplace or in some other way, they have their roots in the feelings people express toward particular sensations. Because of this, feelings are studied experimentally as determinants of preference among various objects or events in the environment of human beings. Since the satisfaction of drives (motives) is usually pleasant, while frustration of them is unpleasant, feelings thus are related to motivation and to the whole field of economic behavior. Thus, the value a human being places on an experience, an object, or a phenomenon is based on: the attitudes he holds toward the commodity; the objects or goals which are motivating him; his preferential ordering of these goals in terms of past feelings about different sensations; and the other learning situations through which he has been processed.

A. H. Maslow has suggested that man's motives fall into an ascending hierarchy beginning with those oriented around his needs for survival, safety, and security and ending with those related to self-actualization which involve the maximum use of all his resources. The satisfaction of lower-level needs leads to a loss or reduction in their motivational power and to a reorientation of motives around the achievement of higher-level satisfactions. Thus, as the simple requirements for survival, safety, and security are satisfied, higher-level satisfactions are increasingly valued and become the basis of an individual's value and behavioral orientation.[3]

Drawing on these basic concepts, it can be said that *those stimuli which lead to feelings of comfort, pleasure, or joy may be referred to as amenities.* Since these feelings may be manifest in situations in which more basic, lower-order human needs are also being satisfied, a system or scale for classifying responses is needed. Because of this, it seems useful to conceive of a scale of human responses which are ordered around man's discernible hierarchy of motives and values, extending from survival at one end to self-actualization, comfort, and joy at the other. Since such a response scale has relevance to stimuli generated by environmental circumstances, it may also be appropriate for the measurement of environmental quality.

In similar terms, Frank Stead has suggested a scale involving four criteria by which environmental quality can be judged:[4] First, does it insure survival? Second, does it prevent disease and accidents? Third, does it help promote efficient or unusual human performance? Fourth, does it promote comfort, pleasure, or joy? In this chapter we will view Stead's fourth criterion in terms of an "amenity scale" along which might be ordered the several types of responses man makes to those circumstances in his environment which generate feelings of comfort, pleasure, or joy. Some of these responses may lead to heightened productivity or to such a relaxation of pressure, tension, and stress that they may be found to increase man's longevity or health. Other responses may be said to have economic value since they motivate the human being to purchase private amenity goods or to support community investments in public amenity goods. Still other higher-order responses may be psychologically valued by the individual but result in no clearly discernible behavioral manifestation, either economic or political.

An example of a simple amenity response system follows:

| | |
|---|---|
| Amenity stimulus generator (or precipitant) | Hilltop bordering on an urban park |
| Respondent | Family in hilltop residence |
| Amenity | View of park<br>View of hill contours<br>Sound of breezes in hilltop trees and shrubs<br>Smell of vegetation<br>Quiet<br>Privacy |
| Amenity response | Purchase of hilltop home<br>Frequent walks on hilltop<br>Potential support for zoning in surrounding area |
| Potential disamenities | Visually insulting introduction of highway through park<br>Visibility-obscuring smog<br>Noise-generating traffic routes<br>Privacy-destroying developments on hilltop |

The example makes clear the several components that are involved in any amenity-response system. The stimulus generator, which we shall call the precipitant (the park), generates a stimulus (a view of the park) which in turn provokes a sensation having affective value (pleasure, joy) to a respondent receiving the stimulus. For the sensation to occur, a respondent having sensitivity to and value for the stimulus must be brought into effective proximity (the hilltop) to the precipitant. In the model, it seems clear that the *view*, not the park or the hilltop, is the amenity. Factors, such as smog, which can interfere with the reception of the amenity (or stimulus) or which affect the capability of the precipitant to give rise to the amenity are here called *disamenities*.

In the model, the willingness of the hilltop resident to pay a higher price for his home there than for one in alternate locations can be viewed in three ways: as a measure of the intensity of his response to the amenities converging on that site; as an expression of his preference for that particular package of amenities versus others purchasable through a comparable investment; and as an indication of his ability to pay for amenity values in his environment. However, these expressions are simply indicators of his favorable response to this set of amenity stimuli, and are not to be confused with the amenity response itself; viz., the feeling of pleasure evoked by the view.

Since a variety of circumstances can lead to amenity responses, or can interfere with the generation and reception of amenity stimuli, an amenity-precipitant typology must include not only disamenities as well as amenities but should also cover several types of precipitants in each case. Thus:

|  | Amenities | Disamenities |
|---|---|---|
| Sociocultural precipitant: | Interactive (e.g., group activities) Artistic Community services | Interactive ("not our kind of people") Aesthetic "insults" Lack of community services |
| Physical precipitant: | Man-made (e.g., architectural artifacts) Natural: basic environmental variables amenity resources areas (ARA's) | Man-made (e.g., junkyards) Natural (e.g., smog, noise, dust) |

In this paper, the principal focus is on natural amenities and the disamenities which threaten enjoyment of them, although from time to time other types of amenities will be brought in for illustrative purposes.

In our view, then, the amenity value of any environmental configuration is determined by the human responses which it engenders. Thus, the concept of amenities relates to an entire system of stimulus-response variables; to the conditions which influence the occurrence of the stimuli—their intensity, extensity, and duration; and to the significance of these stimuli to human beings exposed to them.

In these terms, it becomes necessary to conceptualize the existence of both an "amenity response system" and a "disamenity response system." In one case, the stimulus is an amenity while in the other it is a disamenity. Each has a systemic reference and cannot be defined outside the context of a system consisting of a precipitant, a stimulus, and a respondent.

## AMENITY RESPONSES AND RESPONDENTS

Within the context of the concept of the human stimulus-response system presented above, it is important to recognize that any measurable response attribute may have a wide range of variations. People differ in their response to music and drama, just as they differ widely in their response to the eye-irritating properties of photochemical smog. Where mixed cultural and biological factors are at play, as in the case of human responses to noise, similar wide variations in response patterns are observed. The threshold of amenity or disamenity experience may therefore be hypothesized to vary widely throughout a population, as may the intensity or significance of the experience. The process of socialization to which an individual has been exposed and the values of his family, his region, and his country can be viewed as factors important to the pattern of response he exhibits toward any environmental stimuli. Consequently, an understanding of these variations in human response patterns is a key aspect of urban amenity planning and management.

Since an amenity is measured by the response it evokes from human beings, the values, standards, and tastes of a population must necessarily influence the characterization, as amenities, of those environmental variables which impinge on the life space of that population. Since human perceptions are critical to the root concept, the amenity characteristics of an environmental variable, singly or in combination, may therefore vary from population group to population group, from place to place, and from time to time.

Response curves indicating the distribution of reaction of various population groups to amenity and disamenity precipitants would be helpful for environmental planning and management. However, we have found little hard data which could be used to construct such curves at this time. The task of developing scales of human response to environmental stimuli seems to us to be a most important and challenging one.

The factor of differences in response to amenity stimuli of individuals, groups, and communities might conceivably be measured by:

1. The proportion of exposed population experiencing a response;
2. The distribution of response intensity within the respondent group; and
3. The willingness and capability of the respondent group to pay for any given level of the amenity value as a private good. . . .

## AMENITIES, DISAMENITIES, AND THEIR PRECIPITANTS

As noted earlier (and as detailed in Table 1), it is necessary to distinguish between precipitants (which extend over very many natural and man-made features) and amenities (or stimuli).

Amenity planning and management should be concerned both with the amenity values of the basic natural resources (air, water, and so on) and with those *areas* in which a special juxtaposition of resource endowments and environmental quality characteristics converge at some point in time and space to result in the quality of "being pleasant and agreeable."

The qualitative properties of any basic natural resource, such as water,

151

**TABLE 1.** Amenity Response Patterns within an Amenity Resource Area

| Precipitant(s) | Supporting precipitants | Function/uses | Amenity | Respondent(s) | Potential disamenities | Amenity infrastructure required, if any |
|---|---|---|---|---|---|---|
| Hilltop bordering on a large park | Congenial climate and weather | Site for residential, or commercial and/or industrial development | Views, vistas, panoramas, perspectives of park | Residents of and visitors to hilltop and park | Fumes, odors, smog | Clear trees |
| | "Pure" air | | View of hill contours | Bird-watchers, viewers, walkers, hikers, nature lovers, tourists | Excessive wind | Build roads/tramway |
| | Vegetation, soils, wild life (e.g., trees, wild flowers, birds) | Viewpoint and natural landmark for residents and visitors to the park | The delight of natural sights, sounds, and smells; breezes through trees and song of birds | Campers | Foreground interference from roofs, walls, overhead wires, cars, backyards, trees, structures, signs, poles obstructing or distorting view of park | Install sewers and drainage systems |
| | Unique geological formations (e.g., cliffs, promontories, natural bri ge) | Open area; limited development and use | Natural quiet | | Visibility-obscuring smog | Eliminate disamenities where possible |
| | | Camping and active recreation | Privacy and repose | | | Minor roads to hilltop |
| | | | Natural landmark | | Noise-generating traffic | Hiking, riding, bicycling trails |
| | | | Communion with nature | | | Viewpoints |
| | | | Educational values | | Privacy-destroying developments elsewhere on hilltop | Campsites |
| | | | Flora, fauna, wildlife, etc. | | Levelling and denuding of hilltop | Stores, car parks, picnic areas |
| | | | Being able to get away from it all | | Any development as required for residential, commercial, or industrial use | |
| | | | Active recreation | | | |

may be judged, at least conceptually, by an amenity scale. Similarly, some of the public concern over air pollution is directed at the visibility-reducing characteristics of a polluted air mass, characteristics which are aesthetically offensive to a substantial fraction of the population.

In contrast, the concept of an amenity resource *area* (ARA) is intended to refer to some point in time and space at which a special juxtaposition of environmental amenity precipitants occurs and which exhibits a complex pattern of amenity stimuli and response. Such a complex system is presented in Table 1, which deals with a hypothesized area consisting of a major precipitant, a hilltop bordered by a park. Within the area, a variety of supporting amenity precipitants are also discernible, each influencing detectable respondent groups. The population exposed to these precipitants responds to both single amenity variables and to combinations of those variables. The boundaries of any amenity resource area may be difficult to draw, but nevertheless seem to be prescribed by the pattern of stimuli and human reactions to them exhibited within the system.

Referring back to the question of measurement, these concepts suggest that for any amenity resource area, and for any level of amenity quality, there is:

1. a discoverable exposure group;
2. a discoverable respondent group;
3. a discoverable distribution of response intensity within that group;
4. a discoverable economic demand (value) for the amenity;
5. a discoverable cost for protecting and/or developing the amenity;
6. a discoverable economic gain or loss for protecting and/or developing the amenity.

## The Amenity Decision System

Clearly, any environmental policy strategy for urban communities must be based on the fact of continued urbanization and urban growth and not simply on current situations. The massive city-building effort that yet lies ahead provides us with numerous opportunities to readjust our traditional decisional practices and undeniably would be enhanced by new sets of criteria concerned with the range of consequences to environmental quality and life styles—optional patterns of land use, urban design, population distribution, and other factors. One of the primary virtues of the systems approach is the new visibility it may give to these consequences.

If the approach is to be made operational, however, attention must be given to correction of the most grievous deficiencies of the present decisional system. If the information fed back into the system is confined only to economic criteria, rather than being concerned with the full range of human responses to environmental quality conditions, then it seems likely that the system will behave in the future much as it has behaved in the past, at least in respect to the protection and/or development of natural amenities within our cities. The "social accounting" movement seeks to correct this deficiency.

Also exerting pressure on the existing system is an increasing volume of citizen protestation about the current quality of the urban environment and the lack of public policy concern for our natural amenities. Throughout the country citizen groups have risen in recent years to promote changes in traditional business and public policy practices. Attacks on service station architecture, billboard jungles, aesthetically offensive commercial strips, junkyards, the bulldozer rape of the cityscape, overhead utility lines, and unlandscaped freeways have been mounted by citizen groups throughout the United States and are generating new demands for the public policy system to concern itself with the amenity values of urban natural resources.

Each of these several forces is a part of the "decisional reality" within which the amenity planners will function in the future.

## THE PHYSICAL CONTEXT OF AMENITY DECISIONS

It is our view that urban amenity planning and management must focus on the environmental subsystems, or "cells," which comprise the urban or metropolitan community. This follows Perloff[5] and others who argue that the urban community may be viewed as a set of interacting subsystems. We see man as an environmentally mobile creature who moves from subenvironment to subenvironment (from cell to cell) throughout the course of the day, the week, the year, and his lifetime within the metropolitan community. We have identified the following subenvironments which interface with a metropolitan community: (1) the *residential* environment, including the dwelling unit, its surrounding space, and the agglomeration of other dwelling places comprising any particular cell; (2) the *occupational* environment, including the work place and its surrounding service facilities, both interior and exterior to the structure or site within which the work is performed; (3) the *service* environment, including the institutions, organizations, commercial establishments, and other facilities which dispense commodities to urban man as he performs one or another of the functions associated with the other environmental cells; (4) the *leisure* or *recreational* environment, including all the places, facilities, and areas to which urban man transports himself for pleasure-seeking, rest, and respite—both within the urban environment and outside the urban complex itself, the latter comprising part of what Perloff refers to as "the environment of the urbanite"; (5) the *commuter* environment, including all the pathways followed by the urbanite in transporting himself from his residential environment to other environments within the metropolitan complex and to places such as leisure or recreational areas outside the metropolitan complex itself; and (6) the *background* environment. Each subenvironment is a "setting" for people's lives. The objective of environmental planning and management must be to enhance each of these settings, to bring out and heighten—not to submerge—the character of each subenvironment. The challenge is to produce delight in the whole fabric of the entire metropolitan landscape, not merely to pick out the highlights in the fabric.

The available literature suggests that the intensity and extensity of amenity responses within an urban population varies as a function of the subenvironment in which the response is measured. Thus, Robert L. Wilson suggests that people place more value on the environmental quality of their immediate neighborhood than on environmental quality variables which occur at the scale of the entire community.[6] Since his study focused on two comparatively small communities, these findings may be inapplicable to the giant metropolis; they nevertheless suggest the relevance of examining the significance of amenities as a function of the subenvironment in which they occur and the functions which that subenvironment is to serve, and of manipulating environmental variables on the scale of the subenvironment rather than of the whole city in any effort to increase its livability for most people.

## A MANAGEMENT SYSTEM FOR URBAN NATURAL AMENITIES

As suggested above, the amenity planner/manager must concern himself with certain key factors: the amenity precipitants, the pattern of amenity responses, the subenvironments in which they occur, and the decisional system within which amenity decisions are made.

The information collected and processed by the planner must meet more than some abstract standard of need; it must conform to the requirements of the decisional system in which the planner resides and the appetite of that system for various kinds and quantities of information.

We are currently engaged in a study of decision chains which impinge on environmental quality in several major sections of Southern California. One aspect of that study has been the decision chain through which proposals are processed for the subdivision of raw land, the subsequent development of physical facilities, and other improvements on the land. Results to date suggest that the people within the system have failed to perceive the "systemic" nature of their actions and the broad spectrum of environmental goals to which they might address themselves. Individually, they judge the quality of their decisions in terms of a very limited set of criteria—such as structural safety—and do not customarily concern themselves with other qualitative considerations, which they see as the function of "other professionals" or "other departments."

In view of the low amenity value of residential developments within Los Angeles County, the study suggests that something more is necessary than the insertion of new criteria into the system. If natural amenities are to receive attention, and if the competitive processes of our present decisional system are to act rationally with respect to urban amenities, then it may be necessary to build professional "amenity advocates" into the system. For example, Great Britain utilizes amenity planners whose professional task is to protect and/or develop amenities within the geographic zone of their concern. A similar step may be necessary in the United States if amenities are to receive the attention they deserve.

Operationally, it may be useful to adopt such practices as the conduct of amenity precipitant inventories, amenity demand surveys, attitudinal and opinion surveys of selected groups within the urban population, and research pointed at the development of predictive criteria appropriate for use by amenity planners and decision makers.

## INVENTORY OF NATURAL AMENITY PRECIPITANTS

Before beginning any management system for urban natural amenities it is necessary to obtain information on the features that now exist in the urban or metropolitan community that may be considered potential amenities— in short, the nature, characteristics, and location of the amenity precipitants.

Because natural amenity precipitants are place-bound (since they are a function of the natural environment) and are not ubiquitous throughout the metropolitan community, and because they perform different functions and evoke different human responses depending on their location within the urban community, it would be helpful to inventory them for various subunits of the whole. Two localized differentiations should be considered: (1) within each of the subenvironments noted earlier; and (2) within different geographic settings or scales; e.g., at the scale of the home, neighborhood, community, county, and metropolitan region.

That the function of natural amenity precipitants varies at different geographic scales is most clearly seen in the case of open space. Table 2 illustrates various types of open space amenity precipitants typically found at various geographical scales within a metropolitan region.

The open spaces under (1) are intensively used man-made spaces; e.g., yards, gardens, piazzas, plazas, and so on; those under (2a) and (2b) and some of those under (3) are semideveloped areas; e.g., parks, playgrounds, and so on; and part of those under (3) and practically all of those listed under (4) are basically natural areas and features; e.g., natural preserves, beaches, rivers, undeveloped mountain areas, private farms, ranches, or large grazing areas.

In short, while open space at the street scale is uniquely man-made, regional open space is the opposite, you can only take it the way it comes and that is the chief justification for its preservation. Therefore, it is not possible to specify standards for open space at the regional level. Some regions—e.g., New York, San Francisco, and Los Angeles—have a great variety of natural open spaces at the regional level; in Washington and Philadelphia, nature was somewhat less generous; Indianapolis and the Dallas–Fort Worth area, to cite but two examples, will have to be more inventive.

The open space immediately associated with homes and work places— i.e., at the street scale—is experienced more than all other open space. This is open space in microcosm. It is with us day in and day out. This dominance suggests that it has an impact on the role of other levels of open space. Open space at the street scale is also unique because it is the most man-made, both in its quantity and design. Nature can be of some help

| Scale or level | Examples of open space amenity resources | |
| --- | --- | --- |
| | Land | Water |
| **1. Street scale** | | |
| a) Building site | Yards; courts; gardens (i.e., sites less buildings) | |
| b) Group of buildings | Rights-of-way, streets, pedestrian ways, piazzas, plazas, residential commons, tot lots. | |
| **2. Community** | | |
| a) Neighborhood | School grounds; playgrounds; small parks (up to 10 acres); hillsides; shopping center; squares. | Small lakes (natural or man-made), ponds, streams, lagoons. |
| b) Municipality | Parks up to 100 acres, play fields; civic center and other public squares; recreation roads and bicycling, riding, and hiking trails. | |
| **3. County** | Mountain and valley floor parks — 100-1,000 acres; shoreline parks; streamside preserves; golf courses; minor conservation areas (flood plains, watersheds, wildflower / bird /game preserves); scenic roads (driving, hiking, etc.); reservoir parks. | Large lakes, rivers, bays, inlets, water conservation reservoirs, islands. |
| **4. Metropolitan region** | Mountain and valley floor parks over 1,000 acres; wilderness areas; large conservation areas; private farms, greenbelts, woodland and other land on the urban fringe; coastlines and seacoasts; mountain ranges; milksheds; large institutional open spaces (e.g., university, college, hospital, sports arena, music center); scenic highways; historic natural landmarks. | Major water bodies; e.g., oceans, great rivers, major lakes; marine parks; harbors; islands; tidelands; marshland. |

**TABLE 2.** *Classification of Urban Open Space Amenity Resources by Geographic Scale**

\* Adapted from: Stanley B. Tankel, "The Importance of Open Space in the Urban Pattern," in Lowdon Wingo, Jr., ed., *Cities and Space: The Future Use of Urban Land* (The Johns Hopkins Press for Resources in the Future, 1963), Table 1, p. 61.

here—for instance, a few trees in a subdivision may save it from barrenness, or a location on a hillside certainly has many benefits—but for the most part street-scale urban open space is a creation of man. In particular, it is the creation of our architects, urban designers, and city planners, working within the framework and limitations of municipal zoning and subdivision regulations, and thus poses a challenge to these specialists.

## AMENITY DEMAND CURVES

As Parr and others[7] have suggested, we need to plot the "behavioral topographies" associated with environmental quality variables, both singly and in the aggregate. More objective information is needed on how people actually respond to amenity and disamenity precipitants within the urban community. Can research instruments be developed and utilized by planners to detect changing response patterns? Can predictive criteria be developed by which planners may more precisely determine amenity demand levels, perhaps through inspection of such readily obtainable information as discretionary income levels?

We believe that it is possible to accomplish all this, although a good deal of hard work will have to be done before these planning tools will become available. Several specific targets seem appropriate for such an effort:

1. *Human response curves.* These may be thought of as human value or response scales. They should reveal the fraction of the population which responds to any environmental quality variable, or aggregation of such variables (i.e., amenity resources area); the social, economic, and other characteristics of that population fraction; and the distribution of response type and intensity within the respondent group. For example, a *disamenity-amenity* response scale might be constructed for a single environmental quality variable, such as the loading of suspended particulate matter in a cubic meter of air. At the disamenity end of the scale, human respiratory discomfort and ill health would be measured by a particular range of particulate loadings for a specified respondent group. By relating such loadings to ambient visibility conditions, still further responses could be measured, in terms of human values toward optional conditions of visibility (10 miles, 5 miles, 3 miles, and so on). Through application of paired-comparison methods and other techniques, the utility function of responses to optional visibility conditions might be predicted for specific respondent groups. The intensity of public support for such specific environmental improvement measures as billboard removal, freeway landscaping, protection of primitive areas, and so on, might be measured by these techniques and fitted into the response scales.

2. *Economic demand criteria.* As a special aspect of human responses to amenities, the economic behavior of urban populations in respect to amenity values deserves much more study. It seems clear that a substantial fraction of the public is willing to pay for amenity values as private goods and that substantial citizen support exists for public programs of investment in protecting amenity values and amenity resource areas. Nevertheless, at present it is difficult to compose precise statements that have predictive value to planners and managers in the public and private sector. For example, how much are people willing to pay to protect views now marred by outdoor advertising and overhead utility lines? Of what value to the purchasers in a subdivision is the protection of an adjacent open area, a hiking and riding trail, or a landscaped traffic collector route? Without new or unusual systems of public intervention into the private economic marketplace, the development of answers to these and similar questions would contribute much toward a more rational and socially responsible system of urban amenity management. Frederick Gutheim has pointed out:

In housing economics we have been able to attribute specific values to apartments with balconies, houses with fireplaces, and other design features having little to do with the raw facts of space and structure but much to do with amenity. We know that certain tenants will pay more for these features, and we know how much more they will pay. We also know that location has a specific value, one not always attributable to economic factors, but frequently linked to design. Here we tread more uncertainly; but it should be possible, for example, to compare a house in Georgetown with an identical house in the adjoining community of Foggy Bottom, and to disentangle what parts of the extra value of the Georgetown house are due to its location in a community with definite boundaries, quiet streets, shade trees, ample gardens, historical associations and architectural homogeneity, and what parts are due to its location in a community of high-income families, high property values and accessibility. We can also determine just which families will pay these premiums. Studies of aesthetic value can be usefully pursued at the point of decision when families move in or out, when they buy or sell. They should have a priority second only to experiments and demonstrations in the design of the urban environment itself.[8]

## RESEARCH INTO DECISION-MAKING CRITERIA

Of course, the development of amenity-precipitant inventories, measurement scales, response curves, and predictive economic criteria will not alone provide an improvement in amenity abundance and distribution which many now demand. For such an improvement we must look also at our traditional approach to the "unit" amenity decision. How have we traditionally decided on the allocation of land among competing user groups? How valid are these criteria in the modern urban community?

It is probable that much of the erosion in the amenity value of our urban communities has been produced by our orientation to goals related to short-term economic gains and losses. Given a tidal flat having potential for development either as a small-boat marina and waterfront residential development or as a petro-chemical complex, we often retreat into a "parochial" cost-benefit analysis. If the greatest economic gain accrues to the petro-chemical development, we argue with scientific pride that this is the "preferred" pattern of development. But is this really so?

In John Steinbeck's famous and still unspoiled Monterey–Salinas Valley in California, a recent public conflict focused on this very question. The Humboldt Oil Company desired to locate a major petroleum refinery at Moss Landing, which is located on a small bay at the upper northwestern end of the valley. Construction of the refinery would have resulted in a large economic gain to a limited group of landowners and might have presaged the migration of heavy industry into the valley. In terms of the typical complex of petro-chemical establishments which frequently surrounds refineries, one can predict that construction of the refinery might well have resulted in an enlarged pattern of industrial development throughout the area. Escalating land values, an expanded tax base, enlarged employment opportunities, and a higher level of income for the valley would have been the inevitable result. However, this pattern of development would have destroyed one of the last remaining unpolluted airsheds in California, and one of the most scenically rich resources of the entire state. The valley, and the Monterey Peninsula to which it is linked, are scenic favorites of many Californians residing hundreds of miles from the site. The area has value to these casual users, yet the dollars they leave behind after their infrequent visits probably amount to a much smaller sum than the possible economic gains from industrial, commercial, and intensive residential development of the area. If this area is finally developed, Californians, as well as tourists from the rest of the United States, will have lost a precious resource whose social value simply cannot be measured on an economic scale.

This case suggests that a community of interest may be identified and measurable in respect to any given amenity resource area and that the discoverable community may include nonresidents as well as residents, and casual visitors as well as habitual and frequent nonresident visitors; that, in some cases, the community may even include persons whose life-space is touched by the amenity even though they remain physically remote from it and who would bemoan their loss although they never have, and never will, personally and directly experience it (in short, they represent an "option demand").

In the Moss Landing case, there was a clear need for examination of the broad range of potential costs, benefits, and optional solutions for a variety of groups. Excluding the consideration that this location had an undisputed amenity value for a large group of Californians, how many other sites within the state were appropriate for a refinery complex, and at what incremental costs or benefits? Given the loss of this amenity area, what could be done to replace it? What impact would the loss have on the "quality of lives" of the respondent groups?

These considerations suggest to us that the following dictum might be useful to environmental planners and managers: *Given equivalence in the economic potential of resource areas competing for development, such development should occur last in that area which exhibits the greatest amenity potential and in which the projected pattern of development would most adversely affect the area's amenity potential.*

Assuming that adequate inventories of potential amenity resource areas exist, the adoption of such a precept might permit incremental decision making without a gross dysfunction to amenity values.

Similarly, we suggest that a range of information is available to amenity planners, managers, and decision makers that can help with respect to the two broad clusters of decisional problems they face: (1) those dealing with public investments, and (2) those concerned with the public regulation of environmental quality and/or the allocation of amenity resources among competing users. Although it does not lead to any mathematical model appropriate for judging the final end-state decision, such information would expand our understanding of some of the consequences of our decisions. (See Table 3 for a preliminary classification.)

| Public investment decisions | Allocative and regulatory decisions |
|---|---|
| 1. Cost of acquiring, developing, and /or protecting the ARA in question;<br>  a. Present ($T^1$)<br>  b. Future ($T^n$). | 1. Reproducibility of ARA;<br>  a. Cost of ARA<br>  b. Cost of reproducing ARA at another location ($ARA^1$). |
| 2. Cost of operating the ARA, $T^1$ to $T^n$. | 2. Non-amenity use demands for ARA. |
| 3. Size of potential respondent group;<br>  a. Present ($T^1$)<br>  b Future ($T^n$). | 3. Availability of alternative sites for non-amenity uses;<br>  a. Cost of ARA site<br>  b. Cost of alternative sites. |
| 4. Expected exposure duration frequency distribution of potential respondent group. | 4. Size of ARA potential respondent group;<br>  a. Present ($T^1$)<br>  b. Future ($T^n$). |
| 5. Capital costs per respondent and per respondent exposure ($T^1$ to $T^n$). | 5. Several of the items under "Public investment decisions" also relevant here. |
| 6. Operating costs per respondent and per respondent exposure ($T^1$ to $T^n$). | |
| 7. Comparative value of ARA to respondent group. | |
| 8. Distribution of economic valuation of ARA, per unit of exposure, within respondent group. | |
| 9. Distribution of ability to pay within respondent group. | |
| 10. Absolute cost of developing and operating ARA. | |

**TABLE 3.** *Information for Decision-Making in Amenity Resource Area (ARA) Planning and Management\**
A partial list.

A more rational and socially rewarding system for the planning and management of urban amenities is sorely needed. The main intention of this paper is to emphasize that the development of such a system may be promoted through increased attention to the nature, functions, and systemic qualities of amenities.

# NOTES

[1] Quoted in "A Changing City: Government," *Progressive Architecture* (August, 1967): 123.

[2] Aaron Quinn Sartain, et al., *Understanding Human Behavior* (New York: McGraw-Hill, 1958), p. 81.

[3] A. H. Maslow, *Motivation and Personality* (New York: Harper, 1964).

[4] Frank Stead, "Levels of Environmental Health," *American Journal of Public Health* 50, no. 3 (1960).

[5] Harvey S. Perloff, ed., *The Quality of the Urban Environment* (Washington, D.C.: Resources for the Future, 1969), Chapter 1.

[6] Robert L. Wilson, "Livability of the City: Attitudes and Urban Development," in F. Stuart Chapin, Jr. and Shirley F. Weiss, eds., *Urban Growth Dynamics* (New York: Wiley, 1962).

[7] H. E. Parr, "Mind and Milieu," *Sociological Inquiry* 33 (Winter, 1963); Raymond C. Studer and David Stea, "Architectural Programming, Environmental Design, and Human Behavior," *Journal of Social Issues* 22, no. 4 (1966).

[8] Frederick Gutheim, "Urban Space and Urban Design," in Lowdon Wingo, Jr., ed., *Cities and Space: The Future Use of Urban Land* (Baltimore: The Johns Hopkins Press for Resources in the Future, 1963), p. 130.

# FURTHER READING

## Surveys of Behavioral Aspects of Recreation

Berelson, B., and G. A. Steiner, *Human Behavior* (New York: Harcourt Brace, and World, 1964).

Burton, T. L., *Experiments in Recreation Research* (Totowa, N. J.: Rowman and Littlefield, 1971).

Burton, T. L., and G. E. Cherry, *Social Research: Techniques for Planners* (London: Allen and Unwin, 1970).

Burton, T. L., and P. A. Noad, *Recreation Research Methods*, Occasional Paper no. 3, Center for Urban and Regional Studies, The University of Birmingham Edinburgh (England: R & R Clark, 1968).

Burton, T. L., ed., *Recreation Research and Planning* (London: Allen and Unwin, 1970).

Kerlinger, F. W., *Foundations of Behavioral Research* (New York: Holt, Rinehart and Winston, 1967).

Mercer, D., "The Role of Perception in the Recreation Experience: A Review and Discussion," *Journal of Leisure Research* 3 (Fall, 1971): 261–76.

Meyersohn, R., "The Sociology of Leisure in the United States: Introduction and Bibliography, 1945–1965," *Journal of Leisure Research* 1 (Winter, 1969): 53–68.

Perin, C., *With Man in Mind* (Cambridge, Mass.: M.I.T. Press, 1970).

Proshansky, H. M., W. H. Ittelson, and L. G. Rivlin, *Environmental Psychology: Man and His Physical Setting* (New York: Holt, Rinehart and Winston, 1970).

U.S. Department of Agriculture, Bureau of Outdoor Recreation, *Outdoor Recreation Space Standards* (Washington, D.C.: U.S. Government Printing Office, 1967).

## Concepts and Methods in Behavioral Aspects of Recreation

Baumann, D. D., "The Recreation Use of Domestic Water Supply Reservoirs: Perception and Choice," Research Paper no. 121, University of Chicago, Department of Geography, 1969.

Bull, C. N., "Prediction of Future Daily Behaviors: An Empirical Measure of Leisure," *Journal of Leisure Research* 4 (Spring, 1972): 119–23.

Campbell, F. L., "Participant Observation in Outdoor Recreation," *Journal of Leisure Research* 2 (Fall, 1970): 226–36.

Clark, R. M., J. C. Hendee, and F. L. Campbell, "Values, Behavior, and Conflict in Modern Camping Culture," *Journal of Leisure Research* 3 (Summer, 1971): 143–59.

Fishbein, M., *Readings in Attitude Theory and Measurement* (New York: Wiley, 1967).

Gilbert, C. G., G. L. Peterson, and D. W. Lime, "Toward a Model of Travel Behavior in the Boundary Waters Canoe Area," *Environment and Behavior* 4 (June, 1972): 131–58.

Goldberg, T., "The Automobile: A Social Institution for Adolescents," *Environment and Behavior* 1 (December, 1969): 15–186.

Johoda, M., and N. Warren, eds., *Attitudes: Selected Readings* (Baltimore: Penguin, 1966).

Karlsson, K. A., and M. J. Ellis, "Height Preferences of Children at Play," *Journal of Leisure Research* 4 (Winter, 1972): 33–42.

Kelly, E. L., *Assessment of Human Characteristics* (Belmont, Calif.: Brooks/Cole, 1969).

Peterson, G. L., and E. S. Neumann, "Modeling and Predicting Human Response to the Visual Recreation Environment," *Journal of Leisure Research* 1, no. 3 (Summer, 1969): 219–370.

Shafer, E. L., Jr., J. E. Hamilton, Jr., and E. A. Schmidt, "Natural Landscapes Preferences: A Predictive Model," *Journal of Leisure Research* 1 (Winter, 1969): 1–20.

Stankey, G. H., "The Use of Content Analysis in Resource Decision Making," *Journal of Forestry* 70 (1972): 148–51.

Winkel, G. H., R. Malek, and P. Thiel, "The Role of Personality Differences in Judgments of Roadside Quality," *Environment and Behavior* 1 (December, 1969): 199–223.

# Part Four
## ECONOMICS
## OF RECREATION

# PREFACE

Every time we participate outdoors (or anywhere) we make economic choices. Knowledge of such recreational behavior is useful for planners and managers because monetary and personal values associated with recreation use can help them make choices. Knowing our values for recreational experiences and resources allows such judgments as the comparison of recreation with other uses of the same land area, the desirability of a recreational investment, the relation between the number of users and an entry fee, and the determination of the efficiency and "fairness" of recreation projects.

The demand for recreation (economic behavior) is determined in much the same way as the demand for other things. Although the response to the market price is the factor that economists emphasize, other factors are also important: the satisfaction expected or derived from the recreation experience; the personal situations of residence, income, and leisure time; the "costs" of consuming recreation such as money, inconveniences, and travel time; and the knowledge and availability of alternative ways of using money and time.

The market can determine the values of many products and services, as well as the manner of production, the amount, and the potential audience. The problem for the recreation economist is that no outdoor recreation market exists to answer these questions. Instead, the demand (user responses) and supply (recreational facilities) decisions are reflected through government agency perceptions of the public's demands for outdoor recreation. To provide scarce recreation opportunities (scarce because natural resources and urban lands are under severe competition to provide other demanded services), efficient planning and use of recreation resources is required. Such efficiency involves comparing alternate kinds of recreation as well as alternate kinds of services other than recreation. In addition, the social consequences of the proposed recreational area are important. If land is marked for a recreational site, will it provide the greatest benefits to the people it serves, or could these people benefit more if the land were used for some other purposes? Also, would any segments of society be excluded by virtue of a site's location, its fee structure, or the kinds of activities it offers? Central to studies on efficiency and fairness are the concepts and methods involved in demand and supply.

Two seminal studies, the Prewitt report for the National Park Service and Marion Clawson's study of the demand and value of national parks, are not included here because of space constraints. Both studies were based on travel costs to parks which were assumed to be a substitute for willingness to pay.

The main objective of this Part is to introduce the concept of demand and the various methods and cautions used in measuring it. The secondary objective is to describe the role of the economist, including his reasoning process as well as some problems inherent in his search for value.

CHAPTER

# 11 OUTDOOR RECREATION ECONOMICS
## John V. Krutilla
## Jack L. Knetsch

The basic conceptual approach of economics to outdoor recreation is summarized in this chapter by John Krutilla and Jack Knetsch. Their main concern here is with the efficiency of allocating resources of land, labor, and capital to the management of recreational resources. Central to the efficiency of resource use is the concept of economic value depending on the demand for recreation. In addition, the distribution of income is seen as crucial in determining the efficiency of recreation allocation decisions. Krutilla and Knetsch discuss why methods of valuing recreational resources depending on willingness to pay or to travel are applicable to natural resource dominated recreation; and why these methods are not as valid for urban recreation, even though both kinds of recreation are provided by the public sector.

Outdoor recreation implies different things to different people and admits of a variety of different classifications of activities. From the standpoint of this paper, it will be convenient to make a distinction between two rather general categories that stem from the relative emphasis of their resource, as opposed to market orientation. On the one hand, there is outdoor recreation which depends to a greater degree on or is associated with a particular type of immobile resource environment, for example, mountains, seashores, and their recreational opportunities. Here we think of the resources as the medium for engaging in activities, whether active, like fishing, hiking, skiing, and boating, or passive, like sightseeing or merely relaxing in the sunshine. On the other hand, there is a set of outdoor recreation activities which is more market-oriented, that is, which tends to take place at the centers of population and which may depend for its indulgence more on mobile resources, like capital and labor inputs, which can produce facilities such as playgrounds, parks, recreational programs, and the like, at nearly any site where the population or market may be.

The essential concerns in the economics of outdoor recreation differ little from those of economic concerns generally. We are faced with

Reprinted from *The Annals* of The American Academy of Political and Social Science 389 (May, 1970): 63–70, by permission of The American Academy of Political and Social Science and the authors.

demands on scarce resources which can be used for recreational purposes, and also, in most cases, for alternative purposes, and we desire to allocate or use these productive resources in the ways that are most beneficial. All this is part of the larger problem of maximizing the *net* benefit from all potential combinations of goods, services, and leisure which the economy is capable of producing, given the resources with which it is endowed, the level of technology available, and the preferences of members of the society with respect to alternative goods, services, and leisure. We include leisure because it is an alternative to remunerative activity, and thus, in a sense, an alternative to the consumption of goods and services which could be purchased otherwise with the income which is foregone by opting for more leisure in lieu of remunerative activity. In short, leisure can be traded for goods and services, in spite of the fact that leisure and other commodities are also complementary, that is, consumed together.

Although recreational experiences are often cited as being highly personal and variable among individuals, the economic value is, nonetheless, real and comparable to the economic value of all consumer goods—a value measured by what people are willing to give up to attain them. Thus, the operational definition of the value of outdoor recreation is simply the individual user's willingness to pay for the use of resources rather than go without the opportunities afforded.

This criterion of willingness to pay is fully consistent with the evaluation of all goods and services provided by a market system—the method of organizing production and distribution for the bulk of goods and services in our economy. In a free-market economy, resources are devoted to those uses which are relatively more highly valued, as reflected in the prices that consumers are willing to pay, and are thus diverted from alternative potential uses, reflecting consumers' insufficient willingness to pay the required prices.

In the case of providing outdoor recreation, however, there are two major difficulties that give rise to allocative concern. The first stems from the notion that although the economic value of outdoor recreation is comparable to that of other resource-uses, the demands are not registered in the market. Although a private market does exist in recreation, it caters to only a limited spectrum of the demands, with major provisions made publicly. Although good reasons may underlie this choice, the relative preferences of consumers may not be adequately reflected in the use of many recreational facilities or opportunities.

Another concern with our means of allocating resources has to do with the assumption—an assumption which is particularly crucial for an important area of outdoor recreation—that there is a socially sanctioned distribution of income, that is, the concept of efficient resource-allocation and concomitantly, that the allocative criteria used in weighing the benefits and the costs of any proposal affecting recreation are meaningful only for a given distribution of income. There is a different allocation of resources which is efficient for each different distribution of income among persons with differing tastes. Thus, if a benefit-cost criterion is to be meaningful in application at any particular time in any particular area, the distribution of income relevant to the problem must itself be one which is considered "right," in the sense that it enjoys a social sanction.

It may now be clear why we chose to distinguish between the resource-oriented outdoor recreation activities, on the one hand, and the market- or population-centered activities on the other. In the former, the rules of the "efficiency game" are, to a very considerable extent, applicable. In the latter, when we consider the inner-city ghetto and its related environment, few would maintain that the distribution of national income and social weal to the ghetto residents represents an equitable one, socially judged, or that society, if given, say, an "instant feasible alternative," would sanction such conditions. Accordingly, while economic analysis concerns itself with an efficient allocation of resources in both cases, the rules of how we might want to provide for recreation in the one case are likely to be different from the rules—or, rather, the specific criteria—for the allocation of resources in the other.

## TRADITIONAL JUSTIFICATION FOR NONPRICING OF OUTDOOR RECREATION SERVICES

In a society which sanctions vesting rights to property in private individuals and businesses, the pricing system is relied upon to allocate resources among the nearly limitless possibilities. To the extent that public policy (progressive income-tax structure, inheritance taxes, and the like) retains, for the most part, a sanctioned income-distribution, the free market, with prices as signaling devices, has many advantages. A shift in tastes, reflected by increases in the demand for, or an increase in the willingness to pay (increased price) for, a commodity, will signal to entrepreneurs that higher returns may be possible through increasing production of such commodities as compared with alternative employment of their productive resources. Thus, relatively more resources will be allocated to those activities for which there has been experienced a relative increase in demand, and as prices fall and returns decline, less will be allocated to those from which demand has shifted. In this way, prices of both inputs and product outputs, and hence returns to investment, represent signaling devices which result in a flow of resources continuously adjusting to correspond with changes in relative preferences among consumption goods and services.

The pricing system, however, fails to function properly as an efficient resource-allocator under some technical conditions.[1] Aside from the question of the distribution of income, the factors of production must be divisible to permit more or less continuously variable amounts and proportions; moreover, the output must also be divisible, in the sense that if provided for one consumer, it is not automatically and simultaneously provided for all individuals, irrespective of whether or not they pay for it.

If inputs are not divisible, we get production under conditions such that the cost of serving an additional person is less than the average cost for all consumers. In the case of our national parks and wilderness areas, for

169

example, once the cost of providing the area for recreation has been undertaken, the additional cost of admitting an additional recreationist may be almost zero. Under such circumstances, *maximum* net benefits could not be realized by charging each user the average cost of all use because the savings in costs resulting from excluding some individuals would be less than the loss of benefits from their exclusion. This may be one reason for a policy to charge a nominal or even no price for some recreational-area uses.

When the output or product is indivisible, so that if it is provided for one individual, no other individual can be excluded for failing to pay a price, one would expect that no market would be established. National defense is a classical case of the nonexcludability character of an indivisible product. The same characteristic attaches to the *option value* of irreproducible resources such as unique scenic areas, genetic information of threatened species, and the like. In these cases, we may perceive an important value in retaining an option for future use of such resources, and may, therefore, be willing to refrain from action which would have an irreversible consequence for such irreproducible resources. However, if the option is retained for any individual of society, for example, by protecting a threatened species from extinction, it is equally and simultaneously retained for all members of society. Accordingly, it is not possible to establish markets for options of this sort nor for the adequate provision of commodities or services having as a significant part of their total value such attributes of jointness in supply or product indivisibility.[2]

Although the above limitations of prices and market transactions for leading to optimal resource allocations may have been at the root of pricing policies which historically avoided exacting the users' willingness to pay for services of resource-based recreational facilities, a contributing, if not alternative, reason has, perhaps, been very influential. This is the concept, in societies with an egalitarian tradition, of the "merit-good": that is, the consumption of some goods or services is conceived to be of such overriding significance to the well-being of members of society that their consumption, within limits, by any individual should not be dependent on his income.[3] Put another way, the budget constraint imposed on the consumption of goods and services, in general, is relaxed, in the case of satisfying merit-wants, by providing for them (at least in part) at public expense. Examples of merit-goods in the United States would be public education, public health programs, museums, and the like, as well as outdoor recreation in public playgrounds, parks, and campgrounds.

## LIMITATIONS ON APPLICABILITY OF TRADITIONAL JUSTIFICATION OF NONPRICED RECREATION

When we consider the merit-want rationale in relation to the general problem of deprivation in the inner city or in some outlying areas near urban places, few reasonable persons would maintain that willingness to pay, and related measures of the value of benefits, should be employed as tests for the allocation of resources to improve outdoor recreational facilities or programs in these areas. On the other hand, given the dominant clientele of the typical resource-oriented recreational areas, the applicability of the merit-want, public-subsidy rationale needs to be carefully examined. There is also reason to question the assumption of zero or nominal marginal costs in providing many recreational services, given the congestion encountered within many recreational areas. Moreover, there is a need to recognize the subsidized services' disincentive effects on enrollment of the private sector of the economy in the effort required to meet burgeoning outdoor recreation demands, as well as the allocative distortions within the recreational sector when pricing is dismissed as a matter of convention where it can function effectively as an efficient resource-allocator.

We find that resource-oriented outdoor recreation activity often involves substantial expenditure for equipment that is not inexpensive. At the top of the list is $3,000 to $10,000 for a travel trailer, or for the pickup truck-camper combination which has come increasingly into vogue with "camping" families. But, aside from such touring—rather than camping—expenditures, outlays for outdoor recreation activities involving power boats will rival expenditures on campers and trailers. The expenses involved in obtaining more personal items, such as those associated with skiing, are not inconsequential, and the expenditure required to equip a family for comfortable back-packing activities soon mounts to four figures. To those who are enthusiastic about this kind of activity, travel to and from the sites of immobile resources involves considerable expense. As a consequence, participation in such resource-oriented outdoor recreational activities is restricted predominantly to those income classes well able to meet a comparatively small additional cost of admission. The issue of budget constraints that have an adverse effect on access to merit-goods is not very meaningful for the majority of people who participate in this kind of recreational activity.

Aside from the issue of merit-wants, the subsidization of such recreational services often results in the failure to maximize the net benefits from resources available to the community. Pricing, looked upon from another perspective, is a means by which to allocate scarce resources among alternative uses. Where no scarcity exists (that is, no opportunity returns are foregone), no price is warranted. This applies similarly, then, in cases in which we have facilities with excess capacity. But when excess capacity does not exist and the services of a facility are subsidized, crowding will occur. Here we find, as at Yosemite, the South Rim of the Grand Canyon, and Yellowstone's geothermal attractions, a congestion which is not only destructive of the ecology in the area, but is also likely to have benefit-diminishing disutilities as the recreational site's capacity is exceeded. Even wilderness areas like the Boundary Waters Canoe Area are becoming so heavily used that the atmosphere of remoteness sought in wilderness experience is being eroded rapidly. Under such circumstances, it is no longer meaningful to provide unrestricted access to the most heavily used areas. Rationing by pricing, perhaps coupled with other restraints, not only would reduce the excessive demand, but could be used as a management tool for redistributing activity toward less heavily used areas and times.

As indicated in our discussion of the expenditures necessary for engaging in resource-based outdoor recreation activity, complementary goods, for example, equipment, obtained at substantial cost, are employed in such activities. When the recreational service of the resource on which the activity is based is underpriced, the complementary inputs which combine with it can be expected to be used in excess, reflecting the overuse of the underpriced input. An important, nonefficiency, side-result of such policies is that, as with so many other publicly provided services, the underpricing simply results in the value of those services being capitalized in other assets providing complementary services. Just as underpriced irrigation water results in increases in the value of private lands on which such water is used, so a portion of the value of publicly owned recreation facilities finds its way into expanded sales and profits for firms which sell equipment, and into increases in the value of land surrounding the publicly owned recreational facilities which are provided at nominal user costs.

A final problem associated with failure to use pricing in areas of recreation where the merit-want rationale is inappropriate is the serious disincentive effect it has on provision of adequate resources for these activities. Inasmuch as private suppliers of resource-based outdoor recreation services cannot compete with subsidized, publicly supplied recreational services, there is no incentive for private-resource owners to aid in supplying the burgeoning demand for such services. This failure to enroll the private sector is reflected by the fact that demands for resources outstrip the fiscal capabilities of the public—or, at least, the performance of the appropriation committees of the Congress and state legislatures.

To summarize, then, there is need to depart from conventional pricing policies to the extent that we encounter capacity-limitations and to consider instituting user fees as a means of rationing scarce resources and as management tools to redistribute the load among all facilities more appropriately to their carrying capacities. Second, charging users for such things as National Park, Forest Service, and National Recreation Area campgrounds, boat-launching facilities, and related services would serve as a test of the economic demand for such services and would set in motion an efficiency-inducing effect. In those instances where the demand for such services was quite price-responsive, the numbers of participants and their participation frequency would drop, relieving pressure on such resources through discouraging visitation by individuals for whom the experience has a low marginal value. It would also release needed public fiscal resources for other programs. In cases where the demand was not responsive, so that visitation would not be affected appreciably, the prospect of profitable returns to private-resource owners would be enhanced and could bring about commitment of new resources to these ends, thereby easing the supply constraints without a commensurate demand for public fiscal resources.

## OUTDOOR RECREATION FOR THE CITY

If poverty is a basic and pervasive feature of parts of cities, then tests such as "willingness to pay" and benefit-cost criteria, where the validity of the criterion is related to the social acceptability of the particular income-distribution, are obviously meaningless concepts for the allocation of resources to outdoor recreation programs. Large allocations, or larger allocations, of resources provided through public fiscal measures are clearly in order.

Thus, where such useful notions as willingness to pay, and market tests of correspondence between consumer preferences and kind and quality of services being provided, are unavailing, more explicit recreational planning is required. But inadequacy of notions of willingness to pay and of market tests does not dispel the need to conform to consumer preferences, even if the particular consumption clientele does not have the wherewithal to participate in the "market-voting game."

It is important that we not only respond to the quantity of the recreation services demanded in this fashion, but also that, in doing so, we do not, as a society, persist in providing inappropriate mixes or types of recreational opportunities to different segments of the population. In our new-found enthusiasm for recreational planning, we often find ourselves providing only a narrow range of recreational opportunities, and, furthermore, we have a great tendency to provide increasing quantities of what we have already provided in the past.

A serious error persists in much of our recreation-planning of this kind: we are able to judge the demand for recreation facilities solely by observing present recreational habits and multiplying the current participation rates by anticipated future populations. There is serious danger that the resulting magnitudes are completely meaningless. The participation-rate figures observed are those under prevailing conditions of recreation opportunities. This use of facilities is determined not only by what the population in question demands, *but also by what has been made available to them.* The hazard of short-changing the impoverished by this procedure for determining what they want is real and impending. There is too facile a tendency to beguile oneself with computing ratios and performing arithmetic operations, as a substitute for meaningful recreational-planning activity.

It is in this area that the creative integration of the contributions of economists, social psychologists, and sociologists is needed in order to introduce the concept of consumer preferences meaningfully into the planning of recreational facilities and programs, when that concept must travel independently of the notion of willingness to pay, as conventionally used. The identification of tastes, preferences, and potentials for growth and development of progressively more sophisticated tastes, as opportunities for learning experiences are provided, might all fall within the province of, and present a challenge to, the behavioral scientist.

The demands for outdoor recreation facilities are, with the exception of national biologic and scenic wonders, predominantly local or regional in

173

character. The provision of recreational facilities, therefore, may be viewed primarily as a local public responsibility. But the current state of such provisions raises the serious question of local fiscal capability, and of state and, perhaps more important, federal, responsibility. The question of the nature and extent of the latter's responsibility might be raised. A policy environment of incentives and restraints might be created which would present more efficient and equitable provisions for recreational services. Alternatively, programs can be formulated with equally good intentions that will limit the choices available or guarantee only more acquisition of facilities where more operating programs are more urgently needed. There is great need for careful stock-taking at this juncture.

## NOTES

[1] There may be conditions which cause market failure that are not technical in nature, but we assume for this purpose that government policies with respect to policing monopoly, maintaining high level of employment, redistributing income, and the like, which involve measures other than pricing policy, deal with the questions posed by other conditions of market failure.

[2] The interested reader can refer to perhaps the most comprehensive treatment of the phenomenon of the failure to reveal one's true willingness to pay for goods or services from the consumption of which he cannot be excluded, and of related problems of market failure, in Mancur Olson, *The Logic of Collective Action: Public Goods and the Theory of Groups* (Cambridge, Mass.: Harvard University Press, 1955).

[3] For the original discussion of this phenomenon, under the term "merit wants," see Richard A. Musgrave, *The Theory of Public Finance* (New York: McGraw-Hill, 1959), pp. 9, 13–14.

# 12

# COMPARISONS OF METHODS FOR RECREATION EVALUATION

**Jack L. Knetsch**
**Robert K. Davis**

Several different methods of measuring the economic value of recreation are compared in this study by Jack Knetsch and Robert Davis. The basic problem is attempting to discover an appropriate proxy for the usual market price which is known for other kinds of commodities or services. The use of gross expenditures, costs, and market values as means of approaching recreational value is rejected. Instead, interviews and travel costs are shown to be valid methods since they are based on the concept of demand as exhibited by willingness to pay or to travel. The degree of complementarity between the two approaches is noted in the conclusion.

Evaluation of recreation benefits has made significant headway in the past few years. It appears that concern is increasingly focusing on the hard core of relevant issues concerning the economic benefits of recreation and how we can go about making some useful estimates.

The underlying reasons for this sharpening of focus are largely pragmatic. The rapidly increasing demand for recreation, stemming from the often-cited factors of increasing population, leisure, incomes, mobility, and urbanization, calls for continuing adjustments in resource allocations. This is the case with respect to our land and water resources in general; but more specifically it bears on such matters as the establishment of national recreation areas, setting aside or preserving areas for parks and open spaces in and near expanding urban areas, and clearly on questions of justification, location, and operation of water development projects.

Recreation services have only recently been recognized as products of land and water resource use. As such, they offer problems that do not occur when resolving the conflicting uses of most goods and services—for example, steel and lumber. Conflicting demands for commodities such as these are resolved largely in the market places of the private economy, where users bid against each other for the limited supplies.

Outdoor recreation, however, has developed largely as a non-market commodity. The reasons for this are quite elaborate, but in essence outdoor

Reprinted from Allen V. Kneese and Stephen C. Smith, eds., *Water Research* (Baltimore: Johns Hopkins Press, 1966), pp. 125–42, copyright by Johns Hopkins Press and published for Resources for the Future, Inc., by permission of Johns Hopkins Press and the authors.

recreation for the most part is produced and distributed in the absence of a market mechanism, partly because we prefer it that way and have rejected various market outcomes, and partly because many kinds of outdoor recreation experience cannot be packaged and sold by private producers to private consumers. This absence of a market necessitates imputing values to the production of recreation services. Such economic benefits can be taken into account in decisions affecting our use of resources.

## MISUNDERSTANDINGS OF RECREATION VALUES

Discussions of values of outdoor recreation have been beset by many misunderstandings. One of these stems from a lack of appreciation that the use of outdoor recreation facilities differs only in kind, but not in principle, from consumption patterns of other goods and services. Another is that the market process takes account of personal and varied consumer satisfactions.

It is, furthermore, the incremental values that are important in making decisions relative to resource allocations. The incremental values of recreation developments of various kinds are a manageable concept which can be used for comparisons, in spite of the very great aggregate value that some may want to attribute to recreation. Nothing is gained—and no doubt a great deal has been lost—by what amounts to ascribing the importance of a total supply of recreation to an added increment, rather than concentrating on the added costs and the added benefits.

A similar difficulty arises with respect to questions of water supply. That man is entirely dependent upon the existence of water is repeatedly emphasized. While true, the point does not matter. Decisions necessarily focus on increments and therefore on the added costs and the added benefits that stem from adding small amounts to the existing total.

Further, no goods or services are priceless in the sense of an infinite price. There is an individual and collective limit to how much we will give up to enjoy the services of any outdoor recreation facility or to preserve any scenic resource. The most relevant economic measure of recreation values, therefore, is willingness on the part of consumers to pay for outdoor recreation services. This set of values is comparable to economic values established for other commodities, for it is the willingness to give up on the part of consumers that establishes values throughout the economy.

Failure to understand these value characteristics results in two types of error. The first is the belief that the only values that are worth considering are those accounted for commercially. A second and related source of error is a belief that outdoor recreation experience is outside the framework of economics, that the relevant values have an aesthetic, deeply personal, and even mystical nature. We believe both of these to be incorrect. In particular, the notion that economic values do not account for aesthetic or personal values is fallacious and misleading. Economically, the use of resources for recreation is fully equivalent to other uses, and the values which are relevant do not necessarily need to be determined in the market place. This last condition does indicate that indirect means of supplying relevant measures of the values produced may be necessary. But this is an empirical problem, albeit one of some considerable dimension, and the primary concern of this paper.

The problem of using imputed values for value determination has been met with a considerable degree of success for some products of water resource development. Procedures have been developed to assess the value of the flood protection, irrigation, and power services produced by the projects, even though in many cases a market does not in fact exist or is inadequate for the actual benefit calculations. Without commenting on the adequacy of these methods, it is generally agreed that such measures are useful in evaluating the output of project services.

## NATIONAL AND LOCAL BENEFITS

Discussions of these topics have often been further confused by failure to separate two types of economic consequences or benefit. This has led to improper recognition of relevant and legitimate economic interests, and to inferior planning and policy choices.

There are, first, what we may call primary benefits, or national benefits. Second, there are benefits we may refer to as local benefits, or impact benefits. Both sets of values resulting from investment in recreation have economic relevance, but they differ, and they bear differently on decision.

The primary recreation benefits, or values, are in general taken to be expressions of the consumers' willingness to pay for recreation services. These values may or may not register in the commerce of the region or in the commerce of the nation, but this does not make them less real. When appropriately measured, they are useful for guiding social choices at the national level. The other set of accounts is concerned with local expenditure of money for local services associated with recreation. While outdoor recreation is not marketed—in the sense that the services of parks, as such, are not sold to any great extent in any organized market—money does indeed become involved in the form of expenditures for travel, equipment, lodging, and so forth. The amount of money spent in connection with outdoor recreation and tourism is large and growing, making outdoor recreation expenditures of prime concern to localities and regions which may stand to benefit. Our concern is with measuring the more difficult of the two types of benefit just mentioned—national recreation benefits. While these are measured essentially by the consumers' willingness to pay, in some cases the benefits extend to the non-using general public.

## ALTERNATIVE MEASUREMENT METHODS

There are obvious advantages to evaluating recreation benefits by market prices in the same manner as their most important resource competitors. However, as we have indicated, past applications have been hampered by disagreement on what are the meaningful values. In spite of growing recognition that recreation has an important economic value, economists and public administrators have been ill-prepared to include it in the social or public calculus in ways that lead to better allocations of resources.

The benefits of recreation from the social or community viewpoint are alleged to be many and varied. Some of the descriptions of public good externalities arising from recreation consumption are gross overstatements of the real values derived from the production of recreation services. But recreation benefits do in fact exist. Where externalities are real—as in cases of recreation in connection with visits to various historic areas or educational facilities, or where preservation of unique ecological units has cultural and scientific values—they should be recognized in assigning values to the development or preservation of the areas. However, it is our view that, by and large, recreation is a consumption good rather than a factor of production, and the benefits to be enjoyed are largely those accruing to the individual consumer participating. This is even more likely to be the case with recreation provided by water projects. The large bulk of primary recreation benefits can be viewed as the value of the output of the project to those who use them. This view stems from the concept that recreation resources produce an economic product. In this sense they are scarce and capable of yielding satisfaction for which people are willing to pay. Finally, some accounting can be made of this economic demand.

As the desirability of establishing values for recreation use of resources has become more apparent over the past few years, a number of methods for measuring or estimating them have been proposed and to some extent used. Some of the measures are clearly incorrect; others attempt to measure appropriate values, but fall short on empirical grounds (Crutchfield, 1962; Lerner, 1962; Merewitz, 1965).

## Gross Expenditures Method

The gross expenditures method attempts to measure the value of recreation to the recreationist in terms of the total amount spent on recreation by the user. These expenditures usually include travel expenses, equipment costs, and expenses incurred while in the recreation area. Estimates of gross recreation expenditures are very popular in some quarters; for one thing they are likely to produce large figures. It is argued that persons making such expenditures must have received commensurate value or they would not have made them. The usual contention is that the value of a day's recreation is worth at least the amount of money spent by a person for the use of that recreation.

These values have some usefulness in indicating the amount of money that is spent on a particular type of outdoor recreation, but as justification for public expenditure on recreation, or for determining the worth or benefit of the recreation opportunity afforded, they are of little consequence.

The values we seek are those which show not some gross value, but the net increase in value over and above what would occur in the absence of a particular recreation opportunity. Gross expenditures do not indicate the value of the losses sustained if the particular recreation opportunity were to disappear, nor do they show the net gain in value from an increase in a particular recreation opportunity.

## Market Value of Fish Method

A proposed method for estimating the recreation benefits afforded by fishing imputes to sport fishing a market value of the fish caught. The main objection to this procedure is the implied definition that the fish alone are the primary objective of the activity.

## Cost Method

The cost method assumes that the value of outdoor recreation resource use is equal to the cost of generating it or, in some extreme applications, that it is a multiple of these costs. This has the effect of justifying any contemplated recreation project. However, the method offers no guide in the case of contemplated loss of recreation opportunities, and allows little or no discrimination between relative values of alternative additions.

## Market Value Method

Basic to the market value method measure is a schedule of charges judged to be the market value of the recreation services produced. These charges are multiplied by the actual or expected attendance figures to arrive at a recreation value for the services.

The method is on sound ground in its emphasis on the willingness of users to incur expenses to make choices. However, the market for outdoor recreation is not a commercial one, certainly not for much of the recreation provided publicly and only to a limited extent for private recreation. It is in part because private areas are not fully comparable with public areas that users are willing to pay the fees or charges. It seems, therefore, inappropriate to use charges paid on a private area to estimate the value of recreation on public areas. Also a single value figure or some range of values will be inappropriate for many recreation areas. Physical units of goods and services are not everywhere equally valuable, whether the commodity be sawtimber, grazing, or recreation. Location in the case of recreation affects value greatly. Moreover, differences of quality and attractiveness of recreation areas are not fully comparable or recognized by the unit values.

There are other methods, but few have received much attention. Where does this leave us? The only methods to which we give high marks are based on the concept of willingness to pay for services provided.

## METHODS BASED ON WILLINGNESS TO PAY

We have alluded to two kinds of problems we face in measuring the benefits of outdoor recreation: the conceptual problems and the measurement problems.

Conceptually, we wish to measure the willingness to pay by consumers of outdoor recreation services as though these consumers were purchasing the services in an open market. The total willingness of consumers to pay for a given amount and quality of outdoor recreation (that is, the area under the demand curve) is the relevant measure we seek. Our conceptual problems are essentially that any measurement of effective demand in the current time period, or even an attempt to project effective demand in future time periods, must necessarily omit from the computation two kinds of demand which may or may not be important. These are option demand and demand generated by the opportunity effect.[1]

Option demand is that demand from individuals who are not now consumers or are not now consuming as much as they anticipate consuming, and who therefore would be willing to pay to perpetuate the availability of the commodities. Such a demand is not likely to be measured by observance or simulation of market phenomena. The opportunity effect derives from those unanticipated increases in demand caused by improving the opportunities to engage in a recreational activity and thereby acquainting consumers with new and different sets of opportunities to which they adapt through learning processes. To our knowledge no methods have been proposed which might be used to measure those two kinds of demand for a good.

Notwithstanding the undoubted reality of these kinds of demand, our presumption is that effective demand is likely to be the predominant component of the aggregate demand for outdoor recreation of the abundant and reproducible sorts we have in mind. We further presume that this quantity can be estimated in a useful way, although by fairly indirect means, for we have no market guide of the usual sort. Two methods—a direct interview, and an imputation of a demand curve from travel cost data—currently appear to offer reasonable means of obtaining meaningful estimates.

## Interview Methods

The essence of the interview method of measuring recreation benefits is that through a properly constructed interview approach one can elicit from recreationists information concerning the maximum price they would pay in order to avoid being deprived of the use of a particular area for whatever use they may make of it. The argument for the existence of something to be measured rests on the conception that the recreationist is engaged in the utility maximizing process and has made a rational series of allocations of time and money in order to participate in the recreation being evaluated. Since the opportunity itself is available at zero or nominal price, the interview provides the means for discovering the price the person would pay if this opportunity were marketed, other things being equal.

The chief problem to be reckoned with in evaluating interview responses is the degree of reliability that can be attached to the information the respondent provides the interviewer. Particularly on questions dealing with matters of opinion, the responses are subject to many kinds of bias.

One such bias of particular interest to economists stems from the gaming strategy that a consumer of a public good may pursue on the theory that, if he understates his preference for the good, he will escape being charged as much as he is willing to pay without being deprived of the amount of the good he now desires. This may be a false issue, particularly when it comes to pursuing recreation on private lands or waters, because the consumer may be well aware that the owner could, through the exercise of his private property rights, exclude the user from the areas now occupied. An equally good case can be made that, on state and national park lands to which there is limited access, particularly when at the access points the authority of the state is represented by uniformed park patrolmen, recreationists would have no trouble visualizing the existence of the power to exclude them. This being the case, it is not unreasonable to expect the recreationist to be aware of some willingness to pay on his part in order to avoid being excluded from the area he now uses.

Counterbalancing the possibility that the recreationist may purposely understate his willingness to pay in order to escape charges is the possibility that he may wish to bid up his apparent benefits in order to make a case for preserving the area in its current use, a case equally appropriate on private or public lands and waters.

The problem, to continue the argument, is narrowed to one of phrasing the question in such a way that the recreationist is not asked to give his opinion on the propriety of charging for the use of recreation areas.

It has become something of a principle in survey methodology that the less hypothetical the question, the more stable and reliable the response. By this principle, the respondent ought to be a consumer of the product rather than a potential consumer, thus distinguishing the data collected as pertaining to effective demand rather than to option or potential demand. It may also be preferable to impose the conditions on the interview that it occur at a time when the respondent is engaged in the activity. This may contribute to the accuracy of the responses by reducing the requirement that he project from one situation to another. (Admittedly, it is desirable to experiment with the methodology on this question, as well as others, in order to determine its sensitivity to such variations.)

In sum then, we expect to discover the consumer's willingness to pay through a properly constructed interview, and further, we expect that this measure will be the same quantity as would be registered in an organized market for the commodity consumed by the respondent. In other words, we hold a deterministic view that something exists to be measured, and is a sufficiently real and stable phenomenon that the measurement is useful.

*The interview procedure.* The willingness to pay of a sample of users of a forest recreation area in northern Maine was determined in interviews on the site (Davis, 1963). The interviews included a bidding game in which respondents could react to increased costs of visiting the area. Bids were systematically raised or lowered until the user switched his reaction from inclusion to exclusion or vice versa. At the beginning of the interview rapport was established with the respondents largely through objective questions inquiring into their recreation activities on the area, on other areas, and the details of their trips. The bidding questions were interspersed

181

with a series of propositions for which the respondent was to indicate his opinion in the form of a positive, negative, or neutral reaction. His reactions to increased expenses connected with the visit constituted the essence of the bidding game. Personal questions regarding income, education, and the like were confined to the end of the interview.

The sampling procedure amounted to cluster sampling, since the procedure followed was to locate areas of use such as campgrounds and to systematically sample from the available clusters of users. The interviews were conducted from June through November by visiting areas in the privately owned forests of northern Maine and in Baxter State Park.

The data from the interviews is pooled to include hunters, fishermen, and summer campers. This pooling is defended largely on the grounds that no structural differences between identifiable strata were detected in a multiple regression analysis of the responses.

The procedure imputes a discontinuous demand curve to the individual household which may be realistic under the time constraints faced particularly by vacation visitors and other non-repeating visitors. This rectangular demand curve (see Figure 1) reflects a disposition either to come at the current level of use or not to come at all if costs rise above a limiting value. Its realism is supported by a number of respondents whose reaction to the excluding bid was precisely that they would not come at all. It seems reasonable to view the use of remote areas such as northern Maine as lumpy commodities which must be consumed in five- or six-day lumps or not all. Deriving an aggregate demand function from the individual responses so characterized is simply a matter of taking the distribution function of willingness to pay cumulated on a less-than basis. This results in a continuous demand schedule which can be interpreted for the aggregate user population as a conventional demand schedule.

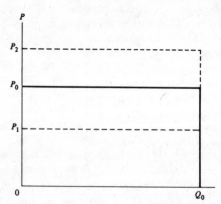

**FIGURE 1.** At prices in the range $O\text{-}P_o$ the constant amount $Q_o$ will be demanded. Above $P_o$ demand will fall to zero. The individual may be in one of three states depending on the reigning price. Consider three individual cases with market price at $P_o$: The user paying $P_1$ is excluded; $P_o$ is associated with the marginal user; and $P_2$ is the willingness to pay of the third user who is included at the reigning price, $P_o$.

For the sample of 185 interviews, willingness-to-pay-per-household-day ranges from zero to $16.66. Zero willingness to pay was encountered in only three interviews. At the other extreme, one or two respondents were unable to place an upper limit on their willingness to pay. The distribution of willingness to pay shows a marked skewness toward the high values. The modal willingness to pay occurs between $1.00 and $2.00 per day per household.

Sixty percent of the variance of willingness to pay among the interviews is explained in a multiple regression equation with willingness-to-pay-per-household-visit a function of income of the household, years of experience by the household in visiting the area, and the length of the stay in the area. (See Equation 1.) While the large negative intercept of this equation necessitated by its linear form causes some difficulties of interpretation, the exhibited relation between willingness to pay, and income, experience, and length of stay appears reasonable. The household income not only reflects an ability to pay, but a positive income elasticity of demand for outdoor recreation as found in other studies. It is also significant that an internal consistency was found in the responses to income-related questions.

$$W = -48.57 + 2.85Y + 2.88E + 4.76L \qquad .5925 \qquad (1)$$
$$\phantom{W = -48.57 + }(1.52) \quad (0.58) \quad (1.03)$$

$$W = .74L^{.76} \ E^{.20} \ Y^{.60} \qquad\qquad .3591^* \qquad (2)$$
$$\phantom{W = }(.13) \ (.07) \ (.17)$$

Standard errors of regression equations: (1) 39.7957; (2) 2.2007.
Standard errors of coefficients are shown in parentheses.
$W$ = household willingness to pay for a visit.
$E$ = years of acquaintance with the area visited.
$Y$ = income of the household in thousands of dollars.
$L$ = length of visit in days.
$F$ = ratios of both equations are highly significant.
* Obtained from arithmetic values of residual and total variances. ($R^2$ of the logarithmic transformation is .4309.)

The significance of years of experience in returning to the area may be interpreted as the effect of an accumulated consumer capital consisting of knowledge of the area, acquisition of skills which enhance the enjoyment of the area, and in some cases use of permanent or mobile housing on the area.

The significance of length of stay in the regression equations is that it both measures the quantity of goods consumed and also reflects a quality dimension suggesting that longer stays probably reflect a greater degree of preference for the area.

Colinearity among explanatory variables was very low. The general

economic consistency and rationality of the responses appear to be high
Respondents' comments indicated they were turning over in their minds the
alternatives available in much the same way that a rational shopper
considers the price and desirability of different cuts or kinds of meat. Both
the success in finding acceptable and significant explanatory variables and a
certain amount of internal consistency in the responses suggest that
considerable weight can be attached to the interview method.

*The simulated demand schedule.* While providing an adequate equation
for predicting the willingness to pay of any user, the results of the interviews
do not serve as direct estimates of willingness to pay of the user population,
because the income, length of stay, and years' experience of the interviewed
sample do not accurately represent the characteristics of the population of
users. Fortunately, it was possible to obtain a reliable sample of the users by
administering a questionnaire to systematically selected samples of users
stopped at the traffic checking stations on the private forest lands. A
logarithmic estimating equation, although not as well fitting, but free of a
negative range, was used to compute the willingness to pay for each
household in the sample. (See Equation 2.) The observations were then
expanded by the sampling fraction to account for the total number of users
during the recreation season.

The next step in the analysis consists of arraying the user population
by willingness to pay, and building a cumulative distribution downward
from the upper limit of the distribution. Table 1 shows the resulting demand
and benefit schedule. The schedule accounts for the total of about 10,300
user households estimated to be the user population in a 450,000-acre area
of the Maine woods near Moosehead Lake, known as the Pittston area.

The demand schedule is noticeably elastic from the upper limit of
$60.00 to about $6.00, at which point total revenues are maximized. The
interval from $60.00 to $6.00 accounts for the estimated willingness to pay
of nearly half of the using households. Total benefits at $6.00 are $56,000.
The price range below $6.00 accounts for the other half of the using
households, but only for $15,000 in additional benefits. Benefits are
estimated as the cumulative willingness to pay or the revenues available to a
discriminating monopolist.

*Willingness to drive vs. willingness to pay.* An alternative expression of
the willingness of recreationists to incur additional costs in order to
continue using an area may be found in their willingness to drive additional
distances. This measure was first proposed by Ullman and Volk (1961)
although in a different version than is used here. (See also Meramec Basin
Research Project, 1961.)

Willingness to drive additional distances was elicited from respondents
by the same technique used to elicit willingness to pay. If there are biases
involving strategies to avoid paying for these recreation areas, then
certainly willingness to drive is to be preferred over willingness to pay as an
expression of value. Analysis of the willingness to drive responses shows
that a partly different set of variables must be used to explain the responses.

| Price | Interview results | | Willingness to drive (interview method) | | Willingness to drive (travel cost method) | |
|---|---|---|---|---|---|---|
| | Household visits | Benefits [1] | Household visits | Benefits [1] | Household visits | Benefits [1] |
| $70.00 | 0 | 0 | | | | |
| 60.00 | 11.36 | $ 747.77 | | | | |
| 50.00 | 15.35 | 983.56 | | | | |
| 40.00 | 44.31 | 2,281.46 | | | | |
| 30.00 | 150.22 | 6,003.19 | 11 36 | $ 384.79 | 165 | $ 3,800 |
| 26.00 | 215.80 | 7,829.71 | | | | |
| 22.00 | 391.07 | 12,027.89 | | | | |
| 20.00 | 536.51 | 15,099.31 | 76.96 | 1,890.12 | 422 | 12,134 |
| 18.00 | 757.86 | 19,275.95 | | | | |
| 16.00 | 1,069.01 | 24,607.81 | | | | |
| 14.00 | 1,497.75 | 31,027.17 | 392.29 | 7,287.06 | | |
| 12.00 | 1,866.41 | 35,802.70 | | | | |
| 10.00 | 2,459.70 | 42,289.68 | 2,157.91 | 28,921.93 | 1,328 | 26,202 |
| 8.00 | 3,100.99 | 48,135.01 | | | | |
| 6.00 | 4,171.89 | 55,794.64 | | | | |
| 4.00 | 5,926.94 | 64,436.36 | 5,721.06 | 53,531.68 | 3,459 | 44,760 |
| 2.00 | 7,866.02 | 70,222.66 | | | | |
| 0.00 | 10,333.22 | 71,460.94 | 10,339.45 | 63,689.99 | 10,333 | 69,450 |

**TABLE 1.** Demand and Benefit Schedules for Pittston Area Based on Alternative Estimates of Willingness to Pay

1. Benefits are computed as the integral of the demand schedule from price maximum to price indicated. Willingness to drive computations are based on an assumed charge of 5¢ per mile for the one-way mileage.

Equation 3 shows willingness to drive extra miles to be a function of length of stay and miles driven to reach the area.

$$Wm = 41.85 + 20.56L + .15M \qquad (3)$$
$$(3.03) \quad (.04) \qquad (R^2 = .3928)$$

$Wm$ = willingness to drive additional miles.
$L$ = length of visit in days.
$M$ = miles traveled to area.

The respondents thus expressed a willingness to exert an additional driving effort, just as they expressed a willingness to make an additional money outlay if this became a requisite to using the area. Moreover, there is a significant correspondence between willingness to pay and willingness to drive. The simple correlation coefficient between these two variables is .5. Because of the correlation with length of stay, the reduction in unexplained variance produced by adding either variable to the equation in which the other variable is the dependent one is not very high. However, willingness to pay was found to increase about 5¢ per mile as a function of willingness to drive additional miles. This result gives us a basis for transforming willingness to drive into willingness to pay.

We may now construct a demand schedule for the Pittston area on the basis of willingness to drive, and compute a willingness to pay at 5¢ per mile. The resulting demand and benefit schedules appear in Table 1. The estimated $64,000 of total benefits is very close to that developed from the willingness to pay interview. While one may quibble about the evaluation of a mile of extra driving and about the treatment of one way versus round-trip distance, the first approximation using the obvious value of 5¢ and one-way mileage as reported by the respondents produces a result so close to the first result that we need look no further for marginal adjustments. The initial result strongly suggests that mileage measures and expenditure measures have equal validity as a measure of benefits in this particular case at least.

There are some differences between the respective demand schedules worth noting. The much lower price intercept on the willingness to drive schedule reflects the effect of the time constraint in traveling as well as our possibly erroneous constant transformation of miles to dollars when an increasing cost per mile would be more reasonable. The travel schedule is also elastic over more of its range than the dollar schedule—also perhaps a result of the constant transformation employed.

This initial success with alternative derivations of the benefits schedule now leads us to examine an alternative method for estimating the willingness to drive schedule.

### Travel-Cost Method of Estimating User-Demand Curve

The direct interview approach to the estimate of a true price-quantity relationship, or demand curve, for the recreation experience is one approach to the benefit calculations based on willingness to pay. An alternative approach has received some recognition and has been applied in a number of limited instances with at least a fair degree of success. This uses travel-cost data as a proxy for price in imputing a demand curve for recreation facilities. (Brown, 1964; Clawson, 1959; Knetsch, 1963; Knetsch, 1964.) As with the direct interview approach, we believe that estimates derived from this approach are relevant and useful for measuring user benefits of outdoor recreation.

The travel-cost method imputes the price-quantity reactions of consumers by examining their actual current spending behavior with respect to travel cost. The method can be shown by using a simple, hypothetical example. Assume a free recreation or park area at varying distances from three centers of population given in Table 2.

The cost of visiting the area is of major concern and would include such items as transportation, lodging, and food cost above those incurred if

| City | Population | Cost of visit | Visits made | Visits/1,000 pop. |
|------|-----------|---------------|-------------|-------------------|
| A | 1,000 | $1.00 | 400 | 400 |
| B | 2,000 | 3.00 | 400 | 200 |
| C | 4,000 | 4.00 | 400 | 100 |

**TABLE 2.** *Visits to a Hypothetical Recreation Area*

the trip were not made. Each cost would vary with the distance from the park to the city involved. Consequently, the number of visits, or rather the rate of visits per unit total population of each city, would also vary.

The visits per unit of population, in this case per thousand population, may then be plotted against the cost per visit. A line drawn through the three points of such a plot would have the relationship given by the equation of $C = 5 - V$, or perhaps more conveniently $V = 5 - C$, where $C$ is cost of a visit and $V$ is the rate of visits in hundreds per thousand population. This information is taken directly from the tabulation of consumer behavior. The linear relationship assumed here is for convenience. Actual data may very well show, for example, that $1.00 change in cost might have only a slight effect on visit rate where the visit is already high in cost, and a large effect on low-cost visits.

The construction of a demand curve to the recreation area, relating number of visits to varying cost, involves a second step. Essentially, it derives the demand curve from the equation relating visit rates to cost, by relating visit rates of each zone to simulated increases in cost and multiplying by the relative populations in each zone. Thus we might first assume a price of $1.00, which is an added cost of $1.00 for visits to the area from each of the three different centers used in our hypothetical example. This would have the expected result of reducing the number of visitors coming from each of the centers. The expected reduction is estimated from the visit-cost relationship. The total visits suggested by these calculations for different prices or differing added cost are given in the following table.

| Price (added cost) | Quantity (total visits) |
|--------------------|-------------------------|
| $0.00 | 1,200 |
| 1.00 | 500 |
| 2.00 | 200 |
| 3.00 | 100 |
| 4.00 | 0 |

These results may then be taken as the demand curve relating price to visits to the recreation area. While this analysis takes visits as a simple function of cost, in principle there is no difficulty in extending the analysis to other factors important in recreation demand, such as alternative sites available, the inherent attractiveness of the area in question or at least its characteristics in this regard, and possibly even some measure of congestion.

A difficulty with this method of benefit approximation is a consistent bias in the imputed demand curve resulting from the basic assumption that the disutility of overcoming distance is a function only of money cost. Clearly this is not so. The disutility is most likely to be the sum of at least three factors: money cost, time cost, and the utility (plus or minus) of driving, or traveling. The total of these three factors is demonstrably negative, but we do not know enough about the significance of the last two components. In all likelihood their sum—that is, of the utility or disutility of driving and the time cost—imposes costs in addition to money. To the extent that this is true the benefit estimate will be conservatively biased, for, as has been indicated, it is assumed that the only thing causing differences in attendance rates for cities located at different distances to a recreation area will be the differences in money cost. The method then postulates that if money cost changes are affected, the changes in rates will be proportional. What this bias amounts to is, essentially, a failure to establish a complete transformation function relating the three components of overcoming distance to the total effect on visitation rates. The resulting conservative bias must be regarded as an understatement of the recreation benefits which the approach is designed to measure.

*Application to Pittston area.* The travel-cost method was applied to the same area as that used to illustrate the interview method of recreation benefit estimation. The same data were utilized to allow at least a crude comparison of the methods. In all, 6,678 respondents who said the Pittston area was the main destination of their trip were used in the analysis.

Visit rates of visitors from groups of counties near the area and from some states at greater distances were plotted against distance. The results were fairly consistent considering the rough nature of the approximations used in estimating distance. A curve was drawn through the points, giving a relationship between visit rates and distance. The demand curve was then calculated, giving a price-quantity relationship based on added distance (or added toll cost) and total visits. It was assumed initially that travel cost would be 5¢ per mile, using one-way distance to conform with our earlier analysis of travel cost by the interview method.

The results at this point were not comparable to the interview method because of a difference in the number of users accounted for. It will be recalled that in the analysis we are now describing only those respondents were used who had specifically stated that the visit to the Pittston area was the main destination of the trip. In order to make this number comparable to the total number of users accounted for in the interview estimate, we counted at half weight the 1,327 respondents who said that Pittston was *not* the primary destination of the trip, and also included in this group the non-response questionnaires and others with incomplete information. In this way we accounted for the same number of users as in the interview estimate. This very crude approximation points out the problems of the multiple-destination visit, but perhaps adequately serves the present purpose.

On the basis of these approximations, the benefit estimates on an annual basis were $70,000, assuming 5¢ per mile one-way distance. While the assumptions made throughout this analysis are subject to refinement, the exercise does seem to illustrate that the procedure is feasible from a practical standpoint and does produce results that are economically meaningful.

## COMPARISON BETWEEN TRAVEL-COST AND INTERVIEW METHODS

Having demonstrated that fairly close results are obtained from both the interview and imputation methods of estimating recreation benefits on the basis of reactions to travel costs, and further that the interview method of directly estimating willingness to pay agrees closely with both estimates based on travel costs, we can now begin to assess the meaning of these results. In some ways the task would be easier if the results had not agreed so closely, for the three methodologies may imply different things about the users' reactions to increased costs. At least, it is not obvious without further probing as to why the agreement is so close.

The interview and imputation methods of estimating benefits on the basis of willingness to incur additional travel costs do not, for example neatly imply the same relationship between distance traveled and willingness to incur additional travel costs. The estimating equation derived from the interviews (Equation 3) suggests that the farther one has traveled, the greater additional distance he will travel. Yet the imputation procedure implies that the willingness to drive by populations in the respective zones does not vary consistently with distance. Furthermore, according to the interviews, responses to the monetary measure of willingness to pay do not attribute any variance in willingness to pay to the distance factor, nor is an indirect relationship obvious. It seems relevant to inquire into the implied effects of these factors to discover why the alternative procedures appear to imply substantially different determinants of willingness to pay.

The superficial agreement in results may be upheld by this kind of further probing, but there are also some methodological issues which should not be overlooked. The travel-cost methods are obviously sensitive to such matters as the weighting given to multiple-destination visits and to the transformation used to derive costs from mileage values. Both methods are sensitive to the usual problems of choosing an appropriately fitting equation for the derivation of the demand schedule. The interview method has a poorly understood sensitivity to the various methodologies that might be employed in its use. Moreover, even the minimal use of interviews in studies of recreation benefits makes the method far more costly than the imputation method based on travel costs.

There are, however, complementarities in the two basic methods which may prove highly useful. In the first place, the two methods may serve as checks on each other in applied situations. One is certainly in a better position from having two methods produce nearly identical answers than if he has to depend on only one. There are also interesting possibilities that interviews may be the best way of resolving the ambiguities in the travel-cost method concerning the treatment of multiple-destination cases and for finding the appropriate valuation for converting distance into dollars. Much can be said for letting the recreationist tell us how to handle these problems.

In sum, we have examined three methods of measuring recreation benefits. All three measure recreationists' willingness to pay. This, we argue, is the appropriate measure of primary, or national, benefits. Furthermore, the measures are in rough agreement as to the benefits ascribable to an area of the Maine woods. This may be taken as evidence that we are on the right track. There are, however, some rough spots to be ironed out of each of the methods—an endeavor we believe to be worthy of major research effort if benefit-cost analysis is to contribute its full potential in planning decisions affecting recreation investments in land and water resources.

## NOTE

[1] These concepts are developed by Davidson, Adams, and Seneca in "The Social Value of Water Recreational Facilities Resulting from an Improvement in Water Quality: The Delaware Estuary," in Allen V. Kneese and Stephen C. Smith, eds., *Water Research* (Baltimore: The Johns Hopkins Press, 1966).

## REFERENCES

Brown, W. G.; A. Singh; and E. N. Castle. 1964. An economic evaluation of the Oregon Salmon and Steelhead sport fishery. Technical Bulletin 78. Oregon State Agricultural Experiment Station, Corvallis.

Clawson, M. 1959. *Methods of measuring the demand for and value of outdoor recreation.* Reprint no. 10. Washington, D.C.: Resources for the Future.

Crutchfield, J. 1962. Valuation of fishery resources. *Land Economics* 38 (2).

Davis, R. K. 1963. The value of outdoor recreation: An economic study of the Maine Woods. Unpublished Ph.D. dissertation, Harvard University.

Knetsch, J. L. 1963. Outdoor recreation demands and benefits. *Land Economics* 39 (4).

Knetsch, J. L. 1964. Economics of including recreation as a purpose of water resources projects. *Journal of Farm Economics*, December.

Lerner, L. 1962. Quantitative indices of recreational values. In *Water resources and economic development of the West.* Report no. 11. Proceedings, Conference of Committee on the Economics of Water Resources Development of Western Agricultural Economics Research Council with Western Farm Economics Association. Reno: University of Nevada.

Meramec Basin Research Project. 1961. *The Meramec Basin.* Vol. 3. St. Louis: Washington University. Chap. 5.

Merewitz, L. 1965. Recreational benefits of water-resource development. Unpublished paper of Harvard Water Program.

Ullman, E., and D. Volk. 1962. An operational model for predicting reservoir attendance and benefits: Implications of a location approach to water recreation. *Papers of the Michigan Academy of Sciences, Arts and Letters*, 1961 Meeting.

# 13

## A NEW APPROACH TO THE EVALUATION OF NON-PRICED RECREATIONAL RESOURCES
### Peter H. Pearse

As an additional valuation method, Peter H. Pearse describes an analysis of big game hunting based upon the concept of consumers' surplus (the difference between total economic value and total revenues—the area between the demand curve and the price line). While this analysis uses travel costs, the method explicitly introduces the use of the income variable rather than ignoring income, as in the travel-cost method just shown.

The concept of consumers' surplus is used as the basis for valuing the recreational resources that support hunting opportunities. Consumers' surplus is still a controversial subject among economists and especially as applied to recreation. One argument against using this concept notes that values above the price cannot be captured because entry fees are not varied by ability to pay. Thus, this measure cannot be used to compare with other services for which only a price is paid. The travel cost method, whether valued via consumers' surplus or maximum revenue, suffers from the assumption of a homogeneous base population.

This chapter has been heavily edited; if additional information is desired the student is referred to the original source.

. . . The last few years have witnessed a flurry of interest among economists in the problem of evaluating nonpriced recreation. The development of techniques of evaluation has proceeded in two directions,

Reprinted from *Land Economics* 44, no. 1 (February, 1968): 87–99, by permission of The University of Wisconsin Press and the author. The theoretical parts of this article have been extensively edited for this volume. The notes and the figure have been renumbered.

This paper is a by-product of a project sponsored by Resources for the Future, Inc. The author is indebted to his colleagues in the Department of Economics at the University of British Columbia for their criticisms of an early draft of this paper at a seminar, and particularly to Professor G. Rosenbluth, who helped clarify several of the methodological issues. The author is entirely responsible for the remaining shortcomings in the analysis.

both of which are directed toward establishing the willingness of recreationists to pay for access to recreation facilities which they actually use without charge. The "direct" techniques attempt to establish a demand schedule by enquiring of the recreationists the most they would be prepared to pay for access to the recreation rather than be excluded.[1] Alternatively they might be asked to declare the minimum amount they would have to be paid (bribed) to willingly abstain from the recreation.[2] It should be noted that these two different kinds of questions would, if answered precisely, give estimates of value which are both defensible on theoretical grounds, but they are unlikely to be equal because they measure two different forms of consumer surplus. In Hicks' terminology, the maximum tolerable price for access measures the "compensating surplus," while the minimum acceptable bribe for abstention measures the "equivalent surplus."[3]

The practical difficulty with these direct techniques lies in obtaining rational and consistent expressions of value from recreationists simply by asking them direct but hypothetical questions, particularly in view of the emotionalism toward the value of recreational resources among many recreationists. Moreover, if recreationists would in fact adjust the amount of recreation they consume in the face of real charges, the results obtained may be spurious.

The second direction of development in techniques is by imputing willingness to pay from indirect evidence relating to recreationists' observed behavior, particularly their willingness to incur costs of travel to the recreational site in question.[4] This approach involves stratifying the total population from which recreationists come by distance zones, within each of which the cost of travelling to the site is fairly consistent (in the more refined applications, the populations are stratified by other variables as well, such as income, family size, and so on). This enables a calculation of an expression relating participation rates to the level of travel cost (among other things). The participation rate from a particular population group under any hypothetical toll is then predicted by referring to the observed participation rate from similar populations with travel costs equal to those of the group in question plus the toll. By applying these predicted participation rates at various levels of toll to the number in the population, a demand schedule can be constructed for each population group, and these can be added to yield an aggregate demand schedule for the recreational resource.

This approach involves a number of important assumptions. First, it implies that the recreationists' response to a toll on access to the site would be exactly the same as an equal addition to the cash cost of travel.[5] Secondly, the costs of travel are incurred solely for the purpose of gaining access to the recreation site. Clearly, if the recreationists gained utility from other activities *en route,* or from the trip itself, it would be inappropriate to attribute travel costs entirely to the on-site recreation experience. Thirdly, all populations are assumed to face identical alternatives to the recreational opportunity under consideration, otherwise it would not be possible to predict different groups' response to costs from a common relationship.

Fourthly, recreationists in all areas are assumed to have the same preference for the site (or if variables other than distance are incorporated in the predictive relationship, these will accurately provide for differences in preference). Finally, there is the critical assumption that not only the recreationists but also the whole populations from which recreationists are drawn have similar characteristics and preferences (or that differences are explained by incorporated variables other than distance). Several attempts have been made to overcome the rigidity of these latter assumptions about similarities in preferences by incorporating variables relating to income levels, availability of substitute areas, congestion, and so on. But specification of the different effects has met with limited success, in large part because of multi-collinearity between such variables as distance, time and costs, and the difficulty of measuring such factors as congestion, availability of alternatives, and quality of the site.[6]

This article presents a new form of indirect approach to the problem of evaluating nonpriced recreational resources which avoids some of the restrictive assumptions of established methods. In particular, it confines the analysis to the recreationists themselves, thus avoiding the necessity of assumptions about the characteristics and homogeneity of the base populations from which recreationists are drawn. . . .

The benefits of a good or service available free of charge are entirely appropriated by consumers in the form of consumer surplus. We need, therefore, a model for analysing recreationists' behavior that will facilitate quantification of their consumer surplus.

The costs of indulging in a particular recreational opportunity are in part fixed, in the sense that they do not depend upon the amount of recreation consumed, and in part variable with respect to the number of days spent at the recreational site. Fixed costs include, among other things, the necessary costs of travel to and from the site. Variable costs are those which depend upon the length of time spent on the site, such as the costs of food and supplies. . . .

The value of the resource to recreationists, in terms of the consumer surplus they enjoy under free access, consists of the sum of the maximum tolls that they would be prepared to pay in addition to their existing fixed costs.[7] This is the area under the demand curve for the resource if the data are analysed in terms of trips rather than numbers of recreationists (if some recreationists take more than one trip in the time period under consideration).

## The Quantification of Consumer Surplus

In order to estimate the amount that recreationists would be prepared to pay in addition to their necessary fixed costs, we compare visitors with similar incomes but differing fixed costs. The required data include the income level and travel costs of visitors (or a representative sample of them) to the area under consideration, and the number of visits made by each.

The relevant "market" to be considered in estimating the effect of a hypothetical toll consists of the population of visitors who participate under free access. Fewer and fewer of them would be expected to purchase access as the toll was raised, and there is no reason to expect others, who did not visit under free entry, to visit under a toll.[8]

We assume at the outset that the recreationists who pursue the activity in question and have similar incomes also have similar preferences for the recreation, and incur similar marginal costs per recreation day. Thus their indifference maps are identical and their market opportunity lines are parallel. It is not necessary to assume that different income groups are similar in these respects.

To quantify the willingness of recreationists to pay for access to a particular site, the data relating to individual visitors are first grouped according to the visitors' income class. Within each class visitors are then ranked by their fixed costs, which will vary primarily with respect to the distance travelled to the recreational site.

The visitor with the highest travel cost in an income class is assumed to break even, in the sense that he enjoys no consumer surplus. . . .

The maximum toll that each visitor would be prepared to bear is the difference between his fixed cost and that of the highest-cost visitor in the same income class. The total of these differences for visitors in all income classes represents the value of the resource in terms of the consumer surplus it generates to visitors under free access.

These data also permit an easy derivation of the demand curve for the recreational opportunity. All visitors, regardless of income class, can be ranked according to the magnitude of their maximum tolerable toll. The number of visitors that would continue to participate under a toll $P$ consists of all those whose maximum tolerable toll is equal to or greater than $P$. Thus by calculating the number of participants for a variety of hypothetical levels of toll, a demand schedule of the conventional form is defined. The total area under this demand curve represents the value of the nonprice recreational resource.[9]

## Some Observations on the Method

The evaluation technique described above falls into the category of indirect methods, and requires the kinds of data that are relatively easy to collect for these purposes. Its greatest advantage over other indirect methods is that it avoids assumptions about the homogeneity of base populations from which recreationists are drawn. This is referred to by Merewitz[10] as the 'vertical cross-section assumption' and is inherent in all the methods which involve predicting participation rates for population groups (or zones) at different prices from observed relationships between participation and the explanatory variables associated with the participating recreationists.

By contrast, the data required for the method proposed here are restricted to observations about recreationists themselves, and the analysis is based only on actual participants. In view of the difficulties in accurately identifying and quantifying all the variables that are likely to influence demand for a particular recreational opportunity, particularly where participants are drawn from widely dispersed population groups, this may be regarded as a significant advantage of the proposed method.

In addition, the technique described above avoids the assumption, inherent in most other approaches, that recreationists faced with an access fee would either consume the same amount of recreation as they do under free access or none at all. If, as the conventional theory of consumer behavior suggests, recreationists would make marginal adjustments in consumption in response to price changes, the results obtained under this assumption would be spurious. The proposed method involves no such assumption about the rigidity of the recreation 'package.'

A related matter is the form in which the hypothetical toll is levied. Most other techniques postulate a toll on a per-day basis, in contrast to the addition of fixed costs postulated here. A per-day charge would change the marginal cost of a recreation day and thereby further weaken the assumption about consumers' lack of response in terms of days consumed per visit.[11]

Nevertheless it is important to recognize the assumptions that this method retains, and their implications for the results produced. First, it is assumed that recreationists will respond to a toll in the same way that they respond to an equal increment in travel costs, and the sole purpose of the journey is assumed to be the enjoyment of on-site recreation. These assumptions are common to all indirect methods. The assumption about consistent response to costs and tolls seems to be a reasonable and not unusual assumption about the rationality of consumers for the purposes of analysis, providing the costs are fully and accurately measured. The sole-purpose assumption is probably not unrealistic for certain categories of recreation, such as hunting and fishing. For campers, tourists, and others who might be expected to be less single-minded about the recreation experience, the assumption is probably more serious. In any event, the validity of the sole-purpose assumption would seem to be easily tested.

The assumptions that are more particular to the technique proposed here are firstly, that recreationists with similar incomes, who have also demonstrated a similarity of tastes to the extent that they have pursued the same recreational experience, are equally willing to pay for the recreation and secondly, that the recreationist with the highest fixed costs in a given income group is a marginal consumer.

This latter assumption deserves further examination, especially because of its implications for the number of income categories selected. At one extreme, if each recreationist was treated as a separate income group, no consumer surplus would be measured. At the other extreme, if all were treated together as a single group, the consumer surplus of recreationists of all incomes would be determined by comparison with the single highest-cost visitor, and this would tend to yield an overestimate of value if willingness-to-pay varies with income as suggested here. Obviously some compromise is necessary between selecting income groups small enough to identify groups within which willingness-to-pay is likely to be similar, and large enough to enhance the likelihood of including an individual near the margin. Clearly, the sample of recreationists and the number of income groups into which they are grouped ought to be selected to minimize variation in income within groups, while including enough observations so that all are not at or near the margin but there is a good probability that at least one is.

The assumed constancy of willingness-to-pay within income groups bears implications for the differing alternative opportunities faced by recreationists with similar incomes. If the recreationists within an income group face differing alternative opportunities, they could not be expected to react identically to a toll on the site under consideration, even though their tastes were similar. The assumption implied in the method is that, within a given income group, participating recreationists are evenly distributed among areas offering substitutes of differing quality, and that the recreationist with highest fixed costs faces alternatives of average quality. This is a very important assumption, but it appears to be the minimum that will allow the analysis to proceed. It is considerably less restrictive than the assumption that not only all participants, but whole populations (of which participants are a part) face identical alternatives, as implied in other indirect techniques.

The rigidity of the assumption about constant willingness-to-pay within income groups might be mitigated if data were available to permit further stratification of recreationists by occupation, age, and other characteristics that may be found significant in determining the strength of demand.

The bias resulting from this assumption in the method followed here is toward an underestimate of resource benefits. High fixed costs are highly correlated with distance travelled, and the greater the distance, the more alternatives are available for the same outlay. The scope of alternatives available at the cost actually incurred tends to be narrower for those who travel shorter distances. The implication of this is that since the highest fixed cost tends to be incurred by recreationists with the widest alternatives, the consumer surplus of the remainder will be underestimated.

Finally, we can assert that the assumption about the marginal status of the highest cost individual in each group means that the calculated value of the resource is in the nature of a lower limit to its real value, particularly if data on only a sample of the population of recreationists are available. This follows from the likely possibility that the highest-cost individual himself is intramarginal in the sense that he enjoys consumer surplus. Again, the likelihood of conservative bias and its magnitude resulting from this assumption will depend upon the number of observations in the group—the larger the number the greater the probability of including a marginal participant.

## AN APPLICATION: BIG GAME HUNTING RESOURCES IN THE EAST KOOTENAY

A detailed statistical survey of big game hunters and hunting activity in the East Kootenay in 1964 provides the data for demonstration of the application of the evaluation technique.[12] The East Kootenay forms the southern part of the Rocky Mountain Trench in British Columbia and has a wide reputation for its prolific and varied populations of big game species. In the analysis that follows we are concerned with the value of these hunting resources to residents of the province of British Columbia.[13]

Detailed information was available on 485 or 3.4 percent of the 14 thousand resident big game hunters who hunted in the area in 1964. The sample was first stratified by six income classes as shown in Table 1. The fixed cost of each hunter was identified as the declared cash cost of travel to and from the area, an allowance for the value of time spent in travel, and other expenses such as hunting licenses, game tags, and so on, which were reported to have been incurred specifically for East Kootenay hunting.

| Income Group | Number of Observations | Highest Fixed Cost | Average Consumer Surplus |
|---|---|---|---|
| less than $ 2,000 | 25 | $ 66 | $ 47 |
| $2,000 to $ 4,000 | 67 | 183 | 149 |
| $4,000 to $ 6,000 | 219 | 287 | 224 |
| $6,000 to $ 8,000 | 109 | 320 | 221 |
| $8,000 to $10,000 | 32 | 267 | 152 |
| over $10,000 | 33 | 355 | 196 |
| Total sample | 485 | (weighted) | $197 |

**TABLE 1.** *Calculation of Consumer Surplus for Resident Big Game Hunters in the East Kootenay in 1964*

Total consumer surplus, all hunters: = total number of resident hunters × average consumer surplus in sample: = *14,346 × $197:* = *$2,900,242.*

The fixed costs of each hunter were then subtracted from the highest observed fixed cost in his income class, to give each individual's estimated consumer surplus.[14] The weighted average consumer surplus over all income classes was $197, which, multiplied by the total number of hunters in 1964, yielded an aggregate value in the form of consumer surplus of $2,900,242. This is the area under the demand curve, shown in Figure 1, which was derived by the method described earlier.

Two procedural problems deserve to be mentioned. The first relates to the evaluation of time spent in travel. To arrive at estimates of the opportunity cost of travel time, the mid-point of each income bracket was divided by 240, which is the assumed average number of working days per year. This provided average values of a day's time for each income category. The value of time spent in travel for each hunter was calculated by multiplying the number of days spent in travel by the per-day value of time for his income group. The cost of time accounted for something in the order of half the total fixed costs.

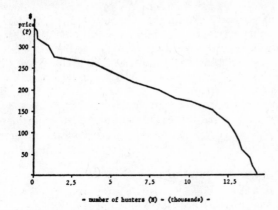

**FIGURE 1.** *The Demand for East Kootenay Hunting*

This procedure obviously provides no more than a rough measure of the opportunity cost of time. Even if the data are accurate, it involves the assumption that each hunter has achieved perfect equilibrium in the allocation of his time (which is assumed to be perfectly divisible) between work, hunting, and other forms of leisure. Moreover, it requires that time spent in travel is a marginal amount. Clearly, the divisibility assumption is more appropriate for certain professional groups whose work schedules are more flexible than for other kinds of labor whose holidays and work-weeks are more rigid.[15] Had data been available, it would undoubtedly have been preferable to reduce each hunter's income foregone by his marginal tax rate. In view of these difficulties and the importance of the time component of fixed costs, improvements in the precision of estimates of value by indirect techniques would seem to depend heavily on better information about expenditures of time and attitudes toward travel.

The second problem concerns the treatment of cases in which individual hunters made more than one visit in the season. The methodology, as outlined earlier, implies that hunters make one hunt each, so that willingness to incur cost for access can be thought of in terms of a single fixed cost. Yet many of the hunters—especially among those that lived in or near the East Kootenay—made several trips each. The relationship between number of hunters and number of visits therefore needs to be clarified. . . .

As long as the hunter who takes two or more trips incurs total fixed costs (for all his trips) less than the highest fixed costs observed in the relevant income class, the estimate of his consumer surplus should be based on the fixed cost of one trip only. It follows from the assumptions of the analysis that this is the maximum amount he would pay rather than abandon the recreation altogether. If he were charged this amount, he would, of course, reduce the number of trips he takes to one, and consume fewer days. If, on the other hand, he is observed to incur fixed costs on all his trips that exceed the fixed costs of any other hunter in the income class, then this should become the measure of maximum costs for that income class, because the maximum tolerable costs should be measured by the highest total fixed costs observed in each income class.[16]

It follows that in cases where multiple trips are involved (as in the East Kootenay example), the quantity variable on the demand schedule is hunters, not numbers of trips.

The statistical information available on East Kootenay hunters enabled an analysis of some of the assumptions inherent in the method. It is instructive to review these, and one or two procedural problems involved in the empirical analysis.

## The Sole-Purpose Assumption

The hunters sampled were asked to report any purposes other than big game hunting in the East Kootenay which influenced their decision to make the trip. Only 5.5 percent indicated other purposes, such as sightseeing, visits with relatives and friends, and business activities. It was not possible to determine the relative importance of hunting and the other activity, where another activity was indicated. However, since hunting was the only purpose in 94.5 percent of the hunts, and was at least a determining factor in the remainder, it appears that the sole-purpose assumption is not unreasonable in this case.

## Dependence of Willingness-to-pay on Income

The assumption that participating hunters with similar incomes would be willing to pay the same amount for access to the hunting opportunity has already been discussed. Some light might be cast on this assumption by examining the consistency within income groups of on-site expenditures. Linear regressions were run to test the correlation between reported variable (on-site) costs of hunting and the number of days spent hunting for the individuals in each income group. The results suggest that one-half to two-thirds of the variation in total variable costs within income groups can be explained by differences in duration of hunt. This degree of consistency within income classes in costs per day incurred tends to strengthen the assumption about willingness to incur similar fixed costs. Moreover, the close relationship between the level of income and the highest observed fixed cost (see Table 1) tends to support the assumption that willingness to pay depends upon income. While the method involves no assumptions about consistency in consumer surplus gained by hunters with different incomes, an orderly relationship between these variables does suggest a significant dependence of willingness-to-pay on the hunters' income level.[17]

## Sources of Bias

It was earlier suggested that a conservative bias in the assessment of value is likely to result from the assumption that the hunter with the highest fixed cost in each income group is marginal, and that this likelihood is increased where the number of observations in a group is small, because of the reduced probability of including a marginal participant. This may be the case, for example, for the $8,000–$10,000 income class in the table where the highest observed fixed cost did not follow the otherwise consistently upward trend with income level.[18] Significantly, the number of observations in this class was relatively small. An alternative procedure might have been to smooth out anomalies by fitting a curve through the highest fixed costs, which would have the effect of increasing the measured consumer surplus.[19] Another source of conservative bias suggested earlier derives from the assumption that hunters within income classes faced similar arrays of alternative opportunities, whereas those that travelled farthest (incurred the highest fixed costs) might reasonably be expected to have a wider array of alternatives.

In this connection it is interesting to note that the East Kootenay hunters tended to hold a higher opinion of the relative quality of East Kootenay hunting the closer they were to it. Half of the local hunters felt that the East Kootenay offers "the very best" in big game hunting available anywhere, compared with less than a third of the other residents with this view. Three quarters of the local hunters considered the area at least "very good" while only two-thirds of the others held so high an opinion.

Since the largest component of fixed costs is costs of travel, the highest fixed costs tend to be incurred by hunters who travel the furthest distances. The hunters' expressed opinions, however, suggest that these distant travellers value East Kootenay hunting relatively less highly than the more proximate hunters. Measuring the consumer surplus of individual hunters by comparing their fixed costs with highest in their income group is likely, therefore, to underestimate the value of the hunting to those closer to the resource.

## NOTES

[1] See Robert K. Davis, "The Value of Big Game Hunting in a Private Forest," *Transactions of the Twenty-Ninth North American Wildlife and Natural Resources Conference* (Washington, D.C.: Wildlife Management Institute, 1964), pp. 393–403.

[2] This is the suggestion of James A. Crutchfield, "Valuation of Fishery Resources," *Land Economics* (May, 1962): 145–54.

[3] J. R. Hicks, *A Revision of Demand Theory* (Oxford, Eng.: Clarendon, 1956). This distinction is discussed further below.

[4] The most important contributions are those of Harold Hotelling in a letter to the Director of the United States National Parks Service (dated 1947), quoted in Outdoor Recreation Resources Review Commission, *Economic Studies of Outdoor Recreation*, Study Report 24 (Washington, D.C.: U.S. Government Printing Office, 1962), p. 56; Marion Clawson, *Methods of Measuring the Demand for and Value of Outdoor Recreation*, Reprint No. 10 (Washington, D.C.: Resources for the Future, 1959); Jack L. Knetsch, "Outdoor Recreation Demands and Benefits," *Land Economics* (November, 1963): 387–96; E. Boyd

Wennergren, "Valuing Non-Market Priced Recreational Resources," *Land Economics* (November, 1964): 303–14; William G. Brown, Ajmer Singh, and Emery N. Castle, *An Economic Evaluation of the Oregon Salmon and Steelhead Sport Fishery*, Agricultural Experiment Station Technical Bulletin 78 (Corvallis: Oregon State University, 1964); Joe B. Stevens, "Recreation Benefits from Water Pollution Control," *Water Resources Research* (Second Quarter, 1966): 167–82; and Marion Clawson and Jack L. Knetsch, *Economics of Outdoor Recreation* (Baltimore: The Johns Hopkins Press, 1966).

[5] Incidentally, none of the applications of this technique has provided for non-cash costs of travel. Yet the cost of time spent in travel (quite apart from other utilities or disutilities associated with the journey) may be highly influential in recreationists' decisions. Failure to consider the full opportunity costs of travel will overestimate the elasticity of the demand schedule and underestimate the consumer surplus. This point is discussed by Anthony Scott, "The Valuation of Game Resources: Some Theoretical Aspects," *Canadian Fisheries Reports* 4 (Ottawa, Canada: Department of Fisheries of Canada, Queen's Printer, 1965), pp. 27–47.

[6] Another type of indirect method is to estimate the saving in travel costs that accrues to users of the recreational opportunity in avoiding the necessity of resorting to the next nearest site with similar characteristics. See, for example, Edward L. Ullman and Donald J. Volk, "An Operational Model for Predicting Reservoir Attendance and Benefits: Implications of a Location Approach to Water Recreation," *Papers of The Michigan Academy of Science, Arts and Letters*, 1961 Meeting (1962): 473–84; also, R. A. Spargo, "Evaluation of Sport Fisheries: An Experiment in Methods," unpublished manuscript, Economics Service, Department of Fisheries of Canada, Ottawa, June 1964. This approach suffers from a number of serious weaknesses. In fact, many recreationists pass what they consider their next best opportunity *en route* to the site in question, in which case their benefit is apparently (but illogically) negative. The method presumably attempts to quantify the locational rent attributable to the site, but it will underestimate value because it takes no account of the site's qualities other than location.

[7] It is worth noting that nearly all the suggested indirect methodologies referred to earlier (see note 4) base the calculation of consumer surplus on average travel costs *per recreation day consumed,* on the assumption that recreationists will not respond to a change in costs *per day* by changing the quantity of recreation consumed during a trip. This assumption underlies the study by Andrew H. Trice and Samuel E. Wood, "Measurement of Recreation Benefits," *Land Economics* (August, 1958): 195–207; and is explicitly recognized in Davis' application of his direct method in Davis, "The Value of Big Game Hunting"; and Jack L. Knetsch and Robert K. Davis, "Comparisons of Methods for Recreation Evaluation," in Allen V. Kneese and Steven C. Smith, eds., *Water Research* (Baltimore: The Johns Hopkins Press, 1966), pp. 125–42. While there are arguments to support the assumption under certain circumstances, it will be recognized that it does not concur with generally accepted theory of consumer behavior.

[8] This might not be the case if changes in the number of participants alter the quality of the experience (for example, if solitude is a quality characteristic). We assume here that interdependency between consumers is negligible over the range of use under consideration.

[9] Marion Clawson ("Methods of Measuring the Demand for and Value of Outdoor Recreation") contended that the appropriate measure of value is represented by the largest rectangle that can be constructed under the demand curve. This view was taken also by Emery N. Castle and William G. Brown, "The Economic Value of a Recreational Resource: A Case Study of the Oregon Salmon-Steelhead Sport Fishery," paper presented to the Committee on the Economics of Water Resources Development of the Western Agricultural Economics Research Council, San Francisco, 1964; and is defended by Joe B. Stevens, "Recreation Benefits from Water Pollution Control," and "Recreation Benefits from Water Pollution Control: A Further Note on Benefit Evaluation," *Water Resources Research* (First Quarter, 1967): 63–64. But while the rectangle represents the maximum revenue obtainable by a nondiscriminating seller of access, it underestimates the value enjoyed by users under free access by an amount equal to the remaining area under the demand curve.

[10] Leonard Merewitz, "Recreational Benefits of Water Resource Development," *Water Resources Research* (Fourth Quarter, 1966): 625–40.

[11] It should be noted that the form of an actual levy can have important welfare implications. A per-day charge would tend to cause recreationists to economize on the number

202

of days consumed, while a fixed access charge, regardless of the number of days consumed, would not. If the social cost of providing a marginal recreation-day were zero, the expected reaction to a per-day charge would be undesirable. On the other hand, if (perhaps because of interdependencies between consumers due to congestion) it was desirable to ration the available capacity among recreationists, a positive per-day charge would be efficient.

[12] Peter H. Pearse and Gary Bowden, *Big Game Hunting in the East Kootenay* (Vancouver, Canada: Price Printing, 1966).

[13] A large number of hunters come to the East Kootenay each year from other parts of Canada and from foreign countries. Nonresident demand constitutes a distinctly separate market because of the different conditions under which nonresidents are permitted to hunt. Moreover, from the point of view of British Columbia, the consumer surplus of nonresident hunters does not constitute a benefit.

[14] Two of the reported highest fixed costs were rejected because their extreme values suggested mistakes in reporting.

[15] A significant number of the East Kootenay hunters sampled reported that they sacrificed income by hunting. Not surprisingly, local hunters, who hunted mostly on one-day trips, sacrificed income much less frequently (8.6 percent) than those who travelled to the East Kootenay from other parts of British Columbia (34.8 percent). These data do not, however, throw much light on the value to be ascribed to time in travel, since time spent in alternative leisure activities should theoretically at least, yield a marginal benefit equal to marginal employment earnings.

[16] In no case, however, was the highest fixed cost used here derived from multiple trips.

[17] A linear regression relating the highest observed fixed cost ($C$) in each income category to the mid-point of the income category ($Y$) yielded the following relationship:

$$T_m = 110.146 + .0218Y \qquad (r^2 = .786)$$
$$(.0065)$$

[18] The decline in average consumer surplus in the upper income groups can be expected to reflect the fact that the wealthier hunters have more consistently travelled the farthest distances, so that higher travel costs have reduced the measured consumer surplus.

[19] An informative exercise would have been to test the sensitivity of results to the income brackets selected, by carrying out the calculations using different income groupings. For this study, however, hunters reported their incomes only according to the ranges shown above, so that it was not possible to allocate them by different income brackets.

# 14

# TRAVEL AND THE NATIONAL PARKS: AN ECONOMIC STUDY
### Ernst W. Swanson

This final chapter in Part Four deals with the valuation of the secondary benefits associated with recreational areas and, as a consequence, differs from the other chapters in this Part which have centered around the concepts and methods for valuing the primary benefits of outdoor recreation. Primary benefits accrue to the demanders in the form of utility or satisfactions derived through participation, while secondary benefits accrue to the surrounding region in the form of spending. Ernst Swanson uses the multiplier—an economic concept which provides an estimate of the amount of final income generated by the original expenditures of the visitors—to measure the amount of expenditures stimulated by the presence of a recreational area. Although Swanson does not calculate the actual value of the multiplier, he does provide a clear example of the application of the multiplier concept to national park expenditures.

This chapter has been heavily edited; if additional information is desired, the student is referred to the original source.

## BASIC ECONOMICS OF OUR NATIONAL PARK SYSTEM

Our most widely accepted measure of economic well-being is income. Hence, our real purpose is to measure the amount generated by the original outlays of visitors to our National Park System. First, therefore, in reviewing the basic economics of the Park System we must get at some of the meanings of income. Income is defined for our purpose as either *personal income* or *gross national product*. Personal income is the accumulation of the amounts of dollars and cents paid out in the form of salaries and wages and their supplements, rents, interest, and net proprietary income. We exclude corporate income, since there are too many delays in the

Reprinted from *Travel and the National Parks: An Economic Study* (Washington, D.C.: National Park Service, 1969), by permission of the National Park Service and the author.

payment of dividends; to adjust these payments to a given period is imponderable. Gross national product is the total net output by society exclusive of interbusiness transactions and certain transfer payments.

It is the total net value added to our well-being in the form of goods and services. In this sense, it may be considered a flow of real goods and services as distinct from a flow of money income. Visitors to our National Park System spend money, but not all this money reaches us as income, because there are interbusiness transactions.

The dollar spent by a park visitor leads, after certain adjustments (to be developed later) to *direct income*. This dollar, as it enters the money flow, first of the region and then of the Nation, generates additional income through the spending process. How much additional income is created depends upon how much of it "leaks" out of the money flow into savings and imports. Savings may not be invested immediately in the form of real goods and services, so that some money lies idle for a time. Imports into a region or nation lead to an income outflow from their economies so that residents of a region or nation are simply exchanging their money incomes for "foreign" goods and services—foreign in the sense that the region does not gain from the production of these goods and services. (This process is not necessarily evil; it may in some situations lead to the best use of money and general resources.)

Both personal income and GNP are composed of *direct* and *indirect* income. This composition arises from the money which remains in a region or a nation, and as it turns over again and again in the spending process, it creates new indirect income in addition to the direct. Again, the amounts so generated depend upon the extent of leakages into savings and imports.

The greater the local production of such goods and services, the greater is the "multiplier" effect upon income. The final total amount so created in the form of income is related to the entry of a dollar (or dollars) into the money flow; and the relationship between the first dollar laid out and the final dollars and cents which the original dollar creates in total is called the multiplier.

Nevertheless, one point must be emphasized at this time. The income figures arrived at do tend to show with good judgment how much parks as a group contribute directly and indirectly in total to the well-being of the regions in which they are situated. Thus, we may say that at Grand Teton National Park travel expenditures find their way into the pockets of merchants and their employees of Jackson Hole and adjacent communities, service station owners and their employees, hotel and motel owners and their employees, restaurant owners and their employees, sightseeing bus owners and their employees, and so on. Moreover, these people spend money in the local area for goods and services which partly generate further income (through the multiplier effects of spending) and for imports of goods and services only a minor portion of which (returns to importing organizations) is gross income to the region. The final "sum" for all parks of the *direct* and *indirect* personal incomes thus provides us an approximation to the localized effects upon the Nation of travel to parks.

Visits to a national park thus have launched chains of reaction, first by the park visits, then spreading to other economic activities so that imports into the region tend to grow at a slower rate, as local entrepreneurs undertake the manufacture of goods at an increasing rate. Once existing and possibly new stimuli develop, there is a tendency for economic growth to become self-generative. Thus, in States such as Arizona, California, New Mexico, Nevada, Florida, and Colorado, travel has induced economic growth and has continued to stimulate it even as new industries develop. Often, these new industries are travel based, but as the region grows, other industries appear. The great value of a travel-based economic structure, especially when individuals with relatively fixed incomes constitute a significant part of the region's business population, is that a floor is built for the region's economy so that spending is fairly stable even during falling business cycles. (Studies by the business research staff at the University of Florida and other universities reinforce this contention. Research papers on the subject have been read at meetings of the Southern Economic Association.)

Hence, we may say that there are perhaps two concepts which permit a pragmatic estimate of the economic impact of tourist expenditure in national parks and monuments. They are: (1) the amount of national (or regional) *personal income* generated by tourist expenditures, and (2) the amount of employment generated in turn by such expenditures. Evidence has it that the employment multiplier matches in size the income multiplier. In those States where recreation is the main activity, the employment multiplier runs as high as 3.5, however.

## COMPUTATION OF INCOME EFFECTS OF VISITOR SPENDING IN THE NATIONAL PARK SYSTEM ON NATIONAL ECONOMY

Given such data as are available, we may now attempt to measure the impact of the park visitor spendings upon personal income. We cannot overemphasize that we are working in essentially virgin territory. In our measurement, we take the following steps:

1. Determine the number of visitors who spent major amounts by staying overnight at or near a given park. (One-day visitors are omitted because we cannot make any valid assumption as to their spending behavior.) The difficulty in effecting such accounting should be patent. But, under presumptions based upon a number of single-park studies as a fair sample of major national parks, and a review by this writer of dozens of park and regional spending patterns, a reasonable average figure may be derived.

To adjust for day visitors, we propose that total visits may be reduced by 25 percent. Thus, transients and double counting may be largely omitted. (In an attempt to be more accurate, the writer assigned weights, ranging from 0.50 to 0.95, to each of the parks' visits, and summed the resulting adjusted visits. No significant difference between this multiple weighting and weighting by the factor 0.75 was found.)

2. Establish expenditures per person who on his trip stays for more than a day in the State in which the park is situated. Such expenditure is a reflection primarily of the average length of stay and the outlay per diem. At the present state of knowledge, some of these data are at best crude. But by comparing the results from their use with totals and averages now known, we may find ourselves on less shaky ground than what at first was supposed. We shall use $15.12 as the daily outlay. (It could very well be larger.)

3. Once adjusted visits are computed they are multiplied by the per-person daily expenditures (for the length of stay) to yield a gross total. This figure might be judged fairly comparable to the debit side of an income and expense account, thus, the variable costs plus some overheads at the receiving end of the spending process. The result is no more than an approximation to total costs of doing business. It is necessary to extract from this total such leakages as imports of goods and services into the region, business savings, and similar items that do not lead directly to personal income (our supposedly best measure of the economic impact of visits). Tax revenues to a State are implicitly considered but the amounts are not necessarily complete, because of tax rate variations. In effect, therefore, the total expenditures arrived at include most major elements of taxes (excise and sales), but not necessarily all. While taxes may be included in the price of goods purchased, they also act to change personal income negatively. Hence, we tend to wash out the tax-revenue effect by our present treatment.

4. Having computed the *direct* personal income, a further step is essential, for we need also to add the *indirect income.* Hence, as stated earlier, we apply a multiplier which reflects the effect of spending out of *direct* personal income upon personal incomes of others who serve the firms in the tourist trade; and so on and on, until leakages (by savings especially) from ensuing expenditures of income finally exhaust the initial outlays of recipients of *direct* income.

Evidence garnered from a host of studies on this subject show that this multiplier varies from 1.12 to around 2.8. As noted earlier, the variation in the multipliers is associated with the size of the region serving a given park.

The multiplier 2.5 used here is an "in-between" value, based upon the findings of several research groups, e.g., Robert R. Nathan Associates, the research groups of the Universities of Utah, Colorado, Memphis State, and Wyoming, and of the Colorado State University at Fort Collins.

For the reader who is not versed in the nature of the multiplier, the following description of it is offered. What happens in an economy, region, or nation, is that as funds from expenditures are first put into operation, they tend to be used over and over again. They help create and lend force to an already existing flow of monies being expended for a vast variety of purposes. An initial outlay is used over and over again until leakages from it become savings and other income-hiding effects. The first spending of $1 contributes $1 to the flow. But if savings, etc., are at a rate such that individual households spend only, say, 70 percent of the incomes received from the initial spending, then the amount returned to the flow is 70 cents. If this rate of withholding of spending (the marginal propensity to consume) continues to operate, then the third amount returned to the flow is, ($0.70) (.70), 49 cents. The fourth amount is, ($0.70) (.49), 34.3 cents, and so on until leakages wipe out the final amount put into the flow of monies.

Given the withholding rate of 0.30, the multiplier turns out to be

$$m = \frac{1}{(1 - 0.70)} = 3.333$$

For our purposes, however, this rate is perhaps much too high. What evidence we gather from a variety of research studies is that the rate of withholding as applies to travel-derived income runs about 0.60. Then, the multiplier we seek is

$$m = \frac{1}{(1 - 0.60)} = 2.5$$

The mathematics for this formula is treated adequately in a number of books on income formation.

We should bear in mind that the multiplier usually treated is called "the investment multiplier," whose effects tend to depart from those of spending for travel and recreation. Ours is stated as a "recreation multiplier."

The analysis of the spending process in the sense of the kinds of expenditures made by travelers and park visitors is subject to debate. Expenditures usually are classified according to income classes. Unfortunately, travel expenditure data so categorized does not afford us an understanding of the expenditures flow in travel and visits to parks. For this reason another mode of classification may be made according to the kinds of lodging sought in travel and visits. Indirectly, we thus note some reflection of income effects, but by this method we get at the spending pertinent to our purpose. The "Montana Study" serves to lay out the broad dimensions of this approach. We turn to it only as illustrative of what may be done in expenditure estimation. But, to get at the nation as a whole we must await findings of additional studies now in progress. Reference is to the research at Colorado State and Denver Universities and at the Midwest Research Institute. These findings will become available within a year or two and should be exceedingly helpful in future expenditure analysis.

The rate of flow of tourists determines the total expenditures in Montana, due in no small part to the presence in the general area of Glacier, Yellowstone, Bighorn Canyon, and similar parks in the National Park System. It should be manifest that the amount which a tourist spends in a State also depends upon the attractions in or adjacent to the State, his income, and the length of his vacation, and how he proposes to divide it among these and other attractions. The best that we can do to place him is to classify him according to the kind of lodgings he used. As noted, luxury or lack of it in lodgings is, in part, a reflection of his income status and his interest in park attractions. In this case, we shall classify the tourist according to whether he stays at a hotel, motel, cabin or cottage, trailer camp, or tourist home.

The confining of this investigation for the moment to Montana, aside from the availability of information, permits us indirectly to reflect some upon the attractiveness of Glacier and Yellowstone National Parks. Although we have before us secondary data only, it still may be possible to derive from these data and additional information on other parks, a measure of income that is fairly plausible.

The experience in Montana in most cases is that motels, cottages and/or cabins, and hotels account for the greater share of stays and services rendered visitors to a park or monument. Evidence suggests that in time the tourist home, a fairly inefficient form of lodging, will disappear, to be superseded by more motels and a growing demand for camping facilities to accommodate trailers and/or specialized camper vehicles. But it is also likely that there may be a saturation point for these last two forms of lodging. This point is determined by the rising depreciation charges of this mode of lodging, and by the fact that the parks can absorb only so many campers, for space is limited. Moreover, there is strong evidence that campers and trailer parties lead to heavy wear and tear on nature, far more perhaps than brought by tourists who stay at motels, cottages, and hotels. What is more, the desire for roughing it is fortunately at a minimum, since a large part of the traveling public increasingly consists of elderly or retired persons who prefer a minimum of physical exertion.

Once having settled upon the most frequent modes of lodging used, we may next classify the tourist according to levels of daily expenditures, as in Table 3. These data are taken from the very fine analysis, *Five Years of Tourist Studies in Montana* (1958–1962), prepared by the Montana State Highway Commission in cooperation with the U.S. Bureau of Public Roads. Table 1 shows the percentages of those who stay in the categories listed above for tourists who visit national parks and monuments and related attractions in Montana. These tables, along with Table 2, lay the foundation for our analysis of the generation of personal income in the State. (No other region or State appears to have come up with such advanced information as is derived from the Montana study and here collated in Tables 1, 2, and 3.)

To bring the Montana findings up to date we shall inflate the expenditures per person per night (Table 3) by the differences in the price level from 1962 to 1967. We multiply the several figures in the column by 110 (percent) on the (fairly reasonable) assumption that the increase in cost of travel has increased by 10 percent over the intervening period (Table 4), and arrive at $10.51 per day per person.

The average of $10.51, however, does not reflect two developments: (1) the high percentage of use and continued rise in use of motels, and (2) the shift to pickup campers and travel coaches, both of which approach the average cost of staying at motels, the predominant mode of lodging.

The preliminary evidence so far garnered from forthcoming studies

| type of lodging* | percent of use, actual | percent of use, normalized** |
|---|---|---|
| camping | 12.6 | 14.2 |
| friends and relatives | 13.4 | 15.0 |
| hotel | 5.6 | 6.3 |
| motel | 48.8 | 54.8 |
| tourist home | 1.7 | 1.9 |
| trailer | 6.9 | 7.8 |
| total | 89.0 | 100.0 |
| average | 14.8333 | |

TABLE 1. *Type of Lodging Used, Montana, 1962*
* Excluded are sleepers in cars and other means, since these constituted but a few, and no exact data on their expenditures are available.
** To adjust "actual" to 100 percent.
From *Tourist Studies in Montana* and checked against the *Cape Cod Tourist Study*, 1963.

supports the proposition that per-person-per-day expenditure is more than $15. We therefore apply a finding based upon an observation of trends in several locales, or $15.12, rather than $10.51.

Let us now track down the relationship of distance traveled to length of stay. According to Clawson, in the case of Glacier National Park, 77 percent of visitors come from homes more than 300 miles distant, and 57 percent come from homes more than 500 miles away. On the basis of those

| type of lodging* | number of nights |
|---|---|
| camping | 3.2 |
| friends and relatives | 5.7 |
| hotel | 3.3 |
| motel | 2.4 |
| tourist home | 4.6 |
| trailer | 5.4 |

TABLE 2. *Nights in State by Types of Lodging, Montana, 1962*
* Users of cars and other types of lodging are omitted.
Other means of overnight sleeping are not included. The average stay is really less than shown here.
From *Tourist Studies in Montana.*

percentages, let us say that, generally speaking, 25 percent could have been visitors who come for 1-day or a few-hours visit. This should be a conservative estimate. To travel 600 miles a day (under the 300-mile radius) and at the same time to visit a park the size of Glacier (or Yellowstone) in

| type of lodging | persons | total expenditures per party | expenditures per person | expenditures per night per person |
|---|---|---|---|---|
| camping | 3.8 | $ 54.52 | $14.35 | $ 4.48 |
| friends and relatives | 3.4 | 177.67 | 52.26 | 9.17 |
| hotel | 2.6 | 121.78 | 46.84 | 14.17 |
| motel | 3.2 | 105.94 | 33.11 | 13.80 |
| tourist home | 3.6 | 191.64 | 53.23 | 11.57 |
| trailer | 3.8 | 86.64 | 22.82 | 4.23 |
| average | 3.4 | | | $ 9.61 |

**TABLE 3.** *Size of Party by Type of Lodging and Reported Total Expenditures by Party and Person, Per Diem, Montana, 1962*
The assumption here is that single overnight visits are on a per person basis, so that persons staying and adjusted visits are essentially equivalent.
From *Tourist Studies in Montana.*

| type of lodging | expenditures per person per night | adjusted figure* |
|---|---|---|
| camping | $ 4.48 | $ 4.93 |
| friends and relatives | 9.17 | 10.08 |
| hotel | 14.17 | 15.59 |
| motel | 13.80 | 15.10 |
| tourist home | 11.57 | 12.73 |
| trailer | 4.23 | 4.65 |
| average | | $10.51 |

**TABLE 4.** *Expenditures Per Night Adjusted to Reflect Price Changes*
* The adjusted figure is equal to the expenditures per person per night times 110 percent.

the same day seems a virtual impossibility. Hence, we may argue with good reason that all who travel at least 300 miles one way will stay overnight in the State or at the park (if possible). It should be added that some authorities consider a 200-mile radius the line of demarcation. For some

States, where road congestion is high, even a 100-mile radius may force an overnight stay, all dependent upon place and traffic patterns. Because of the size of the State, California visitors, for example, stay a night and, more often, several nights.

We are now ready to estimate the total personal income attributable to national parks and monuments. In 1967, total visits to national parks came to 139,675,600. Since this figure is close to 140 million let us use this amount instead, for it will not change our findings noticeably and will make the computations more easily understandable than would the first amount. We multiply 140,000,000 × 0.75 = 105,000,000 net visitors who may be said to make the primary percentage of contributions to the national economy; that is, these net data state the great percentage of spendings. Spending on 1-day visits may run from zero to a few dollars per person. This amount is at its best a pure guess, so evanescent in fact as to only obscure the basic spending. *In effect, we can only treat as pertinent and as valid those visitor expenditures which contribute the highest possible proportional amounts to the visits, now to be regarded as an industry, whose services in a given region are rendered to tourists who live beyond the immediate bounds of day-to-day travel to the locale of a particular park.*

The amount, 105 million visits, supposedly constitutes such visits as denote "real" contributions in the way of exports of services to those visitors whose homes are beyond the relatively immediate vicinity of the park. Let us call these visits the *net or adjusted visits.* They are basically sensitive to the park as is any income-generating tourism.

The choice of the factor, 0.75, has been given much attention by this writer. At first, as noted above, he chose 0.70 as the factor. But after visits to most of the major parks of the National Park System, he concluded that it was too low. In the case of some parks, say, Yosemite, Sequoia, and Kings Canyon, the truly income-generating visitor probably runs no more than 0.55. This factor was accepted by park superintendents and their administrations as the most likely. But in the case of Grand Canyon, Zion, Rocky Mountain, Grand Teton, and Glacier, among others, the real income-generators among visitors run in all likelihood as much as 0.95. Therefore, after a review of all parks, relative to their location away from major population centers, it became apparent that 0.75 is still a conservative deflator, one with which only a few knowledgeable analysts should quarrel. (Indeed, a factor of 0.80 might be deemed plausible.)

The next step involves the multiplication of 105 million by the daily expenditures per person by length of stay. The average daily expenditures are estimated to run approximately $15.12. (Franklin Mullaly has pointed out that this expenditure figure is not far from that chosen by Clawson.) The computation is as follows:

1. Average expenditures per visit for nine different areas are available. But this average has varied with the year of each study. The argument offered here is that the prime changer of the amounts spent is the price level. The averaging of each State average is then subjected to a price level

adjustment. Nine studies for that many areas and their corresponding years are:

| | |
|---|---|
| Arizona, 1954 | Yosemite, 1950 |
| Montana, 1962 | Yellowstone, 1950 |
| Great Smoky Mountains, 1956 | Glacier, 1951 |
| Cape Cod, 1963 | Rocky Mountain, 1952 |

The average expenditures (per person) for each of these are respectively, $9.12, $9.85, $6.32, $9.94, $5.60, $11.17, $11.70, $5.52, and $8.10. The range then is from a low of $5.52 (Glacier) to $11.70 (Yellowstone). We find, in addition, three levels of consistency: (1) $9.12, $9.85, $9.94; (2) $11.17 and $11.70; and (3) $5.60, $5.52, and $6.32. One figure $8.10, for Rocky Mountain National Park, appears to be a maverick. Had there been less visits from the standard metropolitan area of Denver, it could have reached the average of group (2). But why the amount of $5.52 for Glacier is so low as it is, is indeed puzzling. This amount is perhaps a reflection of statistical classifications used, with the result that certain items of expenditure have been excluded. So it and the amount for Denver are omitted in the "inflation" of each average to current price levels.

2. Inflating reflects price level differences arising for the various dates of the studies. Thus, a larger inflator is applied to a 1950 average expenditure than that which is applied to a 1963 average expenditure. The price level has been rising since 1950 so that a 1967 price is much higher than a 1950 price. The inflated data, with the above-stated omissions, are:

| | |
|---|---|
| $ 6.28 | $10.86 |
| 6.32 | 11.94 |
| 9.94 | 16.33 |
| 10.66 | 17.10 |

(Note the average found for these values is $11.18. The reciprocal of the income deflator of the Department of Commerce is used.)

In some cases the arithmetic average of the average expenditures may be a valid representative of this group. Let us, however, make an assumption that may come closer to reality than would the arithmetic average. *We suppose that by 1967, the year we set for the most recent computation, travel prices throughout the United States would have been equalized or might have approached equalization.* Economically speaking, this idea is quite plausible. With the spread of automobile travel through the constantly growing interstate highway system, prices generally should be forced into alignment with the rising demands, even for those parks in relatively low income regions. Hence, let us take the average of the last three values in the array as a plausible national average, or $15.12. This higher value is much more in line with the experience of this writer who over the last two or three decades has moved well into the 100,000-mile class of travelers, and except for Hawaii and Alaska, his visits have been to nearly all major regions of the Nation. Certainly, it is not an extreme value by almost any experience.

3. *Next,* we compute the effects of tourist travel among the national parks and monuments on 1967 national personal income. Three steps are involved.

(a) *The derivation of the adjusted visits* (see above):

$$140,000,000 \times 0.75 = 105,000,000 = \text{net visitors}$$

(b) *The derivation of gross expenditures:* For this purpose, let us use 4 days as the average length of stay in an average locale. This number is based upon several recent studies, notably, the study by Midwest Research Institute, work now in progress at Colorado State University, and data provided by the Fred Harvey Company, all checked against conversations by this writer with members of numerous travel groups. Then: 105,000,000 × $60.48 = $6,350,000,000 gross outlays by tourists, where $60.48 = 4 × $15.12, or the average length of stay times the average per person expenditure.

(c) *The derivation of the direct personal income and indirect personal income:* (1) $6,350,000,000 × 0.30 = $1,905,000,000, the direct income; $6,350 million cannot be considered income. Actually it included purchases by wholesalers, retailers, service stations, and so on, of goods from outside the area. Other items excluded are corporate undistributed profits, or the sale of goods as may be manufactured in the region of the park, and business savings. The amount, $1,905 million, constitutes income payments to merchants, retailers, and service station operators, and all of each of these businesses' employees, rents, and related items.

But direct income is a once-and-for-all amount. Actually, its recipients spend out of it monies to buy goods and services, so that the money income turns over, again and again, until, as argued above, it is completely exhausted by leakages through imports and savings.

The factor 0.30 is based upon the earlier relation, as found between gross outlays and national income. This information is again provided through the analysis of input-output matrices, a highly technical job associated with the process of analyzing income flows. Only net values added may be included as income.

(2) The derivation of direct and indirect personal income. $1,905,000,000 × 2.5 = $4,762,500,000, the total of direct and indirect personal income. As developed earlier, the 2.5 multiplier reflects both the effects of initial spending and the spending which follows as the direct income gets into the money flow of the economy. We could, of course, have selected 2.6 or 2.7 as the multiplier, but since some parts of the nation (the least developed) have small multipliers, and large parts of the nation enjoy multipliers as large as 2.8 or 3.0, it was deemed appropriate to elect 2.5 as the multiplier best representative of the nation. The United States as a whole has a higher pattern of population density and per capita income than do some parts of it. Let us say that 2.5 is an approximation which would reflect a balancing out of the highly developed, populous areas with the poorly developed and sparsely populous areas. In a strict sense, 2.5 is

not an average but a judgment based upon knowledge of the economic conditions of the region where the parks and monuments are located.

Had we selected a multiplier of 3.0, a figure supported by some writers, influenced by their knowledge about the Keynesian multiplier, then the total contribution to *direct* and *indirect* personal income of the national parks and monuments would have reached $5,715 million.

To be sure, all of these estimates are subject to debate, but it is only through debate that the issues involved will be threshed out and the need for better data will be made clear. Refinements in method would take place as data improve.

Until one has traveled to the majority of the national parks, it is difficult to realize how much money is actually spent by the traveling public. To go to Grand Canyon, say, from Washington, D.C., by automobile, to stay at *reasonably* priced motels, to eat at *reasonably* priced restaurants, and to pay more than 40 cents a gallon for gasoline in several regions of the West, two people will find that daily out-of-pocket costs for travel will easily run as much as $30. Two people will barely get away with spending less than $600 for the trip, if a week or so is spent at the park. Of course, depreciation on automobile, camping equipment, and personal property are not included in this estimate. Hence, $15+ is hardly an exaggeration, since relatively few with incomes less than $5,000 travel great distances. (At this income bracket, only a few can afford such outlays.)

## FURTHER READING

### Surveys of Outdoor Recreation Economics

Burton, T. L., and N. M. Fulcher, "Measurement of Recreation, A Survey," *Journal of Economic Studies* 3, no. 2 (1969).

Coomber, N. H., and A. K. Biswas, "Evaluation of Environmental Intangibles: Review of Techniques," Environment Canada, Ottawa, June, 1972.

Miller, K. W., Jr., "Conceptual Frameworks and Methodologies for Applying Benefit-Cost Analysis to Recreation Resources," unpublished thesis, University of California, Berkeley, School of Business Administration, May, 1966.

### Concepts and Methods in Outdoor Recreation Economics

Beardsley, W., "Bias and Non-Comparability in Recreation Evaluation Models," *Land Economics* 47, no. 2 (1971).

Brown, W. G., A. Singh, and E. N. Castle, "An Economic Evaluation of the Oregon Salmon and Steelhead Sport Fishery," Technical Bulletin 78. Corvallis: Oregon State Agricultural Experiment Station, 1964.

Brown, W. G., and F. Nawas, "A New Approach to the Evaluation of Non-Priced Recreational Resources: A Reply," *Land Economics* 48, no. 4 (1972).

Cesario, F. J., and J. L. Knetsch, "Time Bias in Recreation Benefit Estimates," *Water Resources Research* 6, no. 3 (1970).

Cicchetti, C. J., J. J. Seneca, and P. Davidson, *The Demand and Supply of Outdoor Recreation,* Bureau of Outdoor Recreation: Washington, D.C. (1969).

Crutchfield, J. A., "Valuation of Fishery Resources," *Land Economics* 38, no. 2 (1962).

Davis, R. K., "The Value of Outdoor Recreation: An Economic Study of the Maine Woods," unpublished dissertation, Harvard University, Department of Economics, April 1963.

Hines, L. G., "Measurement of Recreation Benefits: A Reply," *Land Economics* 34, no. 4 (1958).

Kalter, R. J., and L. E. Gosse, "Recreation Demand Functions and the Identification Problem," *Journal of Leisure Research* 2, no. 1 (Winter, 1970): 43–53.

Kalter, R. J., and W. B. Lord, "Measurement of the Impact of Recreation Investments," *American Journal of Agricultural Economics* 50, no. 2 (May, 1968).

Knetsch, J. L., "Outdoor Recreation Demands and Benefits," *Land Economics* 39, no. 4 (November, 1963).

Krutilla, J. V., *Evaluation of an Aspect of Environmental Quality,* Reprint no. 93 (Washington, D.C.: Resources for the Future, 1971).

Lee, I. M., "Economic Analysis Bearing upon Outdoor Recreation," Outdoor Recreation Resources Review Commission, *Economic Studies of Outdoor Recreation,* Study Report 24 (Washington, D.C.: U.S. Government Printing Office, 1962).

Lerner, L. J., "Quantitative Indices of Recreational Values," *Proceedings,* Committee on the Economics of Water Resources Development, Western Agricultural Economics Research Council, University of Nevada, August, 1962.

Lessinger, J., "Measurement of Recreation Benefits: A Reply," *Land Economics* 34, no. 4 (1958).

Merewitz, L., "Recreation Benefits of Water Resources Development," *Water Resources Research* 2, no. 4 (1966).

Nelson, J. R., "The Value of Travel Time," S. B. Chase, Jr., ed., *Problems in Public Expenditure* (Washington, D.C.: Brookings Institution, 1966).

Pearse, P. H., "A New Approach to the Evaluation of Non-Priced Recreational Resources: A Rejoinder," *Land Economics* 48, no. 4 (November, 1972).

Seckler, D. W., "Analytical Issues in Demand Analysis for Outdoor Recreation: A Comment," *American Journal of Agricultural Economics* 50, no. 1 (February, 1968).

————, "On the Uses and Abuses of Economic Science in Evaluating Public Outdoor Recreation," *Land Economics* 42, no. 4 (November, 1966): 485–94.

Smith, R. J., "The Evaluation of Recreation Benefits: The Clawson Method in Practice," *Urban Studies* 8, no. 2 (1971).

Stoevener, H. H., and W. G. Brown, "Analytical Issues in Demand Analysis for Outdoor Recreation: A Reply," *American Journal of Agricultural Economics* 50, no. 1 (February, 1968).

Trice, A. H., and S. E. Wood, "Measurement of Recreation Benefits;" *Land Economics* 34, no. 3 (1958).

————, "Measurement of Recreation Benefits: A Rejoinder," *Land Economics* 34, no. 4 (1958).

Wennergren, E. B., "Valuing Non-Market Priced Recreational Resources," *Land Economics* 40, no. 3 (1964).

# Part Five
ENVIRONMENTAL IMPACTS
OF RECREATION

## PREFACE

Recreational activities occur on lands with extremely diverse physical characteristics. These lands differ in their topography, soil, vegetation, and their ability to sustain wildlife. These characteristics can significantly affect the capability and adaptability of the natural resource base to sustain recreational use. For example, a moderately dense timber stand growing on light, well-drained soil is more suitable for the activity of camping than is a dense timber stand on heavy, wet soil. It is important, therefore, to identify how the natural resources base is affected by different types of recreational use. In this way, if the ecological disruption of the landscape is reduced, recreationists can enjoy a recreation experience of higher quality.

Knowledge about the character of recreational resources is useful in planning for the management and use of individual recreation areas in two ways. It enables the recreation planner and manager to define and limit the mix of recreation opportunities that an area can support and it provides the manager with some indication of the costs of offering these opportunities. These costs take the form of direct money expenditures used to maintain the natural resource characteristics indigenous to the recreation area or in the form of indirect costs of recreational resource depletion where there is a change in the actual character of the natural resource.

The objective of Part Five is to present some of the concepts and methods that have been developed to aid the recreation planner and manager in analyzing the environmental impact of recreational activities on the natural resource base.

# 15

# RECREATION AREA PLANNING: SOME PHYSICAL AND ECOLOGICAL REQUIREMENTS
## Eugene Mattyasovsky

This chapter serves as an excellent introductory statement and overview of the complexities associated with recreation and the physical environment. It outlines some of the basic physical and biological concepts that the recreation planner must consider. Again, as with many other studies, the concepts take on added meaning since Eugene Mattyasovsky presents them in conjunction with a case study.

## SCOPE OF THE PROBLEM

Our rapidly growing cities, with their varied land use demands, create a complex planning task in the selection and provision of suitable land for these uses. "Suitable" can mean different things. The criteria used in determining the effectiveness of various uses change over time in response to changes in technology and ideals.

Among these land uses outdoor recreation is increasing rapidly in significance. The demand is growing much faster than the population because the per capita demand is also increasing. According to some U.S. experts, twenty years from now four times as much area will be needed per capita as in 1967.

The "planning" of these areas has many aspects: sociological, ecological, economic, legislative-administrative, transportational, and so on. All are important; we need the help of all of these perspectives for selecting, developing, and maintaining outdoor recreation areas.

Recent research sponsored by the Canadian Council on Urban and Regional Research and conducted by the author concentrates on the problem of "establishing physical and ecological criteria for site selection and maintenance" of outdoor recreational areas outside a city. To translate this into everyday language, the research tries to provide answers to the following questions:

1. What are the basic physical and ecological criteria for selecting and planning regional recreation areas?
2. Specific ecological questions connected with water.

Reprinted from *Plan* of The Town Planning Institute of Canada 8, no. 3 (1967): 91–109, by permission of The Town Planning Institute of Canada and the author. This article has been extensively edited for this volume.

3. Multiple uses. Compatibility of different uses.

4. Positive steps such as erosion control, flood control, preservation of vegetation covering, and so on.

5. How to establish and maintain a so-called "partial ecological balance" or at least a "natural state" within the areas.

6. "Intensity" or "use density" of the various uses to be permitted.

As an experimental research area for studying the questions on the "ground," the outer areas of a fifty-mile radius from Toronto were selected. The existing and potential recreation areas in this belt were examined, excluding city parks, high density use recreation areas, sports fields, and other specific recreation uses. Outdoor recreational areas of fifty acres and above in extent with at least partly natural settings and mixed active and passive uses were identified for research purposes. . . .

A necessary first step was to obtain an overall picture of the present situation in the fifty-mile radius belt, including the more or less accepted proposals of the different authorities. Unfortunately no such compilation was available in comprehensive form so a map had to be made showing all those categories which have any outdoor recreational significance, such as provincial parks, "conservation areas," larger private and municipal parks, hunting and fishing preserves, and so on.

The data of the map and inventory were compared with the existing and expected 1980 population. Without going into details, what is really interesting for us is the overall picture; how the existing recreation areas relate to the users and what the picture will be in—say, 1980, adding proposed (and more or less accepted) future recreation areas, and relating to the projected 1980 population. . . .

To identify or criticize whether [recreational area] is quantitatively adequate or not, was felt to be outside the scope of the research. We omitted it because to determine the measure of adequacy is a question of the standards we apply. These standards are rather arbitrarily determined on assumed bases which include consideration of existing habits and trends in the kind of recreational uses. In other words, they are determined in a cultural, economic, and legislative-administrative context, as well as by ecological considerations. To analyze the standards from all of these different points of view would lead us far from our present task.

Also we feel that—admitting the importance of the quantitative side—the focus should be shifted to the qualitative aspects.

There is a new trend that emphasizes these aspects, such as:

1. The differentiation of their suitability for different recreational uses
2. Esthetic, historic, scientific value of the land
3. Physical and ecological aspects of the outdoor recreation areas

This research concentrated on these qualitative aspects, with particular emphasis on the last one.

In a selected natural setting the following aspects can be considered relevant from physical and ecological points of view:

1. Size
2. Physiography, soil, geology
3. Water
4. Vegetation covering
5. Animal life
6. Management, maintenance practices, recreational demand sought by the public, and so on, as far as they are connected with points 1 to 5.

## THE "PROPER SIZE" OF RECREATION AREAS

. . . It appears reasonable to approach the physical and ecological consequences of the size by attempting to establish either a minimum or an optimum size. The minimum size would be an area where a more or less complex biological community, characteristic of the original setting, can be preserved; and optimally where this community can be preserved in a "balanced" or "self-maintaining" state. Unfortunately, the term ecological "balance" may only be vaguely defined and does not answer the question of whether there should be a "balanced" state at all; the concept cannot be used at the present time as a precise basis to determine size. . . .

So our attitude should be: many different sized areas have to be accepted for practical reasons, and the ecological considerations should be adjusted to the actual size. This implies a very far-going compromise. But to create a possibility for this compromise, "ecological balance," or rather "natural state," is one of the goals of the research.

Of course, even if we accept, in principle at least, that all sizes are acceptable, there are important items to consider:

Certain 40- to 120-acre lands needed for facilities and so on are not easily reducible, which means that in a less than 400-acre area the remaining "natural" part becomes so small that it is nearly impossible to maintain as "natural." The relative length of boundary with adjacent areas becomes proportionately so great that it is increasingly difficult to protect the land from outside threats.

With smaller than 400- to 600-acre areas it would seem better policy to change the character rather than force compliance with a general pattern of providing these areas with all the conventional outdoor recreation facilities in a reduced space. . . .

## VEGETATION COVERING IN RECREATION AREAS

Usually the most conspicuous feature of an outdoor recreation area is its vegetation. . . . The vegetation covering of an existing or prospective recreation area can be examined from the following aspects:

1. General character as it stands
2. The interest, or "demand" of the visiting public, and its relation or effect to certain recreational uses—wildlife, fishing, hiking, and so on.
3. Management practices: possibility of manipulation; policy of management

The first two can be seen together, or the first can be examined from the point of view of the second.

In a passive-type outdoor recreation area the public is looking for a varied, scenic vegetation which gives a natural appearance. The aim is to be "with nature" or to have the illusion of being with nature.

Varied vegetation implies variation in coverage. Open areas vary with patches of dense forest, or with scattered trees and bushes, some water-edge vegetation, and so on. Also the differences in age and size of the trees can add to the variation and the scenic value. This variety of coverage actually exists in many of our areas; the problem is one of preservation, rather than of conscious manipulation.

The case is different where previously cleared farmed land is to be integrated into a recreation area.

Variety in floral composition also adds to the variety of appearance and general scenic value. The following criteria and general management policies can be formulated in this respect:

1. Preservation of the flora found on the establishment of the recreation area in whatever serial stages they are, with a minimum apparent sign of manipulation.

2. Specific consideration of plants with value as food for wildlife or other unique importance for the whole ecology of the area.

3. Preferably, avoidance of the introduction of too many exotic species.

4. Specific consideration (or exception in the above consideration) of strongly diseased or susceptible trees (elm, and so on) and some water vegetation.

## MANAGEMENT PRACTICES AND VEGETATION

There are different views as to the extent to which the natural vegetation should be manipulated within a recreation area.

Extreme "noninterference" can be a workable policy in certain types of recreational parks with an expressed intention of preserving a piece of undisturbed biotic community, although noninterference is an ideal rather than an achievable reality. Some compromise has to be made when human access is allowed.

In other kinds of recreational areas the degree of manipulation of the vegetation varies with the type and intensity of use.

Generally speaking, management practices regarding interference with the natural state or development of plant cover are less conspicuous in large passive types of recreation lands. On the other hand it can be rather artificial in some "high density" city parks. Some observations connected with the management practices in existing recreation areas would be germane:

The predominantly natural vegetation is interspersed with manipulated, "trimmed" sections providing picnic areas, playgrounds, and so on for the public. Though it is sometimes strongly criticized, it is a necessity and a certain degree of artificiality in appearance is unavoidable. One of the most conspicuous interferences is the establishment of lawn or grass covering with its corresponding permanent mowing. Unfortunately the public is inclined to forget that without this mowing the same area would be covered by aster, solidago, and so on—"weed" jungle in only a few years. For these areas the interference is a necessity, the only consideration being how far it should go.

Besides mowing, the use of herbicides can be questioned. This objection is sometimes justified: it depends on the kind of herbicide. Their use may have far-reaching consequences which are sometimes not fully understood. This would suggest a policy of avoiding their use as much as possible.

Another problem is the question of what to do about diseased trees and plants, parasites and plants that are harmful or not desirable from a recreational point of view. It is a subtle question, depending for an answer on how we define our goal. The standard treatments (for example, D.D.T. for elm diseases) can save the tree but at a certain expense to the whole biotic community. To define the desirability of their application is not as easy as in forestry practice. There is much to be said for the view that the removal of the diseased trees rather than the saving of them by chemicals is, in most cases, the proper policy to pursue.

The removal of fallen or dead trees and branches is strongly objected to by those interested in animal life. They are important elements of the habitat. The distribution and density of certain animals is strongly affected by this seemingly simple operation of keeping the area "neat."

On the other hand, barren branches extending out of green healthy vegetation can disturb the esthetic and scenic value of the area, especially in a conspicuous spot. A proper compromise could be the removal of the dead trees or branches in exposed places (picnic areas, edges of open meadow), but to leave the fallen trees where they are in other places with some exceptions for nature trails and highly used areas, or adjacent to pools and streams.

Probably the most important plant management problem is how to establish or re-establish a "proper" covering in previously cleared or other barren areas such as graded or eroded banks. There are many areas of this kind and some are quite extensive. They arise from previous agricultural use, or for other reasons.

Some considerations and guidance for correcting or re-establishing vegetation covering are the following:

1. Similarity or harmony with the original vegetation, "natural" appearance
2. Fast growing, undemanding components
3. Variety, coverage, floral composition, "skyline"
4. Containing food plants for animal life
5. Scenic value

225

6. In some cases, erosion prevention
7. Specific questions of water and water-edge vegetation
8. And—where it exists—preservation and accentuation of the natural historical interest of some feature

We do not have too much experience with this kind of planting. Foresters, landscape architects, recreation area planners, can jointly work out some measures. These measures should fit the specific conditions of the area. On the other hand, if worked out individually, in all cases there will not be a widely applicable measure. The ideal solution would be to work out a few general patterns, and the choice, with perhaps some modification, would be left to the expert applying them in a specific recreation area. No such general patterns or measures were found in the literature presently available. There are such well-proved forestry patterns as erosion protection, wildlife cover, landscape architectural patterns, and so on, but none filling all the above requirements has been yet developed. Perhaps many of the foresty patterns should be integrated in recreation areas.

Some suggestions can be offered for achieving this integration:

1. A "natural landscape plan" should be worked out beforehand.
2. To achieve the above plan, more expensive methods and material can be justified such as: (a) Use of trees or bushes of more advanced age at transplanting, and (b) Soil cultivation, fertilizer application, irrigation, or other cultivation practices should be applied, of kinds normally never used in typical extensive forestry practice, because of much higher initial costs. The application of other cultivation methods would accelerate the growth rate of trees.

## ANIMAL LIFE IN RECREATION AREAS

The questions connected with animal life in the existing parks can be discussed from the following aspects:

1. Faunal (species) composition
2. Their permanency in the area (permanent, transient, migratory, and so on)
3. Their ecological role, density, fluctuation, and so on
4. Habitat and other factors affecting their existence, natural and man-made
5. Desirable policy of management (to encourage, discourage, their increase or presence, and with what measures)
6. Game animals

The composition of "species present" is the easiest and most frequently found "check list" in the published conservation studies. This check list sometimes also briefly refers to permanency or migratory habits and so on. We never know how reliable these lists are. Are they really checked or is this just a list of animals that "should" be there?

The "check lists" give an interesting but limited picture of animal life. We are equally, or even more, interested in their relative density, their role in the biotic community, and so on. Also very interesting, for the same reason, is the role of some prominent insects or other "lower" animals.

The ecological role, density, and fluctuation of numbers of different animals in our parks is to be viewed for our present purpose as an animal ecologist sees them but modified with some comments on the recreational aspects. In other words, the park can be viewed as a piece of undisturbed nature—actually this is what the visitor seeks—or if disturbed, the degree and direction of disturbance may be acknowledged. Some of these disturbances are unavoidable for the maintenance of our parks but fortunately can be managed in a way that does not appear "disturbed" or "unnatural."

The most important representatives of animal life in the parks are the "small" animals. They are present in the greatest numbers and it is easy to interfere with their density, at least with small mammals, but to a less degree with birds.

There is very strong interest in the larger animals—the deer—on the part of visitors. Unfortunately they are, in many cases, transient.

The role of the nature trail is partly to give an opportunity for animal watching. The opportunity for the visitor to watch animals is much less than their actual frequency or density would suggest. Only diurnal animals can be observed by the average visitor; and as many of the mammals are nocturnal, the impression is that there are fewer animals in the parks than there actually are.

Another reason why the users of nature trails are disappointed in their contact with animals is the behavior of those users who are less interested. On the other hand the animals are surprisingly quick in adapting to the presence of man. It is questionable, however, whether in small parks this "taming" of animals should be encouraged. As a result, nonterritorial species or species of wide range, such as deer, become easy victims of hunters in lands outside the parks. With properly regulated use, the nature trails are also the best places to give opportunity for bird watching.

The factors affecting the population density of different animals inside the parks are similar to those outside the parks. Some of these factors are:

1. Use of chemicides within the parks
2. Danger of irruptions in the case of certain species
3. Prohibition of hunting
4. Effect of adjacent lands
5. Effects connected with management practices and recreational use

The danger of population irruptions of certain animals always increases in an area highly protected from external interference where the usual regulating factors are disturbed, and the area is limited.

Considering the complexity, interdependent, and mutually regulating character of biological communities, what is actually more interesting from

227

an ecological point of view than the few observed irruption cases, is the lack of these irruptions.

There is some increase in deer population but nowhere similar to that in some larger parks in the U.S.A. Only in a few exceptional cases has damage caused by deer to foliage been observed.

1. The intensive temporary use of parks (weekend use) apparently does very little damage to habitat. No evidences of adverse effects were observed.

2. The food sources of the habitat are scarcely used up in any trophic level in the Southern Ontario parks (as compared to some cases in the U.S.A. parks). The observations show just the opposite.

3. One very efficient habitat manipulation observed in many parks was the synchronizing of hay or other plant cutting in open areas with the breeding and nesting time of certain mammals and birds.

Other observations of park personnel and ourselves pertaining to factors affecting animal life within parks were collected. Most of them point to direct threats to animal life. Some of these are:

1. Farm practices in adjacent areas
2. Boys with an inclination to disturb birds, or as "conservationists" just collecting birds' eggs, and so on
3. Stray cats, especially where the land is immediately adjacent to residential areas
4. Stray dogs, mostly in remote areas not adjacent to residential areas
5. Highways with considerable traffic adjacent to outdoor recreation areas
6. Hunting in adjacent areas
7. Vandalism, frequently mentioned by park personnel

## WATER

Every recreation survey emphasizes the importance of water. It was found that in most U.S.A. and Canadian parks some form of water proved to be the most critical single factor used or enjoyed by 70–80 percent of park visitors.

To provide water in a recreation area implies many requirements about its physical, chemical, and biological conditions.

The following aspects can be examined:

1. The "forms" of water for recreation areas (flowing water, ponds, reservoirs, and so on)
2. The quantity of water
3. The quality of water for different recreational uses such as swimming, fishing, boating and wildlife habitat
4. Pollution (though it is a "quality" question, for practical purposes it has to be dealt with separately)

5. Compatibility of the above uses
6. Manipulation, regulation, and so on for the above purposes

## "Forms" of Water for Recreation

. . . Of the different categories the following aspects have recreational significance:

1. The quantity and seasonal distribution of water flow. In the case of lake water tables: permanency and other seasonal changes.
2. Quality of water. Chemical and biological characteristics from a recreational point of view. Question of temperature.
3. Characteristic shore or bottom features, not directly water characteristics but relevant for the potential recreational use of the water itself.

These quality and quantity aspects can only be discussed in the broadest outline, characterizing mostly the differences between the different "forms" of water.

The *rivers* emptying their water into the Great Lakes are relatively short water courses with small to medium flow.

Although all have some potential recreational value they differ greatly according to:

1. Seasonal and minimum waterflow
2. Temperature of water
3. Chemical and biological properties of water
4. Degree and kind of pollution affecting the above properties

## The Lakes (Other than the Great Lakes)

There is hardly any other great city on the North American continent better endowed with lakes than is Toronto. Not only lakes but all kinds of lakes, of every imaginable size and quality, are available within a 100-mile radius of Toronto and all have some kind of recreational relevance.

An evaluation of them for recreational use implies a review from two approaches: from the point of view of what is appropriate for both the lakes themselves and the users of the lakes.

The user side, here, means the subjective evaluation of preferences, biases, what body of water should be, and so on. These preferences and biases can be dealt with when evaluating the different lakes.

What kinds of lakes are there in Southern Ontario, and how can they be evaluated for recreation?

The ecologist makes a convenient distinction between "oligotrophic" (poor in life) and "eutrophic" (rich in life) lakes. This categorization explains many things, but needs amplification.

1. The "oligotrophic" lakes are mostly outside our 50-mile radius but their recreational value is so important that they cannot be neglected here. These are the typical lakes of the Shield. Their characteristics are: transparently clear, cold, deep water, generally poor in nutrients and life.

Their further characteristics and dynamisms are thoroughly described by the pertinent literature. Nearly all of their main characteristics have recreational relevance, such as:

a. Their real and apparent clearness appeals to those swimmers who are enthusiasts of the "crystal clear" waters.

b. Temperature affects their value for swimming in a negative way (being usually cold, warming up late in the season, and localization of warming to shallow bays, and so on).

c. Their characteristics do not affect boating practices but do have some affect on water skiing (as for swimming).

d. The natural low productivity of the water adversely affects fishing. (Although some favourite sportfish species such as trout and smallmouthed bass thrive well in these waters, their number per acre of surface water is necessarily low.)

2. The lakes within the 50-mile radius mostly belong to the "eutrophic" group. Their assets or disadvantages are roughly the opposites of the "oligotrophic" category. Swimmers frequently criticize their apparently "unclear" water (opaque because of microscopic algae or other organisms); fishermen object to their excess of coarse fish; and boaters dislike their frequent shallowness and dense water vegetation. On the other hand, the water is warmer, warms up earlier in the season, and potentially can maintain a much higher fish population.

## Great Lakes

There is extensive literature on the Great Lakes which deals not only with general lymnological, ecological, and physical aspects but also their recreational value. The last mentioned has become especially prominent in recent years due to new attention directed toward them as a source of great, barely tapped, recreational potential.

Here are only a few general comments to be made:

1. They show great differences not only in their general characteristics but also in their recreational value. Temperature, degree of pollution, productivity, shore features, and so on, make Lake Ontario, Lake Erie, and Georgian Bay quite different for recreation.

2. There are great differences of opinion about their recreational value. These range from the highest enthusiasm to the most pessimistic view, expressed by authors of different papers.

3. There is an unquestionable trend toward a continuing deterioration of recreational value of waters, mostly in Lake Erie and near great population centers in other lakes. For example, Lake Ontario around Toronto.

4. The most prominent recreational problems are temperature and pollution.

The whole "deterioration" problem of the Great Lakes is one of the main concerns of the surrounding areas. In spite of the tremendous efforts of different institutions, commissions, and government agencies, there seems to be an irresistible trend toward decline. One cannot even say that the problems are not thoroughly studied (sufficient evidence may be assembled through reference to the extensive literature: *Lymnological Survey of Lake Erie*, technical reports of other authorities, and so on). But even where the processes are rather well understood it is difficult to improve them: all the more difficult because the "use pressure" on these waters will rapidly increase in the next few decades. On the other hand, with proper technology the harmful effects can be greatly reduced. The relatively satisfactory situation in the Ruhr Valley waters shows what can be achieved—if we really make the effort.

## Reservoirs

We previously pointed out how well endowed the Toronto area is with lakes. Knowing this, it sounds curious that so many reservoirs are planned partly or mostly for recreational purposes. Quite a few considerable-sized reservoirs are planned within the 50-mile radius. They are flood control reservoirs, with about equal emphasis on recreation. Many are double reservoirs, the upper one acting as a regulator for the lower one. They are not, at least the lower ones, draw-down reservoirs; the levels are kept adequately high even in the late summer when other reservoirs are usually at their lowest.

On examination of the visitor statistics and their trends, there can be little question that these reservoirs are needed and will be well patronized. They are also flood control reservoirs but their multiple use aspects are not discussed here.

From a recreation point of view a reservoir has many advantages:

1. The quality of water can be manipulated.
2. The temperature also can be well manipulated.
3. In the case of a non-draw-down reservoir the shoreline is more or less stabilized and can be developed for recreational purposes.
4. The whole biota can be manipulated.

The most important possibility for manipulation is connected with sport fishing. By a small change of water level the whole species composition can be affected.

## The Quality of Water

Requirements for swimming:

The ideal "swimming water" is clear, has equable pleasant temperature, is the proper size, and has comfortable bottom and shore conditions. These requirements can be found only in an artificial swimming pool. Many of these qualities, such as clear, sterile water, are not compatible with other recreational uses. Consequently swimming water is always a compromise, defined by minimum requirements, rather than absolute criteria. These minimum requirements are mostly connected with health hazards to the user. Unfortunately there does not exist an overall well-defined set of standard criteria. Most authorities, municipalities, and health departments follow different "standards." Water is generally considered unsuitable for swimming if the count of coliforms is in excess of 2,400 per 100 milliliter or if any coliform samples show raw sewage discharge in the water and five-day B.O.D. does not exceed 4 ppm.

This is a somewhat meagre and debatable standard. "Coliform" refers only to the form of the organism, and does not necessarily imply pathogenic qualities. Even less a count than 2,400 coliforms per 100 mill. may contain virulent pathogenic organisms. There is no escape as all natural water contains coliform bacteria and can be used without much health risk. Other criteria of such publications as the "Objectives of Water Quality Control" are rather imprecise and undefined. It puts only in general terms what should not be present in the water such as "highly toxic wastes" or "deoxigenating wastes" (whatever they are). Exceptions are "phenolic type wastes" where exact criteria are given, by not exceeding an average phenol content of 2 ppb. and a maximum of 5 ppb.

There is usually no consideration of the condition of the bottom (broken glass, metal sheets, and so on) or speed of current and other health hazards except sometimes around dams.

Possible proposals are:

1. More uniform standard requirements should be worked out and generally accepted.

2. The artificial swimming areas should be handled independently from the natural ones, applying a much stricter system of standards.

3. Other criteria and "minimum requirements" should be applied also in addition to the coliform bacteria count made by the authorities.

## Requirements for Boating

The quality of the water itself is less important for boating considerations. The boater's interest connected with water is rather (1) the size of the body of water, (2) certain bottom features (rock reaching the surface, and so on), (3) water vegetation conditions, (4) interference with other users, and (5) existence of certain features necessary for the use of boats. These requirements are of a higher order in the case of powered boats than hand propelled boats.

The basic problem with boating, with particular emphasis to power boating, is the question of its compatibility with other recreational uses. Boating is a space-demanding use. Its claim for water, where the area of water is limited, can interfere seriously with other users. This and many other aspects of boating, especially motor boating, make the recreation area planner less concerned with providing the needed space than with protecting other users from interference caused by boats. More correctly: to establish a fair equilibrium between the different demands.

All observations would seem to justify the adoption of policies for the different types of boating in recreational water to be held to well-defined *zones.* This means that high density uses of water such as swimming must be given preference, and boating should be confined to areas where it interferes less with these uses. In some cases where water sources are limited, power-boats can be excluded altogether.

## Sport Fishing and Ecological Criteria of Water Used for Sport

According to statistics, approximately 17–22 percent of recreation area users are fishermen.

But there are different kinds of fishing. Their physical and ecological requirements also differ widely.

To provide and maintain this habitat we have to know our goals. There are also many prejudices, preferences, and so on involved. The so-called "quality" fishing, "coarse fish," and similar notions already express something of this prejudice. To make it more complicated, these prejudices and preferences are most strongly held by those who manage and direct sport fishing activities.

To choose the right habitat, or to manipulate the available ones to provide the most satisfying sport fishing, outdoor recreation area planning has to consider:

1. The water quantity, quality, and temperature requirements of fishing intended to be established in the area and its relation to the available water

2. The bottom, shore, and other physiographic features of the water course or lake bed

3. The manipulability of the water

4. Access to the water

5. Compatibility of other uses, including other recreational uses, using the same source of water

It is extremely difficult to define "water quality requirements" for sport fishing generally. We know a lot about the specific requirements of different sport fish, especially about some of the preferred ones such as trout. A logical approach would be to provide these conditions and assume that everything will be all right. Unfortunately the problem is much more complicated. What can be done with great effort and expense is not always the most desirable. Certain changes and trends are going on irresistibly as consequences of our intensive use of the environment. To reverse them is getting more and more difficult and eventually will be practically impossible.

These changes in the fish habitat are not only due to pollution but also to many other factors which we cannot reverse. The best policy would be to recognize this and reckon with them. They probably create a constellation of conditions where different policies can be accepted.

1. Circumstances where the improvement of conditions for certain desirable fisheries are feasible and will be the right policy

2. Other situations where there should be strong efforts made to improve or reclaim conditions to a certain degree but at the same time to adjust sport fishery to a changed environment

3. Where the main concern is to adjust the fishery to the changed conditions and make the best of them

At the present time point (1) is the general attitude. This is right so far as it is aimed at improving existing waters, fighting against pollution, and so on, where there are reasonable hopes of achieving these goals.

The first attitude is perfectly well justified in many cases, such as middle and upper sections of streams, recreating or preserving the habitat for cold water fish, fighting pollution, and so on. In many cases proper management of these waters needs only stricter implementation of existing legislation, or some very inexpensive improvements, and proper measures to control the use of these waters. . . .

It is, of course, outside the scope of the study to try and debate technical questions. These are the fields of lymnology, fish management, and so on, a well worked out area (although never adequately), and well known by the responsible authorities.

The water requirements differ according to the species of fish and are connected with the quality, quantity, oxygen content and temperature of the water.

In spite of some uncertainty, some generalizations can be risked:

*Temperature.* The requirements are very different. Some fish tolerate a wide range (so called eurythermal) others only a narrow (stenothermal) range. In the case of sport fishing this is a problem only in the colder side, in other words, fish such as the so-called Salamonid group. An important indirect effect of the temperature is that it is connected with the amount of dissolved oxygen.

Another aspect is the temperature requirement for spawning. This can be used in reservoir water level manipulation to influence the fish species composition. For example, pike spawn when the temperature reaches 10° C, perch 12° C, carp above 18° C.

What are the criteria relating to water quality requirements of water organisms, primarily for sport fish? It sounds incredible that after concentrated and substantial pertinent literature one cannot give a definite exact numerical figure about these requirements. Even more discouraging is the summing up of the situation by one of the most authentic experts, Clarence M. Tarzwell, in 1962 in the publication "Development of Water Quality Criteria for Aquatic Life." Although he himself risked giving some criteria in 1956 he now appears to be less sure, emphasizing rather the uncertainties of their selection. He states: "There is a need to know more about the maximum concentrations of dissolved toxicants and the minimum concentrations of dissolved oxygen that fish and other aquatic organisms can withstand for short periods and to what level water temperature may be raised for short or extended periods without adversely affecting aquatic life."

A very generalized set of criteria can be suggested in the following form:

*Oxygen content.* Dissolved oxygen should not be less than 5 ppm. Some warm water fish tolerate even 2 ppm. for a considerable period of time. An overall level of 5 ppm. can be suggested as a minimum.

*Carbon Dioxide.* In lakes, reservoirs, and other more-or-less standing waters the free $CO_2$ concentration can be toxic and at least temporarily harmful for certain organisms. The tolerance here again varies with the species. Generally 5 cc. per litre can be considered as maximum. Other sources give 3 cc. per litre as the higher limit.

*Ammonia.* The decomposing organic matter—the main source of nitrogen compounds or rather the recirculation of nitrogen—contains a considerable amount of ammonium compounds. One of these ammonium compounds, ammonium carbonate, has a relatively high toxicity to many aquatic animals. In natural circumstances in unpolluted water, the ammonium carbonate is well below the toxic level.

*Suspended solids.* The two main sources of the most frequent inorganic suspended materials are erosion and effluents from earthworks and other industrial enterprises. The latter appear to be a growing danger which can—and actually does—destroy aquatic life on considerable sections of water courses.

## Consequences of Pollution for Recreational Uses of Water

The general term "polluted water" covers a wide range of quality conditions, according to the causes of the pollution, the so-called pollutants. Their effect on aquatic life is also widely different.

Possible categorization by origin of the wastes can point the direction of necessary measures. These may include the following:

1. Domestic sewage
2. Industrial wastes, chemicals
3. Industrial wastes, suspended inorganic material
4. Hot water from power plants, boilers, or other sources
5. Washed-in chemicides from adjacent agricultural use
6. Chemicides used in the water for mosquito control
7. Oil products from motor boats
8. Washed-in toxic material from dumped wastes along the water course . . .

## CONCLUSION

In this brief summary, we have tried to find the necessary physical and ecological criteria for the outdoor recreation area planner.

The planner's task in these fields is extremely complex and needs the contribution of specialists and special knowledge. This in itself is not new. Nearly all planning tasks are complex by their very nature. In this case the importance of biological sciences such as ecology came out with strong emphasis. The problem is that most of our planners are not too well prepared in this field. In many respects the best outdoor recreation area "planners" are at present some of the members of the pertinent Authorities (Metropolitan Toronto Conservation Authority, Department of Lands and Forests, River Valley Authorities, and so on). This is "right" to a degree and not unexpected, but as recreation areas are becoming one of the most important land uses around metropolitan areas, their development and control cannot be separated in a vacuum from the overall planning view.

CHAPTER

# 16

## CAMPGROUND TRAMPLING AND GROUND COVER RESPONSE
### Wilbur F. LaPage

This chapter by Wilbur LaPage is a fine follow-up to the preceding chapter, insofar as it presents a specific method that recreation planners might use to determine the degree of trampling that campgrounds receive during recreational use. By using the case study technique to present his method, LaPage helps to provide guidelines for the design and management of campgrounds so that the quality of outdoor recreational experiences can be sustained and even improved.

## TRAMPLING, A THREAT TO NATURAL GROWTH

Trampling of recreation sites frequently has been reported as a serious threat to the natural attractiveness of developed recreation areas (Clawson, 1959; DeVoto, 1953, James and Ripley, 1963). Previous studies of the impact of trampling upon soils and plants have been restricted almost entirely to after-the-fact analyses of forested parks and playgrounds that have been used and over-used for decades (LaPage, 1962; Lutz, 1945; Magill and Nord, 1963; Meinecke, 1929). Much valuable information about species tolerance levels and rates of decline has never been collected because after-the-fact studies make it impossible to reconstruct the appearance of soils and plants at different stages of park use. However, Wagar (1964) made a major advance in gaining information about species tolerance when he studied simulated recreation conditions in which different intensities of recreation use were applied to a narrow range of soils and vegetation to measure their reaction to trampling.

A more useful method of gaining the needed information would be to measure vegetative change concurrently with actual recreation use. Therefore, in 1963, the Northeastern Forest Experiment Station began a continuing study to record changes that occur in the composition and density of ground cover on a series of permanent plots located throughout 17 units of a 40-unit campground in the new Buckaloons camping area in the Allegheny National Forest.

The Buckaloons campground is located on a flood plain of the

Reprinted from "Some Observations on Campground Trampling and Ground Cover Response," U.S. Forest Research Paper NE-68 (1967), pp. 1–11, by permission of the United States Department of Agriculture, Forest Service, Northeastern Forest Experiment Station and the author. This article has been edited for this volume and the figures renumbered.

Allegheny River in northwestern Pennsylvania. The soil here is Chagrin silt loam, a deep, well-drained, and productive soil originating from sediments of sand, silt, and gravel washed down from the glaciated upland. The vegetation present at the time the campground was established was that of a typical abandoned field containing an abundance of grass, moss, violets, goldenrod, asters, and associated species. Parts of the field were overgrown with a fairly dense stand of hawthorn, which provided some screening between camping units, but no shade.

The past three years of observation on these plots have produced several interesting and useful clues about the nature of trampling in an old-field type campground.

## FIRST-YEAR FINDINGS

Just before the campground was opened to the public in June 1963, the low-growing vegetation on all plots was photographed, and plant density and species composition were determined by using a transparent 4-inch-square grid containing 100 evenly spaced dots. Plant density was recorded as the percent of living or dead ground cover (attached vegetation) present on six randomly selected 4-inch-square sampling units within each plot. Before camping use, most of the plots contained a dense 100-percent cover, averaging 11 species per campsite.

Re-examination of the plots in September 1963, after a season of use, revealed a reduction in the abundance of vegetative cover as well as fewer plant species present. The average loss of plant cover for all campsites was found to be 45 percent. Campsites that had received 150 camper-days of use throughout the summer averaged less than a 10-percent loss in vegetative cover. However, loss of vegetative cover increased to 60 percent for 300 camper-days of use.

The logarithm of camper-days use and reduction of ground cover provides the best description of the relationship and explains 78 percent of the variation in ground cover present at the end of the first year. This curvilinearity indicates, for this site at least, that restricting the average amount of use to 200 campers or fewer per season might be a feasible way of minimizing native cover loss.

Such severe restrictions are hardly an economic use of developed resources and may only be prolonging the inevitable anyway. Subsequent observations made during the second and third years suggest that the original ground cover composition is probably destined for replacement by more resistant species.

Reductions in the number of species making up the ground cover were not significant during the first year. Throughout the 17 sites, the average number of species declined from 11 to 9. Three campsites actually showed a slight increase in the number of species present.

The plants most seriously reduced at the close of the season were the larger species such as goldenrod and asters. Those specimens that remained were usually restricted to a single basal rosette. Also, large carpets of moss, present in the spring, were badly damaged by fall.

A fairly distinct size rule seemed to be operating in favor of the smaller annual plants during this first year. Small-leaf plants such as yarrow, sheep sorrell, and oxalis fared better than violets and cinquefoil, but not as well as the narrow-leaved grasses. Even among the grasses, the size rule seemed to operate, with orchard grass showing less tolerance to trampling than bluegrass or bent grass. This superior tolerance of grasses over dicotyledonous herbs agrees with the findings of Wagar (1964) on plant response to simulated recreation use in Michigan, and with that of Bates (1935) on the vegetation of compacted footpaths in England.

## SECOND-YEAR FINDINGS

From the fall of 1963 to the spring of 1964 the study sites received little use and recovered nearly half of the vegetation lost during the previous camping season, leaving them approximately 26 percent barren at the start of the second summer. By fall, cover losses had again increased, but only to 37 percent of the area. This 9 percent gain in cover over the previous fall occurred during an exceptionally dry summer when camping use had increased from an average of 237 days in 1963 to 351 days per site in 1964.

The variation present in campsite cover conditions by the fall of 1964 reflected a direct relationship with total campsite use, but showed no relationship with second-year use-intensity alone. Apparently the strong effect of the first year of use on the area continued to be evident after two years of cumulative use. However, as the barren ground became revegetated with a more resistant cover, the relationship between barren ground and cumulative man-days of use weakened and disappeared entirely by the end of 1965.

Most of the original species present in early 1963 had become less abundant by the fall of 1964. . . . The average number of species per campsite was reduced to six by the end of the second season.

## THIRD-YEAR FINDINGS

The relationship between use intensity and campsite condition became even more erratic in 1965. Under increasing pressures of use, some sites continued to lose ground cover, others gained, and still others barely changed.

Average campsite use increased to 368 camper-days, and average barren area stood at 31 percent in the fall after a recovery to 26 percent in the spring (see Figure 1). The change in campsite condition from the end of the second to the end of the third camping season reflected a general pattern of increasing cover occurring simultaneously with increasing use. This general improvement in campsite condition was clearly the result of more resistant species taking over the barren ground previously occupied by the original plant community.

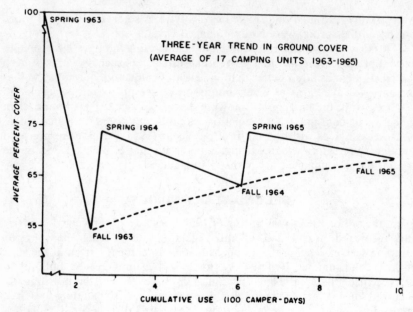

**FIGURE 1.** *Annual and Seasonal Change in Average Ground Cover on 17 Campsites Subjected to Normal Camping Pressures*

Although occasional specimens of the broad-leaved community have survived, and a few pioneer species have appeared, the total number of species has declined steadily during these three years of campground use. Both the total species represented and the average numbers of species per campsite have been reduced by more than 50 percent.

By an annual ranking of species according to their frequency of occurrence (maximum frequency would be 17) it is possible to arrive at

|  |  | Total species (No.) | Average per site (No.) |
|---|---|---|---|
| 1963: |  |  |  |
|  | Spring | 37 | 11 |
|  | Fall | 29 | 9 |
| 1964: |  |  |  |
|  | Spring | 31 | 11 |
|  | Fall | 23 | 6 |
| 1965: |  |  |  |
|  | Spring | 19 | 6 |
|  | Fall | 17 | 5 |

some tentative conclusions concerning the relative tolerance of various species to trampling (see Table 1).

Among the relatively tolerant species, bluegrass moved from a rank of three in 1963 to seventeen in 1965; path rush appeared on two sites in the fall of 1963 and spread to nine sites two years later, and bent grass was one of the three most abundant species every year. Among broad-leaved plants, clover was the only species to demonstrate any real tolerance of trampling.

Rapidly declining species that were originally abundant were cinquefoil, goldenrod, wild strawberry, and fescue, which were all eliminated; and yarrow, oxalis, sheep sorrel, and moss, which were seriously reduced over the three-year period.

## DISCUSSION

Maintenance of a vigorous ground cover is probably not a primary concern of most campground managers. However, trampling, as it affects long-term recreation-management goals has an undeniable influence on site preservation. And this campground with its abundant and varied ground cover provides an ideal opportunity to study campground ecology. Although only three years of observation have been compiled, several interesting and potentially useful aspects of trampling have been uncovered.

Ground cover losses were generally higher on camping units with stationary picnic tables. Movable tables apparently help to spread the wear and prevent the early formation of paths between fireplace, table, and parking space.

Revegetation with bent grass, bluegrass, and path rush was often best in areas where large patches of moss had died, but where enough stems had remained to trap the wind-blown seed and hold it against bare soil. Campground management could probably duplicate this effect by spreading a thin layer of straw on bare spots immediately after the Labor Day weekend. A logical extension of this revegetation process would be the direct seeding of these grasses, accompanied by restrictions on use during the late fall and early spring months when sites are damp and most easily compacted.

Some of the most lightly used campsites were also the ones that experienced the greatest loss of ground cover. In each of these cases some unusual circumstance of campsites use was evident as the probable cause of accelerated wear. Loose, abrasive, gravel that had strayed from the campground roads, from the built-up tent pads, or from crumbling fireplaces was frequently found on campsites that had experienced an unusually heavy cover loss. Other sites used lightly, but effectively screened from sun and air for extended periods of time by plastic ground cloths and canvas tent floors, also experienced excessive loss of vegetation.

These observations indicate that trampling, expressed simply as man-days of use, is not an adequate measure of the impact of camping on

| Species [1] | Frequency | | | | | |
|---|---|---|---|---|---|---|
| | 1963 | | 1964 | | 1965 | |
| | Spring | Fall | Spring | Fall | Spring | Fall |
| Cinquefoil *(Potentilla)* | 14 | 5 | 10 | 2 | 1 | 0 |
| Yarrow *(Achillea)* | 14 | 10 | 10 | 5 | 5 | 3 |
| Bent grass *(Agrostis)* | 13 | 15 | 16 | 13 | 16 | 13 |
| Fecue *(Festuca)* | 13 | 10 | 4 | 3 | 1 | 0 |
| Goldenrod *(Solidago)* | 12 | 4 | 9 | 0 | 0 | 0 |
| Hair-cup moss *(Polytrichum)* | 11 | 8 | 13 | 9 | 8 | 3 |
| Wood sorrel *(Oxalis)* | 10 | 7 | 9 | 1 | 0 | 1 |
| Sheep sorrel *(Rumex)* | 9 | 11 | 12 | 5 | 5 | 4 |
| Speedwell *(Veronica)* | 9 | 4 | 10 | 3 | 1 | 0 |
| Violet *(Viola)* | 9 | 9 | 11 | 5 | 7 | 4 |
| Wild strawberry *(Fragaria)* | 8 | 7 | 7 | 1 | 0 | 0 |
| Timothy *(Phleum)* | 6 | 0 | 2 | 3 | 3 | 3 |
| White heath aster *(Aster)* | 5 | 3 | 0 | 0 | 0 | 0 |
| Buttercup *(Ranunculus)* | 4 | 3 | 3 | 2 | 4 | 1 |
| Loosestrife *(Lythrum)* | 4 | 2 | 3 | 0 | 0 | 0 |
| Plantain *(Plantago)* | 3 | 5 | 6 | 5 | 6 | 4 |
| White campion *(Lychnis)* | 3 | 6 | 4 | 4 | 6 | 3 |
| Clover *(Trifolium)* | 3 | 3 | 10 | 7 | 8 | 9 |
| Orchard grass *(Dactylis)* | 3 | 1 | 3 | 2 | 4 | 2 |
| Bluegrass *(Poa)* | 3 | 11 | 12 | 14 | 15 | 17 |
| Sedge *(Carex)* | 2 | 2 | 2 | 1 | 0 | 0 |
| Nettel *(Urtica)* | 2 | 0 | 1 | 0 | 0 | 0 |
| Foxtail *(Setaria)* | 2 | 2 | 4 | 0 | 0 | 0 |
| Heal-all *(Prunella)* | 2 | 2 | 0 | 0 | 0 | 0 |
| Milkwort *(Polygala)* | 2 | 0 | 0 | 0 | 0 | 0 |
| Grapefern *(Botrychium)* | 1 | 0 | 0 | 1 | 0 | 0 |
| Dandelion *(Taraxacum)* | 1 | 1 | 0 | 0 | 0 | 0 |
| Hawthorne *(Crataegus)* | 1 | 1 | 2 | 0 | 0 | 0 |
| Field mint *(Mentha)* | 1 | 0 | 0 | 0 | 1 | 0 |
| Hawkweed *(Hieracium)* | 1 | 1 | 1 | 1 | 0 | 0 |
| Bindweed *(Convolvulus)* | 1 | 1 | 0 | 0 | 0 | 0 |
| Wild rose *(Rosa)* | 1 | 0 | 1 | 0 | 0 | 0 |
| Wild onion *(Allium)* | 1 | 0 | 0 | 0 | 0 | 0 |
| Wild carrot *(Daucus)* | 1 | 1 | 3 | 0 | 0 | 0 |
| Field madder *(Galium)* | 1 | 0 | 0 | 0 | 0 | 0 |
| Wild parsnip *(Pastinaca)* | 1 | 1 | 1 | 0 | 0 | 0 |
| Elder *(Sambucus)* | 1 | 0 | 0 | 0 | 0 | 0 |
| Path Rush *(Juncus)* | 0 | 2 | 3 | 6 | 8 | 9 |
| Chickweed *(Cerastium)* | 0 | 0 | 4 | 2 | 3 | 2 |
| Bluet *(Houstonia)* | 0 | 0 | 1 | 0 | 0 | 0 |
| Fall panicum *(Panicum)* | 0 | 0 | 2 | 5 | 2 | 4 |
| Mustard *(Brassica)* | 0 | 0 | 0 | 0 | 0 | 1 |

**TABLE 1.** *Plant Species Present and Their Frequencies of Occurrence during Spring and Fall Examinations for 3 Years of Camping-Use*

[1] All species identifications are tentative because specimens were often badly mutilated by trampling and could not be removed from the plots for detailed examination without damaging the study's basic objective of determining plant survival under actual trampling conditions.

vegetation. Some measure of the quality or character of recreation use is needed that will explain the destruction of ground cover more realistically than simple use intensity does.

The following conclusions have resulted from observations on this study to date:

1. An initial and inevitable heavy loss of ground cover follows the onset of camping use, and the extent of the loss is strongly related to the intensity of first-year use, expressed as camper-days.

2. The plant species composition of the original cover undergoes a gradual rearrangement, in which the more compaction and drought-resistant species become increasingly abundant.

3. During the second, third, and following years the recreation-tolerant species advance while the original less-resistant species continue to retreat, with the result that the cover does not respond to continued trampling in the same direct way that it did during the first year.

At present a more resistant ground cover is spreading over these campsites. From observations at other recreation areas it seems inevitable that this second growth will also decline under sustained trampling. Continued observation will make it possible to document the rate and nature of this decline.

But, similar studies will be needed of other sites and cover types. Ideally, these studies should include three distinct phases. During the initial phase those plant species of the original community that have the highest natural tolerance to trampling are identified. Second, by observing the subsequent decline of these species, it will be possible to determine their limits of endurance. This information should be of value in formulating realistic recreation-site management objectives. And, in the third and final phase, various methods of site rehabilitation can be tested to provide remedial measures for those recreation areas where plant tolerance limits have been exceeded.

These findings, along with those from similar studies on different sites, will help to provide guidelines for the design and intensive management of campgrounds to improve their ability to provide a sustained supply of high quality outdoor recreation experiences.

## REFERENCES

Bates, G. H. 1935. Vegetation of footpaths, sidewalks, cart-tracks, and gateways. *Journal of Ecology* 23: 470–87.

Clawson, M. 1959. The crisis in outdoor recreation. *American Forests* 65 (3): 22–31, 40–41.

DeVoto, B. 1953. Let's close the national parks. *Harpers* 207 (1241): 49–52.

James, G. A., and T. H. Ripley. 1963. Overuse—a threat to our developed recreation areas. *American Recreation Journal* 4 (3): 5–6.

LaPage, W. F. 1962. Recreation and the forest site. *Journal of Forestry* 60: 319–21.

Lutz, H. J. 1945. Soil conditions of picnic grounds in public forest parks. *Journal of Forestry* 43: 121–27.

Magill, A. W., and E. C. Nord. 1963. An evaluation of campground conditions and needs for research. U.S. Forest Service Research Note PSW-4. Berkeley.

Meinecke, E. P. 1929. *The effect of excessive tourist travel on the California redwood parks.* Sacramento: California State Printing Office.

Wagar, J. A. 1964. The carrying capacity of wild lands for recreation. *Forest Science Monograph 7.*

# 17

# USE OF SOIL SURVEYS IN PLANNING FOR RECREATION
## P. H. Montgomery
## Frank C. Edminster

P. H. Montgomery and Frank C. Edminster approach the physical parameters of recreational use of the environment by looking specifically at soil surveys as a method for improved recreation planning. This chapter is particularly significant because it not only discusses the major characteristics and qualities of soil behavior under specific recreational use, but it also attempts to present the interrelationships between the different soil characteristics themselves. Upon reading this chapter, one recognizes the significance of a good soil survey as a prerequisite for sound recreation facility planning.

. . . There are many considerations, physical and economic, that determine the potential of an area for outdoor recreation. The kind of soil dictates to a large degree the type and location of recreational facilities. Some soils are not desirable sites for campsites, play areas, picnic grounds, cabin sites, or natural study areas; other soils are very desirable sites for recreational use. Knowledge of the soils of an area—a farm, ranch, community, watershed, or county—provide fundamental information needed in recreation planning. . . .

In the survey area soil units are recognized, defined, and delineated on aerial photo maps to show the location, size, and slope of the soil areas. The mapping is done at different degrees of intensity depending upon the uses to be made of it. On high- and medium-intensity soil surveys, phases of soil series are the common map unit. These map units are classified, named, and correlated within the national system of soil classification.[1] Low-intensity, or reconnaissance, surveys have limited value for recreational planning.

The same soil properties that affect agricultural uses of soil are the ones that affect their use for recreation. All soils can be used for recreational activities of some kind. Some have no soil limitations for specific kinds of recreational use; others have moderate to severe limitations for certain uses. In fact, some kinds of soil are dangerous if used for certain recreational activities, such as camping. The use of soils subject to flash flooding or landslides can lead to loss of life and property.

Reprinted from L. J. Bartelli, A. A. Kingebiel, J. V. Baird, and M. R. Heddleson, eds., *Soil Surveys and Land Use Planning* (Madison: Soil Science Society of America, 1966), Chap. 10, by permission from the Soil Science Society of America and the authors. This article has been edited for this volume and the notes renumbered.

The effects of a given soil property often vary with different uses. The following are some of the soil properties that singly or in combination with others commonly affect recreational uses of soils.

Soils subject to flooding have severe limitations for use as sites for camps and recreation buildings. If soils subject to flooding are not protected by dikes, levees, or other flood prevention structures they should not be developed for campsites or vacation cottages. These soils are better suited for hiking or nature study areas, or for greenbelt open space, if the flooding is not too frequent.

Soils that are wet all year, even if not flooded, have severe soil limitations for campsites, recreational roads and trails, playgrounds, and picnic areas. Soils that are wet only part of the year or those that have a water table that moves up and down without reaching the surface are not easily detected by most people. These soils have severe limitations for most recreational uses. Soils that dry out slowly after rains present problems where intensive use is contemplated.

Droughty soils also have limitations for many recreational uses. On such sites, grass cover needed for playing fields is difficult to establish and maintain. Access roads may be excessively dusty. Vehicles are easily mired down in sandy soils and soil blowing is common. Knowledge of these soil problems enables planners to use corrective conservation practices, such as irrigation, or to choose alternative locations.

The ability of a soil to support a load is important in many kinds of recreational activities. Some soils when wet fail to support structures such as access roads, trails, and buildings.

Slope affects the use of soils for recreation. Nearly level, well drained, permeable, stone-free soils have few or no limitations for use as playgrounds, campsites, sites for recreational buildings, roads, and trails. Soils with steep slopes often have severe limitations for most recreational uses. On the other hand, steeply sloping soils are essential for ski runs and are desirable for hiking areas, scenic values, and vacation cottage sites "with a view." Of course, deep, gently sloping, and moderately sloping soils can be leveled for campsites, playgrounds, and building sites where the cost is justified. Where this is done it is especially urgent that effective soil conservation practices be applied and maintained based on the specific conditions.

Soil depth affects many uses. Soils underlain by bedrock to shallow depths cannot be leveled for playgrounds and campsites except at high cost. Roads, trails, and basements are very difficult to construct on these soils. It is difficult to establish vegetation on soils shallow to impervious soil layers or rock thus making them poor locations for playing fields and other intensive use areas.

Surface texture is an important soil property to consider. High sand or clay content in the surface soils is undesirable for playgrounds, campsites, or other uses that involve heavy foot traffic by people or horses. Soils high in clay become sticky when wet and do not dry out quickly after rains. On the other hand, loose sandy soils are undesirable as they are unstable when dry. Sandy loam and loam surface textured soils that also have other favorable characteristics are the most desirable for recreational uses involving heavy use by people.

The presence of stones, rocks, cobbles, or gravel limits the use of some soils for recreational uses. Very stony, stony, rocky, or gravelly soils have severe to moderate limitations for use as campsites and playgrounds. In some instances it is feasible to remove the stones, thus eliminating the hazard. Rounded gravels and stones present hazards on steeply sloping soils used for foot trails.

Sanitary facilities are essential for most modern recreational areas and septic tanks are often the only means of waste disposal. Some soils absorb septic tank effluent rapidly and other soils absorb it very slowly. Soils that are slowly permeable, poorly drained, shallow to rock, subject to flooding, or steeply sloping all have severe limitations for septic tank filter fields.[2] In some cases where soils cannot handle the volume of waste involved, sewage lagoons can be used. These also are feasible only in soils that meet the special requirements for sewage lagoons.

Productive capacity of soils for vegetation of different kinds is closely related to the feasibility of many recreation enterprises. The ability of soils to grow sods that can take concentrated human traffic has already been noted as a factor in such areas as playgrounds and campsites. The development of such vegetative conservation practices as shade tree plantings, living fences, plant screens, and barriers to trespass is guided by soil conditions. The capacity of an area to produce economically harvestable crops of game is dependent, in part, on the productive ability of its soils.[3]

The suitability of the soil for impounding water reflects, in considerable measure, the kind of soil at the impoundment site as well as in the watershed above the impoundment. Fertile soils, or soils capable of effective use of artificial fertilizers, generally make fertile waters. And fertile waters produce good fish crops which, with good management, produce good fishing. On the other hand, extremely acid soils associated with a proposed water impoundment may be a critical limitation to the development of good fishing.

Thus we find that basic soil qualities and characteristics are closely associated with the various types of outdoor recreation activities. By knowing the characteristics and qualities of the different kinds of soils and their behavior, and with the aid of a soil map soil scientists and other specialists can develop soil interpretations for recreational uses. Interpretations for recreational uses can best be made locally by those familiar with the soils and conditions in the area. Soils in an area are normally grouped into three or five groups according to their limitations for a specific recreational use.

1. None to slight soil limitations—Soils relatively free of limitations that affect the intended use or the limitations are easy to overcome.

2. Moderate soil limitations—Soils with moderate limitations resulting

| Soil items affecting use | Degree of soil limitation | | |
|---|---|---|---|
| | None to slight | Moderate | Severe |
| Wetness | Well to moderately well drained soils with no ponding and with water table below 3 feet | Moderately well drained soils with water table less than 3 feet and somewhat poorly drained soils with no ponding | Well drained, moderately well drained and somewhat poorly, with occasional ponding of short duration, poorly, and very poorly drained soils |
| Flooding | None | None | Subject to flooding during season of use |
| Permeability† | Very rapid to moderate | Moderately slow | Slow and very slow |
| Slope | 0-8% | 8-15% | 15% + |
| Surface soil texture | sl, fsl, vfsl, l, and ls with textural B horizon. Not subject to soil blowing | cl, scl, sicl, sil, ls, and sand other than loose sand | Organic, c, sic, c, loose sand, and soils subject to severe blowing. |
| Coarse fragments < 10'' | Less than 15% | 15-50% | 50% + |
| Stoniness or rockiness‡ | None | Classes 1 and 2 | Classes 3, 4, and 5 |

**TABLE 1.** *Soil Limitations for Camp Areas (Intensive Use)\**

\* Based on soil limitations during use season. † In low rainfall areas soils may be rated one class better. ‡ For definitions see Soil Survey Manual, pp. 217–221.

| Soil items affecting use | Degree of soil limitation | | |
|---|---|---|---|
| | None to slight | Moderate | Severe† |
| Wetness | Well to moderately well drained soils not subject to ponding or seepage Over 4 feet to seasonal water table | Well and moderately well drained soils subject to occasional ponding or seepage Somewhat poorly drained not subject to ponding. Seasonal water table 2-4 feet ‡ | Somewhat poorly drained soils subject to ponding. Poorly and very poorly drained soils |
| Flooding | Not subject to flooding | Not subject to flooding | Subject to flooding |
| Slope | 0-8% | 8-15% | 15% + |
| Rockiness§ | Class 0 | Class 1 | Classes 2, 3, 4, and 5 |
| Stoniness§ | Classes 0 and 1 | Class 2 | Classes 3, 4, and 5 |
| Depth to hard bedrock | 5 feet + | 3-5 feet‡ | Less than 3 feet |

**TABLE 2.** *Soil Limitations for Buildings in Recreational Areas\**

\* Soil limitations for septic tank filter fields, hillside slippage, frost heave, piping, loose sand, and low bearing capacity when wet are items not included in this rating that must be considered. Soil rating for these items have been developed.

† Soils rated as having severe soil limitations for individual cottage sites may be best from an aesthetic or use standpoint but they do require more preparation or maintenance for such use

‡ These items are limitations only where basements and underground utilities are planned.

§ Based on definitions in Soil Survey Manual, pp. 217–221.

from the effects of slope, wetness, soil texture, soil depth, plant growth deficiencies, stones, and so on. Normally the limitations can be overcome with correct planning, careful design, and good management.

3. Severe soil limitations—Soils with severe limitations resulting from the effects of steep slopes, high water table, stream flooding, unfavorable soil texture, acidity, large numbers of stones, rocks, and so on. Soils rated as having a severe limitation are severe enough to make the use of the soil doubtful for the proposed use. Careful planning and above-average design and management are required. This often includes major soil reclamation work.

| Soil items affecting use | Degree of soil limitation | | |
|---|---|---|---|
| | None to slight | Moderate | Severe |
| Wetness | Well and moderately well drained soils with no ponding or seepage | Well and moderately well drained soils subject to occasional ponding or seepage of short duration. Somewhat poorly drained soils | Somewhat poorly subject to ponding, poorly, and very poorly drained soils. Too wet for use for periods of 1-5 weeks during season of use |
| Flooding | None during season of use | Subject to occasional flooding. Not more than once in 3 years | Subject to more than occasional flooding during season of use |
| Permeability* | Rapid, moderately rapid and moderate | Moderately slow | Slow and very slow |
| Slope | 0-2% | 2-8% | 8% + |
| Surface soil texture | sl, fsl, vfsl, l and ls with textural B horizon | cl, scl, sicl, sil, ls, and sand | sc, sic, c, organic soils and sand and loamy sand subject to blowing |
| Depth to hard bedrock | 3 feet + | 2-3 feet† | Less than 2 feet |
| Stoniness‡ | Class 0 | Classes 1 and 2 | Classes 3, 4, and 5 |
| Rockiness | None | Class 1 | Classes 2, 3, 4, and 5 |
| Coarse fragments | Free of coarse fragments | Up to 15% coarse fragments | 15% + |

**TABLE 3.** *Soil Limitations for Play Areas (Intensive Use)*

* In arid regions soils may be rated one class better.

† These soils have severe limitations if slope is greater than 2%. ‡ As per definitions in Soil Survey Manual, pp. 217–221.

When five interpretive groupings are used instead of three the soils are rated as having none, slight, moderate, severe, and very severe limitations. Essentially this involves dividing the first and last groups in the three class system.

The guides set forth in Tables 1, 2, 3, 4, and 5 are suggested for use in developing soil interpretations for picnic areas, intensive play areas, buildings in recreational areas, intensive camp areas, and for paths and trails.[4]

| Soil items affecting use | Degree of soil limitation | | |
|---|---|---|---|
| | None to slight | Moderate | Severe |
| Wetness* | Well and moderately well drained soils with seasonal water table below 3 feet | Well and moderately well drained soils subject to seepage or ponding and somewhat poorly drained soils. Seasonal water table 1-3 feet | Poorly drained and very poorly drained soils |
| Flooding* | Not subject to flooding during season of use | Subject to occasional flooding. May flood 1 or 2 times during season of use | Frequent flooding during season of use |
| Slope† | 0-15% | 15-25% | 25% + |
| Surface texture‡ | sl, fsl, vfsl, l | sil, sicl, scl, cl, sc, ls | sic, c, sand, and soils subject to severe blowing |
| | Gravelly and non-gravelly | | All very gravelly, very cherty, very cobbly, very channery soils |
| Surface stoniness or rockiness§ | Classes 0, 1, and 2 | Class 3 | Classes 4 and 5 |

**TABLE 4.** *Soil Limitations for Paths and Trails*

* Season of use should be considered in evaluating these items. † Soil erodibility is an important item to evaluate in rating this item. Some adjustments in slope range may be needed in different climatic zones. ‡ In arid and subhumid climates some of the finer textured soils may be reduced one soil limitation class. § Based on definitions in Soil Survey Manual, pp. 217–221.

| Soil items affecting use | Degree of soil limitation | | |
|---|---|---|---|
| | None to slight | Moderate | Severe |
| Wetness | Well and moderately well drained soils not subject to ponding | Well drained, moderately well drained soil subject to occasional ponding. Somewhat poorly drained not subject to ponding | Poorly drained & very poorly drained soils. Somewhat poorly drained soils subject to ponding. Too wet for use for periods of more than 4 weeks during season of use |
| Flooding | None during season of use | May flood 1 or 2 times for short period during season of use | Floods more than 2 to 4 times during season of use |
| Slope | 0-8% | 8-15% | 15% + |
| Surface soil texture | sl, fsl, vfsl, l and ls with textural B. Not subject to blowing | cl, scl, sicl, sil, ls, and sand other than loose sand. * | sc, sic, c, s, organic soils and soils subject to severe blowing. |
| Stoniness† | Classes 0, 1, and 2 | Class 3 | Classes 4 and 5 |
| Rockiness | Classes 0, 1, and 2 | Class 3 | Classes 4 and 5 |

**TABLE 5.** *Soil Limitations for Picnic Areas (Intensive Use)*

* In arid and subhumid climates fine textured soils may be classified as having a moderate limitation. † See definition in Soil Survey Manual, pp. 217–221.

These guides are useful in evaluating each kind of soil to be grouped into soil limitation classes for different recreational uses. It is recognized that interactions, in different major land resource areas, among some of the soil qualities listed in these guides may be great enough to change the soil limitation rating by one class. Soils having the same soil name and occurring in the same land resource area normally will have the same rating.

It is not anticipated that all of these interpretations will be needed in all areas. Interpretations for other recreational uses should be developed locally as needed.

It is important that the proper perspective be placed on the use of soil interpretations in recreational planning. They are based on soil features only and do not include other factors such as location, aesthetic values, and nearness to population centers. A soil survey properly interpreted is a useful guide for general recreation planning and in site selection, planning, and design of recreational facilities.

## NOTES

[1] Soil Survey Staff, "Soil Classification, A Comprehensive System, 7th Approximation," Soil Conservation Service, U.S. Department of Agriculture, 1960; and Soil Survey Staff, "Soil Survey Manual," U.S. Department of Agriculture Handbook No. 18, Washington, D.C., 1951.

[2] William H. Bender, "Soils Suitable for Septic Tank Filter Fields," U.S. Department of Agriculture, Agriculture Information Bulletin No. 243.

[3] Philip F. Allan, Lloyd E. Garland, and Franklin R. Dunga, "Rating Northeastern Soils for Their Suitability for Wildlife Habitat," Trans. 28th North American Wildlife and Natural Resources Conference.

[4] Credit is given to a number of soil scientists in the Soil Conservation Service who developed early drafts of these guides.

# 18

# SILVICULTURE FOR RECREATION AREA MANAGEMENT

**Paul O. Rudolf**

The role of the professional forester in the planning and development of recreation facilities has a long history. On the other hand, managing the forest itself through selective cutting for recreation purposes is new. This chapter by Paul Rudolf is an excellent example of how silviculture methods can be used to provide "variety, harmony, and contrast to satisfy the recreationist."

. . . To many people timber management practices and recreational use of forest land are incompatible. "T'aint necessarily so," however. The cultural practices for producing and tending forests usually can be so applied or so modified as to provide, maintain, or improve recreational values. Silviculture probably is most concisely defined as "the theory and practice of controlling forest establishment, composition, and growth" (S.A.F., 1958). Some ideas on how silvicultural practices can be used for developing recreational areas are described here.

## SOME BASIC ASSUMPTIONS

Before elaborating the main theme, let us set up some basic assumptions.

1. Outdoor recreation areas usually contain trees and whether they be commercial forests (where wood production is the prime use), roadside strips, parks,[1] picnic areas, campgrounds, portages, lakeshores, or what have you, they must be maintained and managed to have aesthetic appeal. This may require the assistance of specialists such as landscape architects, arboriculturists, or ecologists; but the silviculturist, with his understanding of trees and their interrelationships as stands and as biotic communities, will play a vital role.

2. Before any management practices are undertaken, there should be a set of specifications for both the functional use of the area and the requirements for management of the vegetation so that a logical plan will be developed and followed. Such plans should provide, among other things, for the rotation of intensive-use areas (campgrounds, picnic areas, and some hiking trails) and for placing facilities such as picnic tables away from

Reprinted from the *Journal of Forestry* 65, no. 6 (June, 1967): 385–90, by permission of the *Journal of Forestry* and the author. This article has been extensively edited for this volume.

specimen trees to minimize soil compaction, root exposure, and other damages to these trees.

3. Management practices must be applied to potential as well as existing recreation sites, scenic vistas, roadside areas, and wildlife openings. Cultural treatments need, therefore, to be planned and applied in advance so that stand conditions on these sites and areas will be ready when scheduled for recreational development or establishment.

4. The management priorities will differ between kinds of areas. In commercial forests, wood production will be the prime use, but there can be considerable dispersed recreation such as hiking, hunting, fishing, and enjoyment of the scenery. In natural parks and in roadside and waterway strips, recreation or aesthetic values will be stressed, but many such areas can still be managed for some wood production as well.

5. Foresters must be willing to accept a more comprehensive role in managing the forest environment for all its products, including aesthetic aspects. Although there have been numerous instances of aesthetic application of timber management practices, the majority of foresters (silviculturists) have shown few accomplishments and little imagination in this direction—this, even though the timber management instructions under which many public foresters operate provide latitude and often give guidance for many aesthetic practices.

## HOW SILVICULTURE CAN BE APPLIED
## TO RECREATION AREAS

Outdoor recreation areas usually are partly wooded and frequently include lakes or streams or special features of scenic or wildlife interest. Many of them include both areas of intensive use, such as roads, trails, picnic sites, and campgrounds, and other areas of more extensive use that should maintain the appearance of wildland. Managed strips along highways and waterways, including scenic vistas and openings, can add to the pleasure of travelers by bringing out the natural beauty of the region. . . .

While developing silvicultural prescriptions for timber production, silviculturists have acquired fundamental knowledge that enables them to predict what will happen when these prescriptions are altered. Thinning, improvement cutting, pruning, harvest cutting, brush control, and regeneration measures both natural and artificial—all are silvicultural practices involved in these prescriptions and all are as essential in recreation areas as they are in timber production forests. Many of the objectives are different, however, and hence the application of the silvicultural practices may differ. Nevertheless the management of cover in recreation areas is not a separate and distinct art, but an offshoot of *silvicultural* knowledge as it is applied to the growing of timber crops.

### Thinning and Improvement Cutting

Desired stand density is determined by the function of the area. In some recreation areas, stands denser than are desired for wood production may be preferred for such purposes as protecting watersheds, providing refuge for wildlife, directing human traffic, or screening undesirable views. In other areas, low stand densities may be most suitable for providing more typical "park-like" appearances, letting in more light for development of lower vegetation, promoting development of browse for wildlife or berry and nut crops for animals and men, opening up picnic areas and campgrounds, and for similar purposes.

The primary objective of thinnings and improvement cuttings will be to enhance the recreational qualities rather than to achieve maximum timber growth; therefore, the criteria for selecting trees to be left often may be different than for wood production. If crooked trees with heavy crowns or species of low timber value have more scenic and functional value (for shade, flower, and fruit production, and so on) than straight, smaller crowned trees of high timber value, they will be favored. For many recreation uses, intermediate cuts will aim to develop healthy trees with large crowns and big diameters.

Intermingled dense and open stands, instead of rather uniform stands, may provide more attractive surroundings and improved wildlife habitat. By the same token, intermediate cuttings for recreation purposes often should favor a variety of species, especially mixtures of hardwoods and conifers; sometimes hardwoods should be favored for shade.

Special consideration must be given to developing wind firmness, particularly in areas of intense use such as picnic areas and campgrounds. This may require unusually early cuttings where relatively open stands are the desired goal.

Brush, often detrimental in a timber stand, can serve useful purposes in a recreation area. It can also be undesirable. To encourage tree reproduction or to provide scenic vistas, there may be situations where brush should be removed, or one shrub favored over another. Hazardous plants such as poison ivy or poison sumac may require elimination. Unwanted shrubs may be controlled by manipulating stand density, cutting the brush, or spraying with chemicals either general or selective as the case may demand.

## Pruning

On recreational areas pruning often will be desirable, more for safety, better visibility, and improved appearance and health of individual trees than for the development of knot-free wood. Wherever stands are in relatively constant view, such as along roads, trails, or waterways, or in picnic areas and campgrounds, attractive appearance of trees is especially important. Heavy partial cuttings often may expose trees with numerous dead branches or unsightly stubs. Careful pruning can help to eliminate unsightliness and the danger from falling limbs and may be an effective sanitation measure as well. On the other hand, pruning scars can be unattractive. Normally, therefore, only dead or hazardous limbs should be removed on intensive-use recreation areas.

## Harvest Cuttings

For many recreation purposes, large old trees are especially desirable. This will mean growing trees as long as they will stand without providing unusual hazards. Often they will be retained long beyond the accepted rotation ages. In many situations defect will not be a disadvantage so long as there is no danger to people and no serious loss of wind firmness, attractive appearance, or tree vigor. Some defect may even be desirable for fostering nesting facilities for birds, such as wood ducks, and dens for animals, such as raccoons and squirrels. For safety reasons and to avoid interference with recreational use, harvest cuttings on such areas normally should be done during the offseason.

The selection system of harvesting probably will be the most widely applicable for maintaining existing recreation areas. Most often tree selection may be preferred over group selection. Shorter cutting cycles and lighter cuts than for timber management may be used. In application there may often be a fine line between harvest cuttings and sanitation cuttings. In intensive-use areas all cutting will be of a sanitation or salvage nature, since there is no intention of growing a crop to be harvested. In extensive-use areas, there may actually be a planned timber harvest, modified to permit recreational use.

More drastic cutting will be needed to develop those areas in which some of the less tolerant species or open vistas are desired. Here the shape and dimensions of clearings need to be considered. Clearcutting, seed tree methods, or shelterwood cuttings, where required to obtain desired species, probably will have to be confined to rather small areas of irregular shape, either strips or patches; and recreational use will have to be integrated with cutting cycles.

## Regeneration Measures

In scenic zones, long-term management can utilize natural regeneration through manipulation of stand density and control of ground cover. Where harvest cuttings do not produce sufficient natural regeneration, where type conversion is considered desirable, where fires or other catastrophes have destroyed the stand, or where new species are to be introduced, artificial regeneration will be needed. Although in some recreation areas direct seeding will be desirable, normally the quicker and more certain responses from planting will be preferable.

Sometimes the trees and shrubs left on picnic grounds or campsites may not be able to survive the soil compaction, physical damage, or other results of heavy use; or it may be desirable to bring more variety into the stand (introduce conifers into deciduous stands and vice versa), to introduce shrubs for their foliage color, flower, or fruits, to soften the lines of vistas, and so on. In some areas where human traffic is to be discouraged, attractive thorny plants may make useful borders. All these requirements can be met by planting.

On most recreational areas, ground disturbance must be kept to a minimum, so spot or informal group planting may work out best. Informal rather than regular spacing usually will be preferable. Sometimes much larger stock than that used in regular forest plantings may be necessary to create desired conditions with less delay. Special measures (repellent sprays, fences, cages, and so on) to protect the plants from damage (by wildlife species, insects, and human use) may be required during the establishment. Unfortunately, as yet we know little about the resistance of many of our tree and shrub species to the impact of intensive human use of plant communities.

For extensive-use recreation areas developed in natural forests, any necessary planting probably should be done with native species. For some uses this might include special forms (fastigiate, dwarf, procumbent, and so on) that have been selected within the native species by horticulturists or forest geneticists. However, well-adapted exotic species of trees or shrubs may be most effective in artificial stands or in intensive-use areas. . . .

Compared to practices on timber production areas, some of those needed on recreation areas will be more intensive and may verge upon arboriculture and horticulture. In developing prescriptions for recreation areas the prudent silviculturist will consult other experts such as park, wildlife, and watershed managers, landscape architects, arboriculturists, horticulturists, soil specialists, ecologists, entomologists, and pathologists.

It seems obvious, too, that the development of detailed and reliable silvicultural prescriptions for recreation areas will require (1) reinterpretation of existing information on tree growth and development in the light of recreation management goals, and (2) new research on (a) the requirements and responses of some of the minor tree species, shrubs, herbs, and grasses (usually not favored in stand treatments) to stand manipulation, fertilizers, herbicides, and pest control, (b) nursery and planting practices for a number of trees and shrubs not commonly planted in the past (horticultural research should be studied to see what applicable work may be underway there), and (c) calculations of the loss in growth, yield, timber quality, and financial return associated with the modification of silvicultural practices for recreational use to provide a rational basis for making decisions.

Conducting the research and developing and applying the silvicultural prescriptions required for the successful management of recreation areas may seem like an unwanted burden to some silviculturists. There will, however, be a growing need for such knowledge and such management, and the silviculturist is the best man to develop it. I believe the acceptance of this responsibility can be rewarding to silviculturists and that out of it will come silviculture knowledge highly useful in the more conventional bounds of silviculture. We may, after nearly a century's delay, follow further along the course that von Salisch pointed out to us in the waning years of the nineteenth century.

## NOTE

[1] We are concerned here primarily with "natural" parks of the type usually administered by federal, state, or county agencies. The highly developed, intensively used parks usually found in urban areas are not included, except those which are well wooded.

## REFERENCE

Society of American Foresters. 1958. Forestry terminology, 3rd ed. Washington, D.C.: Society of American Foresters.

# 19

# PROPOSED METHODOLOGY FOR AN INVENTORY AND CLASSIFICATION OF LAND FOR RECREATIONAL USE

**Gordon D. Taylor**
**Clarke W. Thomson**

This chapter outlines a basic method for inventorying and classifying land for recreational use. Gordon Taylor and Clarke Thomson do not propose to solve all of the problems associated with classifying recreation land, but the study is significant here because it serves as the basis for the present Canada Land Inventory classification system which is used to identify potential recreational areas across Canada.

Recent events[1] in the United States and Canada have placed a priority on the development of a system for assessing the capability of all land with respect to its suitability for recreation. There is little precedent in the field of recreation for such a broad scale of operation. As a result we have had to develop a system almost from a fresh start. To do this we have set two major objectives: (1) to suggest a relatively simple system of inventory that will indicate the potential of the physical landscape for recreational land use; and (2) to suggest an approach that will allow for a logical sequence in varying the scale of intensity of that inventory.

## APPROACH TO THE PROBLEM

It is our opinion that the problems can best be handled through a four-stage approach to both inventory and classification. The approach suggested proceeds from the general to the specific and then to the general again. Our reasoning is outlined in diagrammatic form (see Table 1). At stage one only the potential of units of the landscape would be presented. The potential which would be based upon the combined effect of water, topography, and cover should be outlined for all areas included in the coverage. Although this stage would provide the information and the framework for broad areal or regional analysis, it would not have the detail for site evaluation. It would point out, however, on a national basis those areas that warrant

Reprinted from the *Forestry Chronicle* (June, 1966): 153–59, by permission of the Canadian Institute of Forestry and the authors.

This paper was presented to the Annual Meeting, West Lakes Division, Association of American Geographers.

closer attention. This stage would provide a grouping of areas based on readily available data and would be the initial step in a sophisticated approach to classification.

```
STEP
    1--Preliminary Analysis of all Lands
    2--Preliminary Analysis of Best Areas
    3--Detailed Site Analysis
    4--Generalized Use Classes
```

**TABLE 1.** *Concept of Classification*

Stage two would provide information at an intermediate level of detail on specific areas. These areas would be selected on the basis of their ranking in stage one. The inventory aspect would be concerned with the number and kind of attractions for selected types of recreation land use. As demonstrated by Fischer (1962) such attractions can be ranked, albeit empirically, for each type of recreation. Inventories using this concept have a particular advantage in that they allow for regional differences in the significance of various physical criteria (Taylor, 1965). The resulting inventory would not only serve as an elaboration of stage one, but also it would reflect the regional significance of particular units of the landscape and serve to further narrow the search for areas requring on-site analysis.

Site analysis could be accomplished through the implementation of a third stage of inventory. At this stage the level of detail would be sufficient to: (a) permit boundary limits to be drawn for each site, and (b) permit decisions to be made with respect to rejection or selection for utilization for various types of recreation use. The only limit to both number of sites selected and detail of the inventory would be money and personnel.

A fourth step would permit the detail amassed at stage three to be generalized into a classification.

We readily admit that the above approach has problems. We feel very strongly, however, that any objections will be outweighed by the advantages of the system. It allows for the most efficient use of limited financial and human resources; it can, with careful selection of criteria, not only satisfy the need for a simplified classification providing blanket coverage but also provide a two-stage base for site analysis in selected areas. At each stage the degree of detail provided by the inventory can be consistent with the scale of generalization required for classification and mapping.

## METHODOLOGY FOR STAGE ONE

The key to successful implementation of the entire approach hinges on the selection of significant criteria and ranges of criteria at stage one. Selection of water, topography and cover is based on personal experience in examining land for park and other recreational purposes. This decision, however, is strongly supported by others who have also been concerned with selecting elements of the natural resource base necessary or most desirable for outdoor recreation.

## MAJOR ELEMENT

### Water
1. Sea, lake or major river; lake exceeds 320 acres; river more than half a mile wide.
2. River from 100 feet to half a mile in width.
3. Lake, river or stream; lake less that 320 acres; river less than 100 feet in width.
4. Lacks a water body.

### Cover
1. Tree cover exists.
2. No tree cover.

### Slope
1. 30-70% of area in slope less than 10%.
2. Less than 30% of area in slope of 10% or less, more than 70% of area in slope of 10% or less.
3. No level land; or all level land.

### Relief
1. From 100 feet to 500 feet in square mile.
2. Less than 100 feet in square mile.
3. Exceeds 500 feet in square mile.

**TABLE 2.** *Critical Limits in Recreational Land*

To keep the system manageable it was necessary to concentrate on one, or at the most two, aspects of each of those elements.

In the case of water we suggest the most important aspect is whether or not water is available for those types of recreation that are specifically water oriented; namely bathing, fishing, boating, water skiing and scuba diving. It has also been possible to include a crude reference to size along with availability. Vegetation is considered only in the light of whether or not the potential to grow cover for shelter exists. Admittedly, extent and type of cover may be influential in the selection of sites for specific locales. In such instances, however, the role will be more apparent in stage two. A single most important aspect of topography is difficult to determine. Recreation areas where space is needed for parking, for roads and for buildings, require gentle slopes. On the other hand, snow skiing, scenic lookouts, hiking, and so on require a variety of relief and slope. We, therefore, decided to use both slope and relative relief.

These elements and their control limits which appear in Table 2, are the basis of our identification system. The interpretation of these factors into an areal analysis has had to be empirical and subjective (see Table 3). Our guiding principles have been:

1. water is the key element and as water conditions become less important the limitation of the area for recreation increases;

2. tree cover has been made permissive and has not placed a severe limitation on the area;

3. a variety of slope and relief conditions provide the most suitable background for recreational uses. Land too flat or too steep presents limiting factors;

4. that recognition should be given to areas that lack usable water but have other suitable characteristics.

| Type Areas | Water | Cover | Element Complex Rating[1] Slope | Relief |
|------------|-------|-------|-------|--------|
| A | 1 | 1 | 1 | 1 |
| B | 2 | 2 | 1 | 1 |
| C | 2 | 2 | 2 | 2/3 |
| D | 4 | 2 | 2 | 2/3 |
| E | 3 | 2 | 2/3 | 2/3 |
| F | 4 | 2 | 2/3 | 2/3 |
| G | 4 | 2 | 3 | 2/3 |

**TABLE 3.** *Areal Analysis of Recreational Land*
Note: To be included in the appropriate class, no element rating may be below that shown.

The type areas are arranged in descending order of significance and reflect the degree of limitation offered by the criteria. The significance is based upon the limitations offered to development for recreational use. Areas with excessively steep slopes, of high local relief, and lacking both water and tree cover are considered least desirable. Environments suitable for limited types of development, or suitable only for single special uses, fall into intermediate categories. Apart from these considerations our break-down into the seven classes is largely a matter of convenience.

The sole purpose of this proposed areal analysis is to determine the location of the recreational potential of the country. It does not cover all recreations, as has already been made clear, but only certain mass recreations that have common physical requirements. The type category assigned to an area will indicate the possibility of finding the type of recreation site that is required, and the limitations therein.

The system as outlined will not identify individual recreational sites, but it will indicate the probability of finding suitable sites (see Table 4).

## METHODOLOGY FOR STAGE TWO

At the conclusion of stage one, broad areal designations will have been made. It is now necessary to proceed towards a more detailed examination of areas designated as Class A or those that are of interest in lesser classes

| Type Areas | Probability of Locating Recreational Site | Physical Limitations that may exist |
|---|---|---|
| A | Excellent | None |
| B | Good | Little |
| C | Fair | Moderate |
| D | Fair | Moderate |
| E | Fair | Moderate |
| F | Poor | Severe |
| G | Poor | Severe |

**TABLE 4.** *Application of the Areal Analysis*

because of a pressing demand. At this stage of the inventory interest will shift from broad areas to the identification of smaller areas suitable for park and/or recreational purposes.

As Fischer (1962) has pointed out, the element that gives a site its recreational character is an attraction. Amongst the possible attractions that should be considered are beaches, waterfalls, canyons, ravines, rapids, unique geologic features, spectacular views, and so on.

By assigning priorities to the types of recreation, the attractions can be ranked one against the other; or, by using associated physical criteria such as slope, materials, and drainage, attractions in one area can be ranked against similar attractions in other areas.

We do not suggest that this concept of attraction eliminates all the problems connected with selection and ranking. Both the number and kind of attractions will vary with the type of recreation being considered. Attractions for intensive uses are not necessarily the same as those for dispersed types of recreation.

## METHODOLOGY FOR STAGE THREE

After possible sites have been selected by the operation of stage two, a detailed analysis of these is essential. There are many ways of carrying out this type of analysis. The one that any specific agency will use will depend upon the scale of the operation and the time and personnel available for the task. It is not our purpose to outline systems of detailed site analysis at this time.

## METHODOLOGY FOR STAGE FOUR

Our system has proceeded from the identification of broad areal possibilities to the detailed examination of site characteristics. It is now necessary to begin to organize the vast body of data that will have become available into a classification system. The classification should consist of categories of declining capability and it must cover all areas of land.

The classification of land for recreation must be based on the physical resources. There is a danger in the development of any classification that the attempt may be made to classify recreation rather than land. Any such attempt to deal with recreation would put the classifier in a position of saying that one form of recreational land use is more valuable than another. As recreation is a highly personal thing and the benefits of any one activity to one individual are probably different than to another, any such classification would be based on weak assumptions. The essential basis of the classification is that the highest category is one that includes all lands that are highly suitable for recreation and so on. In this way, lands that have very different characteristics could be included within one class.

An approach to classification would be through precise valuations being placed on the following variables: physical quality, attraction, size, and the opportunities for recreational use. The grouping of these variables into a classification would be based on the assumption that as each of them decreases in quality, the capability of the land for recreation also decreases. Measurable divide points would need to be established to indicate the decrease in quality (see Table 5).

Judgment will always play an important role in classification, but the more precise limits that can be placed upon the criteria, the less variation due to individual bias there should be in the results. Any procedure which reduces variations of this kind and as a result increases reliability should be thoroughly tested. It's one thing to say that precise limits should be set; it is quite another to set them. These limits can only be suggested at this time. As experience in handling the data increases, an adjustment of the limits will certainly be needed.

The problem now becomes one of combining the variables into a system of classification. One way would be to place equal value on each variable and sum over the four items. Classes could then be estimated by a grouping of sums. Another method would be to apply a weighting system to the variables. Any system of weighting would require a good deal of experimentation but a possible one would be: Class $= (B) (C) + A + D$.

This combination would have the effect of dropping the rating more rapidly as a result of limits on physical quality and attraction than as a

| Rating scale | A Size | B[1] Physical quality | C[1] Attraction | D[1] Recreational use |
|---|---|---|---|---|
| 1. | Exceeds 1,000 acres | No limitations; or very minor. | Major attraction e.g. sand beach in excess of 1 mile. | Will support many activities. |
| 2. | 501-1,000 acres | If water oriented lake size less than 640 acres, cover lacking, slope at or near critical limits. | Some limitation, e.g. sand beach, ½ - 1 mile; long beach, in excess of 1 mile, broken by headland, etc. | At least one activity limited by other factors, e.g. cold water and swimming. |
| 3. | 51-100 acres | Outside No. 1 in slope table | Sand beach 300 ft.- ½ mile; long beach, but sand areas broken. | At least three activities limited. |
| 4. | 10-50 acres | Lakes less than 100 acres, slope poor or cover lacking | Small beach less than 300 feet. | Several activities limited. |
| 5. | Less than 10 acres | Many limitations | Lacks beach | Few activities possible. |

**TABLE 5.** *Suggested Limits of Capability Variables*

[1] The limits suggested here do not cover all the factors that should be considered. These elements are used to illustrate the idea of fixed limits.

result of limits on size and recreational use. The highest ranking possible would be

$$3 = (1 \times 1) + 1 + 1.$$

The lowest ranking would be $35 = (5 \times 5) + 5 + 5$.

Between these two extremes as many classes as were required for the classification could be established.

## CONCLUSION

We have attempted to outline a logical preparation for the inventorying and classification of recreational land.[2] All the necessary detail that could be required for any decision has been fitted into a single system that leads from broad areal designation to finite detail on a specific site and then to a classification. Our approach has been analogous to the concepts of situation and site in location theory.

We have made no claim of infallibility or of an all-pervading knowledge. We have attempted to take the current state of recreational knowledge about landscape and recreation and translate it into a usable system of land classification.

## NOTES

[1] In the United States—the need for State Comprehensive Outdoor Recreation Plans; and in Canada—The Canada Land Inventory of ARDA.

[2] We are indebted to Mr. R. Bourassa, Department of Game and Fisheries, Province of Quebec, for valuable discussion on these ideas.

## REFERENCES

Fisher, W. F. 1962. Methods of evaluating lands for recreational use. Recreation in Wild-land Management, University of California, Agricultural Experiment Station.

Taylor, G. D. 1965. An approach to the inventory of recreational lands. *Canadian Geographer* 9 (2): 84–91.

## FURTHER READING

### Surveys of the Impact of Outdoor Recreation on the Environment

Isard, W., *Ecologic-Economic Analysis for Regional Development* (New York: Free Press, 1972).

Lime, D. W., and G. H. Stankey, "Carrying Capacity: Maintaining Outdoor Recreation Quality," *Recreation Symposium Proceedings*, Northeastern Forest Experiment Station, Upper Darby, Pennsylvania (1971).

McHarg, I. L., *Design with Nature* (New York: Doubleday, 1969).

Rutledge, A. J., *Anatomy of a Park* (New York: McGraw-Hill, 1971).

### Concepts and Methods Related to the Analysis of the Impact of Outdoor Recreation on the Environment

Beardsley, W. G., and J. A. Wagar, "Vegetation Management of a Forested Recreation Site," *Journal of Forestry* 69, no. 10 (October, 1971): 728–31.

Burden, R. F., and P. E. Randerson, "Quantitative Studies of Effects of Human Trampling on Vegetation As an Aid to the Management of Semi-Natural Areas," *Journal of Applied Ecology* 9 (1972): 439–57.

Chuff, M., ed., *Proceedings of the 1971 Snowmobile and Off the Road Vehicle Research Symposium*, Technical Paper 8, Recreation Research and Planning Unit, Department of Parks and Recreation Resources, College of Agriculture and Natural Resources, Michigan State University (1969).

Cordell, H. K., and G. A. James, "Supplementing Vegetation on Southern Appalachian Recreation Sites with Small Trees and Shrubs," *Journal of Soil and Water Conservation* 26, no. 6 (November–December, 1971): 235–38.

Cressman, D. R., and D. W. Hoffman, "Classifying Land for Recreation," *Journal of Soil and Water Conservation* 23, no. 3 (1968): 91–93.

de Vos, A., and R. H. Bailey, "The Effect of Logging and Intensive Camping on Vegetation in Riding Mountain National Park," *The Forestry Chronicle* 46, no. 1 (February, 1970): 49–55.

Fabos, J. G., "An Analysis of Landscape Assessment Techniques," from "An Analysis of Environmental Quality Ranking Systems," *Recreation Symposium Proceedings* (1971), pp. 40–55.

Federal Water Pollution Control Administration, *Water Quality Criteria*, Report to the National Technical Advisory Committee to the Secretary of the Interior (Washington, D.C.: U.S. Government Printing Office, 1968).

Fischer, A., and J. V. Krutilla, "Determination of Optimal Capacity of Resource-Based Recreation Facilities," *Natural Resources Journal* 12, no. 3 (July, 1972): 417–44.

Frissell, S. S., Jr., and D. P. Duncan, "Campsite Preference and Deterioration in the Quetico-Superior Canoe Country," *Journal of Forestry* 63, no. 4 (April, 1965): 256–60.

Goldin, K. D., "Recreational Parks and Beaches: Peak Demand, Quality and Management," *Journal of Leisure Research* 3, no. 2 (Spring, 1971): 81–107.

Goldsmith, F. B., R. J. C. Munton, and A. Warren, "The Impact of Recreation on the Ecology and Amenity of Semi-Natural Areas: Methods of Investigation Used in the Isles of Scilly," *Biological Journal of the Linnean Society* 2, no. 4 (December, 1970): 287–306.

Hamill, L., "Classification of Forest Land for Recreational Potential and Scenery," *The Forestry Chronicle* 47, no. 3 (June, 1971): 149–53.

Heinselman, M. L., "Vegetation Management in Wilderness Area and Primitive Parks," *Journal of Forestry* 63, no. 6 (June, 1965): 440–45.

Juurrand, P., *Wild Rivers Survey 1971: Quantitative Comparison of River Landscapes*, Special Report 72-1 (Ottawa, Canada: Department of Indian Affairs and Northern Development, 1972).

Litton, R. B., Jr., "Forest Landscape Description and Inventories," U.S.D.A. Forest Service Research Paper PSW-49, 1968.

Magill, A. W., "Five California Campgrounds: Conditions Improve after Five Years' Recreation Use," U.S.D.A. Forest Service Research Paper PSW-62, 1970.

Ripley, T. H., "Recreation Impact on Southern Appalachian Campgrounds and Picnic Sites," U.S.D.A. Forest Service Research Paper no. 153, November, 1962.

Settergren, D. D., and D. M. Cole, "Recreation Effects on Soil and Vegetation in the Missouri Ozarks," *Journal of Forestry* 68, no. 4 (April, 1970): 231–33.

# THE PROSPECT

There are three generations of books that a student concerned with the environment can look forward to reading. In recent years the market has been flooded with first generation books; the books of Carson, Commanger, and the Erlichs are examples. Although these books have served the vital purpose of creating a much needed concern for planet earth, they are not books that are of great use in training the concerned or aroused in how to do something about the environment.

We believe that this book is a concrete example of a second generation book. A second generation book should give to the student (1) an appreciation of the disciplinary derivation of the important concepts and methods as they relate to particular environmental issues, (2) a meaningful integrative system or framework for relating the various disciplinary materials together in a meaningful way and (3) definite tools that can be used by the researcher or manager in attempting to answer specific problems.

It is to be hoped that a third generation book dealing with land and leisure will soon emerge. If we are now at the stage that we are concerned, and we have a grasp of the basic "tools of the trade," there then arises a need for a book that attempts to evaluate existing and emerging concepts, methods, and practices in environmental planning and management. Such an evaluation could result in current practices being rejected, changed, or enhanced. It is at this stage that the innovative and creative mind will make useful and original contributions to the field of environmental studies.

Much of what has become standard practice in outdoor recreation is very much in need of review and evaluation. Recreational land use planning and management has been dominated by a very functional approach. Beyond "lip-service" there has been a very real lack of concern for social and ecological considerations. The case of scenic or recreational roads is a case in point. William H. Whyte has pointed out how statistics on volume or frequency of driving could be used to justify another decade of highway development.

> To justify a new recreational roads program, much has been made of the findings of the Outdoor Recreation Resources Review Commission that driving for pleasure is the most frequent form of recreation for Americans. Few statistics have been so widely quoted or so misinterpreted. If Americans find driving their most important recreation, the reasoning goes, and if more Americans are going to do more driving, then the best way to provide people with more recreation is to provide them with more recreational roads.
>
> It does not follow. The ORRRC finding was significant as far as it went, but it should be extrapolated no further. What it boils down to is that when a sample of Americans were shown a list of twenty-three activities they said "driving-for-pleasure" was the activity they did the most of. They did not say why they did it or when, or on what kinds of roads.[1]

Whyte could have gone on to ask: if, in fact, "driving-for-pleasure" is a satisfying recreational experience, what basic human needs does it accommodate? Given other opportunities or a range of recreational options would pleasure drivers pleasure drive? This is but one example of how, time after time, "experts" involved in recreational planning unwittingly bring a narrow bias into play. In dealing with recreational roads, the landscape architect assumes that pleasure driving is the same as scenic driving. For the engineer, recreational roads provides a *raison d'être* for building more roads. For the recreationists the need for yet more and more recreational land has been further justified.

Traditional concepts, methods, and tasks that have now become part and parcel of recreational land use studies are such things as benefit cost, multiple use, sustained yield, land classification and so on. How useful are these concepts? Should they be refined, or discarded? New concepts and concerns are emerging. Do they represent progress or are they just another set of "buzz-words"—environmental impacts, ecosystems, carrying capacity, systems planning, eco-planning, advocacy planning and so on? What is the utility of such concepts to outdoor recreation? Should they be adopted, adopted with modifications, or, rejected?

Considering all these existing and emerging concepts and methods, are there still questions that are left begging. Are we still a long way off from answering the basic problem of a shrinking land resource and increasing leisure time? Is there a need for new approaches and new techniques to effectively combat these rapidly increasing problems?[2]

The study of recreational resources offers unlimited scope for the concerned and the curious. The path to the resolution of these particular environmental issues has become more and more complex. Pressure on the good earth continues to increase and change by quantum leaps as our population grows and becomes increasingly urban.

The study of recreational resources is an appropriate entree into environmental studies—the study of the relationship between man and his environment. The concepts, methods, techniques, and practices employed or implied in the planning, design, and management of recreational resources should provide the future environmentalist with a multiplicity of tools to use in the resolution of many urban and rural environmental problems.

## NOTES

[1] William H. Whyte, *The Last Landscape* (New York: Doubleday & Co., Inc., 1968), p. 335.

[2] National Academy of Sciences, *A Program for Outdoor Recreation Research* (Washington, D.C.: National Academy of Sciences, 1969).

973102     **RECREATION BIBLIOGRAPHIES**

Anderson, D. M., and W. Munro, "An Initial Bibliography on Outdoor Recreation Studies in Canada with Selected United States References," Canada Land Inventory, Department of Regional Economic Expansion, 1970, Ottawa.

Canadian Government Travel Bureau, *Bibliography of Tourism Research Studies* (Ottawa: Information Canada, 1970).

Carroll, M. A., *Open Space Planning: A Selected Bibliography* (Urbana, Ill.: Bureau of Community Planning, Department of Urban Planning, University of Illinois, 1965).

Ditton, Robert B., *Water-based Recreation: Access, Water Quality, and Incompatible Use Consideration*, Exchange Bibliography no. 159, Council of Planning Librarians, 1970.

"Dissertation: Their Author and Titles," Contemporary Research in American and Canadian Universities Related to Recreation, *Parks and Recreation* 42 (May, 1959): 222–29.

Lime, David W., and George H. Stankey, *A Selected Bibliography of Literature Related to Recreational Carrying Capacity Decision-Making*, prepared for the Forest Recreation Symposium, Syracuse, N.Y., 1971.

Pinkerton, James R., and Marjorie J. Pinkerton, *Outdoor Recreation and Leisure: A Reference Guide and Selected Bibliography* (Columbia, Mo.: Research Center, School of Business and Public Administration, University of Missouri, 1969).

U.S. Department of Agriculture, Forest Service, Division of Forest Environment Research, *Forest Recreation Research Publications 1942–1966*, and supplements to 1972 (Washington, D.C.: U.S. Government Printing Office, 1972).

U.S. Department of Commerce, The Office of Regional Economic Development, *Tourism and Recreation: A State-of-the-Art Study* (Washington, D.C.: U.S. Government Printing Office, 1966).

U.S. Department of the Interior, Bureau of Outdoor Recreation, *Outdoor Recreation Research, A Reference Catalog, 1970* (Washington, D.C.: U.S. Government Printing Office, 1971).

U.S. Outdoor Recreation Resources Review Commission, *Outdoor Recreation Literature: A Survey*, Study Report 27 (Washington, D.C.: U.S. Government Printing Office, 1962).

Van der Smissen, Betty, and Donald J. Joyce, *Bibliography of Theses and Dissertations in Recreation, Parks, Camping, and Outdoor Education* (Washington, D.C.: National Recreation and Park Association, 1970).

DATE DUE